INTERNATIONAL DEVELOPMENT IN FOCUS

Undernutrition in the Philippines

Scale, Scope, and Opportunities for Nutrition Policy and Programming

NKOSINATHI V. N. MBUYA, GABRIEL DEMOMBYNES,
SHARON FAYE A. PIZA, AND ANN JILLIAN V. ADONA

WORLD BANK GROUP

1818 H Street NW, Washington, DC 20433
Telephone: 202-473-1000; Internet: www.worldbank.org

1 2 3 4 24 23 22 21

ISBN: 978-1-4648-1701-4
DOI: 10.1596/978-1-4648-1701-4

Cover photo: © Aver Justin Parado. Used with permission of Aver Justin Parado; further permission required for reuse.
Cover design: Debra Naylor / Naylor Design Inc.

Contents

Boxes

Figures

Maps

Tables

Acknowledgments

This report was prepared by a World Bank team led by Nkosinathi Mbuya and Gabriel Demombynes and comprising Sharon Faye A. Piza and Ann Jillian V. Adona, all of whom contributed as coauthors for specific chapters. Regina Calzado and Jeramie Mercado Caballes provided administrative support throughout this study.

The local-level estimates of stunting in chapter 2 are based on the analytics of small-area estimation conducted by a team comprising Alemayeha Ambel, Kasper Brandt, and Thomas Pave Sohnesen. Chapter 4 is an abridged version of the analyses conducted as part of this study and also published as a Policy Research Working Paper by Mario V. Capanzana, Gabriel Demombynes, and Paul Gubbins. Chapter 5 is based largely on background work led by Felipe Dizon and Zetianyu Wang. Chapter 6 is an abridged version of research conducted as part of this study and published as a World Bank Health, Nutrition, and Population Discussion Paper with Nkosinathi Mbuya, Iman Sen, Gabriel Demombynes, and Varun Gauri as authors. Cecilia Acuin conducted the background review for and is coauthor for chapter 7; she also provided insightful comments on all of the chapters. Chapter 8 is based on a policy note prepared by a World Bank team led by Yoonyoung Cho and comprising Jorge Avalos, Yasuhiro Kawasoe, and Ruth Rodriguez.

Appreciated guidance throughout the execution of this study was given by the Nutrition Study Technical Advisory Group, comprising Mario Capanzana (director, FNRI), Ma. Anna Rita Ramirez (senior science research specialist, FNRI), Cielito Habito (professor, Department of Economics, Ateneo de Manila University), Bernie Flores (assistant secretary, NNC), Roehlano Briones (senior research fellow, PIDS), Joris van Hees (nutrition specialist, UNICEF), and Jutta Neitzel (head of programme, WFP). The team also benefited from inputs from Alejandro Herrin, Lubina Qureshy, Toby Monsod, Emmanuel Skoufias, Robert Oelrichs, Vida Gomez, Jed Friedman, Maribeth Villorente, Eeshani Kandpal, Anuja Kar, Steven Jaffee, and Eli Weiss. The authors are grateful to peer reviewers Dr. Azucena Dayanghirang (executive director, NNC), Alice Nkoroi (nutrition manager, UNICEF-Philippines), and Kyoko Shibata Okamura (nutrition specialist, World Bank) for providing technical guidance and a quality review of this report. The authors would also like to thank our government counterparts for their guidance and encouragement: Rosemarie Edillon (undersecretary, NEDA), Dr. Mario Capanzana (FNRI), Bernie Flores (assistant secretary, NNC), and Azucena Dayanghirang (executive director, NNC).

The government of Japan provided financial support for this work through the Japan Trust Fund for Scaling Up Nutrition.

About the Authors

Ann Jillian V. Adona has more than eight years of experience contributing to research in health, education, labor, poverty, trade, economic uncertainty, infrastructure, and information technologies. She has worked as a consultant for the Campbell Collaboration and the Asian Development Bank in the Macroeconomic Research Division, and she previously served as an analyst at the Philippine Institute for Development Studies, the think tank of the government of the Philippines. Her research interests include nutrition and education, econometrics, and development policy. Ann received her master's degree in development economics from the University of the Philippines. She is a member of the Early Years Fellowship, where she is refocusing her research on human development and furthering her studies in economics.

Gabriel Demombynes is the World Bank's Practice Leader for Human Development for Colombia and Venezuela, based in Bogotá. Previously, he has held positions based in Hanoi, Manila, and Nairobi. He led preparation of the Philippines COVID-19 Emergency Response Project and Systematic Country Diagnostics for the Philippines and Vietnam. Other prominent examples of his work include critiques of the Millennium Villages Project evaluation, innovative approaches to surveys in South Sudan, and studies of crime in Latin America and South Africa. His work has been cited in the *Financial Times, The Washington Post*, and *The Economist*. Gabriel has taught at the Johns Hopkins School of Advanced International Studies and was Economic Policy Adviser to Howard Dean during his 2003–04 U.S. presidential campaign. He holds a PhD in economics from the University of California–Berkeley and bachelor's degrees in civil engineering and humanities from the University of Texas at Austin.

Nkosinathi V. N. Mbuya is a Senior Nutrition Specialist in the East Asia and Pacific (EAP) Region of the World Bank. He has led the World Bank's nutrition engagement in the Lao People's Democratic Republic, the Philippines, and Vietnam as well as other regional initiatives. Before joining the EAP Region, Nkosi was the headquarters-based nutrition focal person for the South Asia Region. For the Africa Region, he has supported the Burundi, Madagascar, Sierra Leone, and Zambia health teams in their nutrition engagement. Nkosi led the preparation of the EAP Region Multisectoral Strategy and Action Plan to Reduce the Double Burden of Malnutrition (2015–20) and also the South Asia Regional Assistance Strategy for Nutrition (2011–16), as well as a wide range of analytical work in Afghanistan, Bangladesh, and Sri Lanka. Before joining the World Bank, he was the Impact Assessment Advisor for Save the Children's UK Hunger Reduction Team, based in London. He has also worked for the Ministry of Health and Child Welfare in Zimbabwe as a provincial nutritionist and as a nutrition lecturer at the Institute of Food, Nutrition, and Family Sciences at the University of Zimbabwe.

Sharon Faye A. Piza is a poverty economist for the Philippines, based in the World Bank's Manila office. She has been with the World Bank as a consultant since 2012 and joined as staff in January 2016. She has worked on various analytical reports pertaining to growth, poverty, and inequality. Before joining the World Bank, she also undertook various research work with other multilateral organizations as well as policy analysis for various Philippine government offices. Sharon holds a master's degree in economics and a bachelor's degree in statistics, both from the University of the Philippines.

Executive Summary

ABSTRACT This report presents a comprehensive analysis of undernutrition in the Philippines. It describes high rates of undernutrition among Filipino children and provides evidence of why it is critical for the government of the Philippines to prioritize tackling this persistent challenge. The report assesses the determinants and causes of childhood undernutrition and reviews current policies and programs directed at addressing this problem. Based on these analyses, the report provides recommendations of how national policies and programs can be strengthened to reduce the high rates of undernutrition in the country. The report is aimed at policy makers, development practitioners, researchers, and the general public. It sets out to inform the debate on the causes and potential solutions of undernutrition, while identifying high-priority policy and policy commitments for action.

WHY DOES NUTRITION MATTER?

Undernutrition robs Filipino children of their chance for a bright future. Viewed through the lens of the World Bank's Human Capital Index (HCI)—an index developed to link the human capital of children today quantitatively with future economic outcomes—the country's 2020 HCI of 0.52 predicts that the future productivity of a child born today will be 48 percent below what that child might have achieved if he or she had enjoyed a complete education and full health.

High levels of childhood undernutrition can lead to a staggering loss of a country's human and economic potential. Undernutrition affects economic growth through three key channels. First, it elevates the risk of morbidity and mortality, with the potential for transmission across generations. Second, it is associated with decreased lifelong income-earning potential and labor force productivity in both the short and long terms. Stunting is associated with cognitive delays and lower educational attainment. A closely related association is the relation between stunting in childhood and reduced height and productivity as an adult. Third, undernutrition is associated with an increase in the cost of health care and social safety nets—costs borne largely by the public sector—and a reduced efficacy of investments in education. Childhood undernutrition places a heavy burden on the Philippine economy, estimated at US$4.4 billion, or 1.5 percent of the country's gross domestic product (GDP) in 2015 (UNICEF 2017).

High Burden of Undernutrition in the Philippines

For nearly 30 years, rates of both wasting and stunting have been nearly flat. The rate of stunting[1] among children under five recorded for 2019 (28.8 percent) was only slightly lower than the level in 2008—the prevalence of underweight[2] in 2019 was 19 percent, and the prevalence of wasting was 6 percent.[3] Based on the World Health Organization's classification of undernutrition rates, the prevalence of stunting in children in the Philippines is of "very high" public health significance. The 29 percent stunting rate also places the Philippines fifth among countries in the East Asia and Pacific region with the highest prevalence of stunting and among the 10 countries globally with the highest number of stunted children.

Moreover, these national aggregates mask wide inequalities, with far worse outcomes in some regions than in others. Pockets of population with high levels of stunting, sometimes exceeding 40 percent of the population, are found throughout the country. The highest rates are in the Autonomous Region in Muslim Mindanao (ARMM, 45 percent), MIMAROPA (41 percent), Bicol (40 percent), Western Visayas (40 percent), SOCCSKSARGEN (40 percent), Zamboanga Peninsula (38 percent), and Central Visayas (37 percent).[4] In addition, stunting rates are notably higher in rural areas (30.4 percent) than in urban areas (26.4 percent), according to the 2019 Expanded National Nutrition Survey (ENNS) (FNRI 2019).

Beyond these visible anthropometric differences (stunting, underweight, and wasting), micronutrient undernutrition—so-called hidden hunger—is also highly prevalent in the Philippines. The most recent available data show alarmingly high rates of anemia both among children (38 percent among infants 6–11 months old, down from 48 percent in 2018, and 26 percent among children 12–23 months old) and among pregnant women (20 percent). According to the 2018 ENNS, nearly 17 percent of children 6–59 months old suffer from vitamin A deficiency, of which children 12–24 months old have the highest prevalence (22 percent), followed by children 6–12 months old (18 percent) (FNRI 2018).

Effects of the COVID-19 pandemic

The global social and economic crisis triggered by the COVID-19 pandemic poses grave risks to the nutritional status and survival of young children. Initial indications show that hunger in the Philippines rose sharply following the start of the pandemic. Social Weather Stations (SWS) has collected data on self-rated hunger going back to 1998. The SWS survey asks how often a family had experienced hunger or not had anything to eat during the 30 days preceding the survey. Results from the September 2020 survey show that 30.7 percent of families were suffering hunger by this measure and 8.7 percent were suffering severe hunger—in both cases the highest levels recorded in more than 20 years. These results make it likely that the levels of childhood undernutrition will rise in 2021. Millions of Filipino children who survive these deficits will suffer the consequences of poor school performance and low productivity as adults unless immediate action is taken.

A narrow critical window of opportunity

There is only a narrow window of opportunity for adequate nutrition to ensure optimal health and physical and cognitive development. It spans the first 1,000 days of life, beginning with the day of conception through to the child's second birthday. Any undernutrition occurring during this period can lead to extensive, largely irreversible damage to physical growth, brain development, and, more broadly, human capital formation. Therefore, interventions to improve nutritional outcomes must focus on children in this age group and on women of child-bearing age.

Economic returns from investing in nutrition

In 2013 *The Lancet* published a comprehensive review of interventions to address undernutrition and micronutrient deficiencies in women and children. It identified a package of high-impact, nutrition-specific interventions[5] to accelerate improvements in nutrition outcomes. The interventions are complementary and mutually reinforcing, with some addressing the prenatal period and others the postnatal period. It is therefore recommended that persons living with a high burden of undernutrition receive the full package of interventions rather than only a partial or piecemeal package. In addition, delivering these interventions as a package and at scale (with at least 90 percent coverage) will result in very high economic returns. In 2017 the World Bank estimated the rate of return from 90 percent coverage of this package of high-impact, nutrition-specific interventions in 34 countries, including the Philippines, that together account for 90 percent of the world's stunted children. According to these estimates, the Philippines would have one of the highest rates of return, reflecting the country's low cost per capita to deliver this package, high rate of return to education, and high rate of GDP growth. Under a certain set of assumptions,[6] for every US dollar that the Philippines invests in this package of high-impact, nutrition-specific interventions, adult income would increase an estimated US$66, compared with US$2 for Malawi, US$13 for Ethiopia, and US$48 for Vietnam.

WHAT ARE THE KEY DRIVERS OF UNDERNUTRITION IN THE PHILIPPINES?

The key determinants of undernutrition are multisectoral. First outlined in the United Nations Children's Fund (UNICEF) conceptual framework of child undernutrition in 1990, the determinants fall into three categories: immediate, underlying, and basic. At the immediate level, a child becomes undernourished because of inadequate or inappropriate dietary intake, ill health, or both—these two factors often negatively affect one another. These immediate factors stem from household or community deficits in food security (for example, lack of access to a diverse diet); inadequate care and feeding practices for mothers and children; and inadequate access to health and environmental services. These three deficits or lack of access, often summarized as "food, health, and care," also interact and are themselves underpinned by more basic causes related to the amount, control, and use of resources in society.

Intermediate determinants of undernutrition

Inadequate nutrient intake

To meet their increasing nutritional needs after six months of exclusive breastfeeding, infants should receive safe, age-appropriate, and nutritionally adequate complementary foods combined with continuous breastfeeding in order to achieve optimal growth. However, many Filipino children do not. Overall, 58 percent of children ages 0–6 months are exclusively breastfed, and only 10 percent of children 6–23 months old were reported to have been fed a nutritionally adequate diet in 2019.[7]

Ill health

Illnesses have a bidirectional relationship with undernutrition. Poor nutrition impairs children's immune response, increasing their susceptibility to infection; fever and other signs and symptoms of infection break down the body's reserve of nutrients more quickly and escalate the requirements. Diarrhea and parasitic infestation from soil-transmitted parasitic worms have long been known to affect nutrition through the loss of nutrients from malabsorption. In the Philippines, the prevalence of diarrhea among children under five is 6.1 percent. By age group, the prevalence of diarrhea is highest among children 6–11 months old (9.4 percent), followed by children 12–23 months old (9.0 percent), according to National Demographic and Health Survey (NDHS) data for 2017. However, Field Health Services Information System (FHSIS) data for 2018 reported that less than half (47 percent) of children up to 59 months of age with diarrhea received oral rehydration solution with zinc and only 45 percent of sick children ages 12–59 months were given vitamin A supplements when treated in health facilities.

Underlying determinants of undernutrition

Access to health services

Prenatal care services provide pregnant women with essential nutrition services, including iron and folic acid supplementation, energy and protein supplementation for undernourished women, and nutrition counseling to promote optimal infant and young child feeding practices. However, only 53 percent of pregnant Filipino women are reported to have made the recommended four prenatal care visits, and only 54 percent had received iron with folic acid.

Inadequate access to diverse foods

Currently, poorer Filipinos eat a diet heavy in rice, with low levels of diversity and limited animal protein. According to 2015 data from the Family Income and Expenditure Survey (FIES), Filipinos consume 159 percent of the recommended consumption of starchy staples (particularly rice), but only 22 percent of the requirement for vegetables, 10 percent for fruits, 12 percent for eggs, 79 percent for meat and pulses, 33 percent for milk, and 29 percent for fats and oils (PSA 2015). Moreover, a healthy diet is expensive in the Philippines. Applying the cost of the recommended diet (CoRD) methodology to 2015 FIES data found that the minimum cost of the recommended diet substantially exceeds what households spend on food, on average. In 2015 the CoRD was ₱68 per adult per day. In contrast, households spent approximately ₱48 per adult per day on food.

Unhealthy household environment

The more well-established consequences of unhealthy environments are childhood diarrheas, which occur more frequently among households without improved toilets and access to safe drinking water as well as those practicing open defecation, which is still seen in marginalized areas of the country. Childhood environmental enteric dysfunction (EED) is less recognized but is known to cause subclinical gastrointestinal infections that prevent nutrient absorption even in the absence of diarrhea. EED has been linked to unsanitary physical environments and contributes to childhood stunting. According to the 2017 NDHS survey data, while 94.7 percent of Philippine households have access to improved sources of drinking water, only 83.7 percent of households in the poorest quintile and 70.9 percent of ARMM households have such access. Unimproved sanitation facilities are used by 24.3 percent of households on average, but this share is much higher (31.6 percent) among ARMM households. Handwashing and household-level food preparation and storage require behavior change interventions.

Inadequate care and nutritional practices for women

Early deficits in fetal and child growth usually stem from inadequate maternal macronutrition and micronutrition before and during pregnancy. In the Philippines, 22.9 percent of pregnant women in 2019 were "nutritionally at-risk." Early marriage and adolescent pregnancy can lead to higher maternal and neonatal mortality, low birthweight, and stunting of children. Adolescent fertility and childbearing are on the rise in the Philippines. In 2017 the adolescent fertility rate was about 54 births per 1,000 women ages 15–19 years. Furthermore, pregnant women under the age of 20 are more likely to be deemed nutritionally at-risk than women above the age of 20 (28.5 percent and 22.3 percent, respectively), according to the ENNS for 2019 (FNRI 2019).

Basic determinants of undernutrition

Poverty

One of the most important basic causes of undernutrition is poverty. In the Philippines, 42.4 percent of children from households in the poorest quintile are stunted compared with 11.4 percent of children from households in the wealthiest quintile (FNRI 2019). The Philippines is an archipelago that is vulnerable to natural calamities such as typhoons, earthquakes, and volcanic eruptions—"emergencies" that can lead to displacement and loss of livelihood, compromising the nutritional well-being of infants and young children.

Governance structures

Governance also poses significant challenges for the country's efforts to combat undernutrition. Municipalities, particularly municipalities with a high prevalence of childhood undernutrition, face several problems in the effort to implement nutrition interventions. Chief among them are the limited budget allocated for nutrition programs; the lack of a full-time provincial, city, or municipal nutrition action officer; and the scarcity of health personnel. Nutrition often must compete with a long list of other infrastructure projects in the budget priorities of local government units (LGUs).

HOW IS THE PHILIPPINE GOVERNMENT TACKLING UNDERNUTRITION?

The reviews conducted for this study reflect national commitment and the government's understanding that nutrition is foundational to the country's economic development. For example, the Philippine Development Plan for 2017–22 has an explicit nutritional goal: to reduce the prevalence of stunting in children under five to 21.4 percent by 2022 (NEDA 2017). The Philippine Plan of Action for Nutrition (PPAN) for 2017–22 is the government's blueprint of actions for nutrition improvement and is consistent with the Ten-Point Economic Agenda of the Duterte administration and the Health for All Agenda of the Department of Health (DOH) (NNC 2017). PPAN is a results-focused plan designed to achieve outcomes on various forms of malnutrition: stunting, wasting, micronutrient deficiencies, high adult body mass index, and obesity. It has four main strategies: (a) focus on the first 1,000 days of life; (b) offer a complement of nutrition-specific and nutrition-sensitive programs; (c) intensify the mobilization of government units, prioritizing the 38 areas with the highest burden of stunting; and (d) harmonize national and local government action.

The national strategy is to establish an organizational structure at all levels of government. In this structure, the operational platform for delivering and managing nutrition-specific and nutrition-sensitive activities is anchored in LGUs, which serve as the focal points for planning, coordinating, and implementing nutrition and nutrition-related activities across the concerned sectors. LGUs have the administrative autonomy to raise local revenues, to borrow, and to determine local expenditures, including expenditure on health and nutrition. Although the LGUs' rhetoric conveys broad political commitment to nutrition programs, in practice they do not show sufficient understanding of the importance of adequate financing for these programs or accord them high budgetary priority. LGUs that strongly support nutrition programs, with adequate financing and more structured nutrition planning sessions, tend to perform better and to have a low prevalence of undernutrition among children under five.

Overall, although the government is implementing nutrition-specific and nutrition-sensitive interventions targeting women and children, progress on improving the nutrition status of children has been very slow. The lack of a clearly defined minimum comprehensive package of evidence-based interventions has contributed to fragmented implementation of these interventions at a local level. Moreover, the low coverage of these interventions and other government programs to date accounts for their suboptimal impact on nutrition outcomes. Stronger financial as well as human resources and institutional capacity are needed to implement high-quality nutrition-specific and nutrition-sensitive government programs at scale.

HOW CAN THE GOVERNMENT OF THE PHILIPPINES ACCELERATE THE REDUCTIONS IN CHILDHOOD UNDERNUTRITION?

In line with the experience of countries that have successfully tackled childhood undernutrition, the Philippines can undertake the following policy and programmatic actions to address the development challenge of undernutrition in the Philippines.

Policy recommendations

Secure adequate financing for nutrition

Critical to tackling undernutrition at scale are better and higher levels of nutrition investments as well as adequate domestic financing for nutrition-related programs to achieve the nutrition goals for vulnerable populations. Priority should be given to advocating for increased direct government funding for LGUs to augment current support for a comprehensive package of interventions to reduce stunting that are applicable to women and children. Increasing the budget allocation and providing a separate budget for nutrition would demonstrate strong support for the nutrition agenda. Nutrition programs can only be implemented and sustained if they have an adequate, dedicated budget. At the national level, the National Nutrition Council (NNC) requires sufficient resources to provide technical and supervisory oversight and to draw together the multiple sectoral as well as administrative responses in a comprehensive, cohesive manner.

Build a strong and more coordinated partnership for nutrition

At the national level,

- The NNC is the country's highest policy-making and coordinating body on nutrition, but it is dependent on the commitment of the 10 agencies on its Governing Board.[8] The NNC needs to have sufficient resources to enable it to influence meaningful change at the national level as well as across concerned sectors.
- Cohesion and interaction are needed between the NNC and LGUs. The exchange needs to go beyond advocacy and policy. The NNC has to be strengthened to provide the supervisory and oversight capacities needed for programs to run effectively and efficiently and be enabled to respond to gaps in program implementation.

At the local level,

- High priority and strong support for nutrition should be on the agenda of both the executive and legislative bodies in the municipalities. As indicated in the case studies conducted for this report, LGUs that strongly support nutrition programs perform better and have a low prevalence of undernutrition among children under five.

Programmatic recommendations

Implement at scale well-proven direct nutrition interventions

Substantial progress has been made in developing policies and strategies for an integrated approach to nutrition, but an evidence-based package of nutrition-specific interventions must be defined and made available to all LGUs with a high burden of stunting through primary health care facilities and relevant community platforms. This recommendation should include the following specific actions:

- Adopt an evidence-based package of nutrition-specific interventions and make it available to each household in all high-priority LGUs.
- Formulate a comprehensive, behavior change communications strategy targeted at policy makers, health workers, and households and use it to

underpin media campaigns, community educational materials, and events to improve the nutrition of women and children.

- Formulate more innovative and competency-based training of Barangay Health Workers, Barangay Nutrition Scholars, and their supervisors. It is imperative that these health workers command adequate knowledge of nutrition, shift beliefs toward acceptable practices, and are able to communicate their knowledge effectively so as to bring about sound behavioral change.

Address the determinants of nutrition through multisectoral approaches

Although it is important to address the direct routes to optimal nutrition through the previous recommendations, success in improving maternal and child nutrition indicators will be enhanced and sustained by using multisectoral approaches to address the underlying determinants of nutrition. Significant gaps remain in the provision of essential evidence-backed nutrition-sensitive interventions, and closing these gaps is critical to addressing the underlying causes of undernutrition. Key actions should be targeted primarily at LGUs with a heavy burden of stunting and could include the following:

- Promote the diversification of production in agriculture and expand the sector, with a focus on adding value and specialization in key regions as well as developing channels of access to markets, in effect enhancing the food environment to improve consumer access to nutritious, safe food.
- Ensure that maternal and child health programs have explicit, measurable nutrition outcomes as well as coordinated human resources and logistical support to take advantage of synergies and potential for integration.
- Ensure that the conditional cash transfer program serves the most nutritionally vulnerable populations—pregnant women and young children. Targeting can be improved by adopting the updated registry to identify vulnerable populations and by developing a more dynamic system to update beneficiary information frequently. In addition, create the necessary incentives to report pregnancy and newborns for monitoring under the program, renew the health and nutrition messages of the family development sessions, and improve the program's delivery and monitoring systems.

Establish geographic convergence of key sectors

In order to address the multisectoral determinants of undernutrition in the Philippines, it is essential to achieve geographic convergence—down to the household level—of critical sectors and programs in LGUs with a heavy burden of stunting and to focus on delivering a basic package of nutrition-specific and nutrition-sensitive interventions. The geographic convergence would include the Department of Health, Department of Agriculture, Department of the Interior and Local Government, Department of Social Welfare and Development, and Department of Education. These entities would ensure that sector interventions in agriculture; education; health and nutrition; social protection; water, sanitation, and hygiene; and poverty reduction—albeit delivered in parallel—reach the same households to maximize their contribution to reducing stunting.

Strengthen the systems for data collection and monitoring and evaluation

Nutrition data and information systems play a critical role in ensuring that valid, reliable, and timely nutrition data are available, accessible, and used by key nutrition stakeholders to inform decision making. Hence the inclusion of standard, reliable, and high-quality monitoring and evaluation systems in every nutrition and health-related program will be useful in assessing the effectiveness of intervention programs at the local level. Relatedly, for effective implementation of Operation *Timbang* Plus, standard and appropriate weighing scales (with regular calibration and maintenance) and height boards should be procured. Implementation must be accompanied by appropriate development of the skills of volunteers who take these vital measurements. A priority for the first 1,000 days of life is to include adolescent girls in nutrition surveillance and to develop the capacity of health workers to assess maternal weight gain during pregnancy and act on its interpretation.

A local nutrition information system that is linked to the national system will provide LGUs with access to their own data. They need to be enabled to manage data and be responsive to the information provided as well as to seek and obtain assistance if the needed response is beyond their capacities. Overall, national-level information systems could be streamlined and made more efficient to trigger timely and facilitative action.

NOTES

1. *Stunting* reflects chronic undernutrition, a consequence of a cumulative process that starts in pregnancy and continues in infancy and early childhood, as repeated episodes of illness (such as diarrhea, malaria, or acute respiratory infection), combined with insufficient dietary intake, cause a child's growth to falter. It is measured by height-for-age (or length-for-age). Children whose height-for-age (or length-for-age) is more than 2 standard deviations below the median of the reference population are considered short for their age and are classified as moderately or severely stunted. Those whose height-for-age (or length-for-age) is more than 3 standard deviations below the median are classified as severely stunted. Height growth and brain development that are not achieved during the first 1,000 days of life (from conception to two years of age) are largely irrecoverable and are associated with measurable negative consequences for health, cognition, productivity, and income across the life course.
2. *Underweight*, low weight-for-age, is the least specific and most difficult indicator to interpret. Underweight can be the result of small body size (stunting) or small body mass (wasting).
3. *Wasting*, measured by weight-for-height (or weight-for-length), describes the recent or current severe process leading to significant weight loss, usually a consequence of acute starvation or severe disease. It is a preferred indicator for use in emergency situations such as famine.
4. Regional prevalence is from the 2015 Updating Survey (FNRI 2015).
5. Salt iodization; multiple micronutrient supplementation in pregnancy, including iron and folate; calcium supplementation in pregnancy; energy-protein supplementation in pregnancy; vitamin A supplementation in childhood; zinc supplementation in childhood; breastfeeding promotion; complementary feeding education; and management of severe acute malnutrition.
6. The estimates account only for individual returns through improved health, education, and cognition, not for market effects. The estimates also assume that, once people accrue education and health, they will be valued in the labor market.

7. In terms of the quantity (number of feedings) and quality (number of different types of food).
8. The agencies on the Governing Board are the Department of Health, Department of Agriculture, Department of the Interior and Local Government, Department of Education, Department of Social Work and Development, Department of Trade and Industry, Department of Labor and Employment, Department of Science and Technology, Department of Budget and Management, and National Economic Development Authority.

REFERENCES

FNRI (Food and Nutrition Research Institute). 2015. *2015 Updating Survey Results.* Taguig City: Department of Science and Technology, FNRI.

FNRI (Food and Nutrition Research Institute). 2018. *Expanded National Nutrition Survey: 2018 Results.* Taguig City: Department of Science and Technology, FNRI.

FNRI (Food and Nutrition Research Institute). 2019. *Expanded National Nutrition Survey: 2019 Results.* Taguig City: Department of Science and Technology, FNRI.

NEDA (National Economic Development Authority). 2017. *Philippine Development Plan 2017–2022.* Pasig City: NEDA.

NNC (National Nutrition Council). 2017. *Philippine Plan of Action for Nutrition 2017–2022: A Call to Urgent Action for Filipinos and Its Leadership.* Taguig City: NNC, Department of Health.

PSA (Philippine Statistical Authority). 2015. *Family Income and Expenditure Survey 2015.* Quezon City: PSA.

UNICEF (United Nations Children's Fund). 2017. *The Economic Consequences of Undernutrition in the Philippines: A Damage Assessment Report.* New York: UNICEF.

Abbreviations

AIDS	acquired immunodeficiency syndrome
ARMM	Autonomous Region in Muslim Mindanao
BARMM	Bangsamoro Autonomous Region in Muslim Mindanao
BCG	Bacillus Calmette–Guérin
BHW	Barangay Health Worker
BMI	body mass index
BNS	Barangay Nutrition Scholar
CALABARZON	Cavite, Laguna, Batangas, Rizal, and Quezon
CAR	Cordillera Administrative Region
CCM	cultural consensus modeling
CCT	conditional cash transfer
CHEF	care, health, environment, and food
CLHNS	Cebu Longitudinal Health and Nutrition Survey
CoRD	cost of the recommended diet
DOH	Department of Health
DOST	Department of Science and Technology
DSWD	Department of Social Welfare and Development
DTP	diphtheria, tetanus, pertussis
e-DCS	electronic data collection system
EED	environmental enteric dysfunction
EMR	electronic medical record
ENNS	Expanded National Nutrition Survey
EPI	Expanded Program on Immunization
FDS	family development session
FHSIS	Field Health Services Information System
FIES	Family Income and Expenditure Survey
FNRI	Food and Nutrition Research Institute
GDP	gross domestic product
HAZ	height-for-age *Z* score
HCI	Human Capital Index
HDDS	household dietary diversity score
HFIAS	household food insecurity access status
HIV	human immunodeficiency virus
ICP	International Comparison Program

IMCI	integrated management of childhood illness
IQ	intelligence quotient
IUGR	intrauterine growth restriction
IYCF	infant and young child feeding
LGU	local government unit
MCCT	modified conditional cash transfer
MIMAROPA	Occidental Mindoro, Oriental Mindoro, Marinduque, Romblon, and Palawan
MNAO	municipal nutrition action officer
NCR	National Capital Region (Metro Manila)
NDHS	National Demographic and Health Survey
NEDA	National Economic and Development Authority
NGO	nongovernmental organization
NNC	National Nutrition Council
NNS	National Nutrition Survey
OPT	Operation *Timbang* (also OPT Plus, Operation *Timbang* Plus)
PIDS	Philippine Institute for Development Studies
PIMAM	Philippine Integrated Management of Acute Malnutrition
PPAN	Philippine Plan of Action for Nutrition
RCP	relative calorie price
RCT	randomized control trial
RDD	regression discontinuity design
SDG	Sustainable Development Goal
SOCCSKSARGEN	South Cotabato, Cotabato, Sultan Kudarat, Sarangani, and General Santos
SWS	Social Weather Stations
TRAIN	Tax Reform for Acceleration and Inclusion
UNICEF	United Nations Children's Fund
VAD	vitamin A deficiency
WASH	water, sanitation, and hygiene
WFP	World Food Programme
WHO	World Health Organization

1 The Country Context

INTRODUCTION

The Philippines is situated in Southeast Asia in the Western Pacific Ocean, on a large archipelago composed of more than 7,100 islands and spanning a total area of 300,000 square kilometers (map 1.1). These tropical islands are broadly categorized into three geographic areas: Luzon in the north, Visayas, and the large southern island of Mindanao. The islands and groups are divided into administrative classes of 17 regions, 81 provinces, 146 cities, 1,488 municipalities, and 42,046 barangays, the smallest political unit. The Philippines is a democratic republic with a president, governed through its executive, legislative, and judicial branches. It is highly decentralized, such that local government units impose taxes, enact legislation, and deliver services.

POPULATION AND DEMOGRAPHY

One of the most populous countries in the world, the Philippines had a population of 106 million in 2018 and is still growing annually at a rate of 1.4 percent. The population is young, with an average life expectancy of 71 years. The country has a fertility rate of 2.7, the highest among its regional peers, such that even as that rate declines, the population will continue to grow rapidly. The population pyramid shows a very bottom-heavy demographic (figure 1.1). With a young population and a high fertility rate, the Philippines remains in the early phases of the demographic transition, far from realizing its demographic dividend. Only 5 percent of the population is over age 65, while 31 percent is under age 15. The Philippines does not yet face the risks of a rapidly aging population that are challenging China, Thailand, and Vietnam.

Population density has almost quadrupled since the 1960s, from 91.1 persons per square kilometer to 358.7 persons per square kilometer in 2018. The population is distributed largely unevenly across regions, however. According to the 2015 Population Census, more than half of the population resides in Luzon (PSA 2015). In 2015 population density was 20,785 persons per square kilometer in the National Capital Region and 71,263 persons per square kilometer in the country's capital, Manila, followed by the CALABARZON region (870 per

MAP 1.1
The Philippines

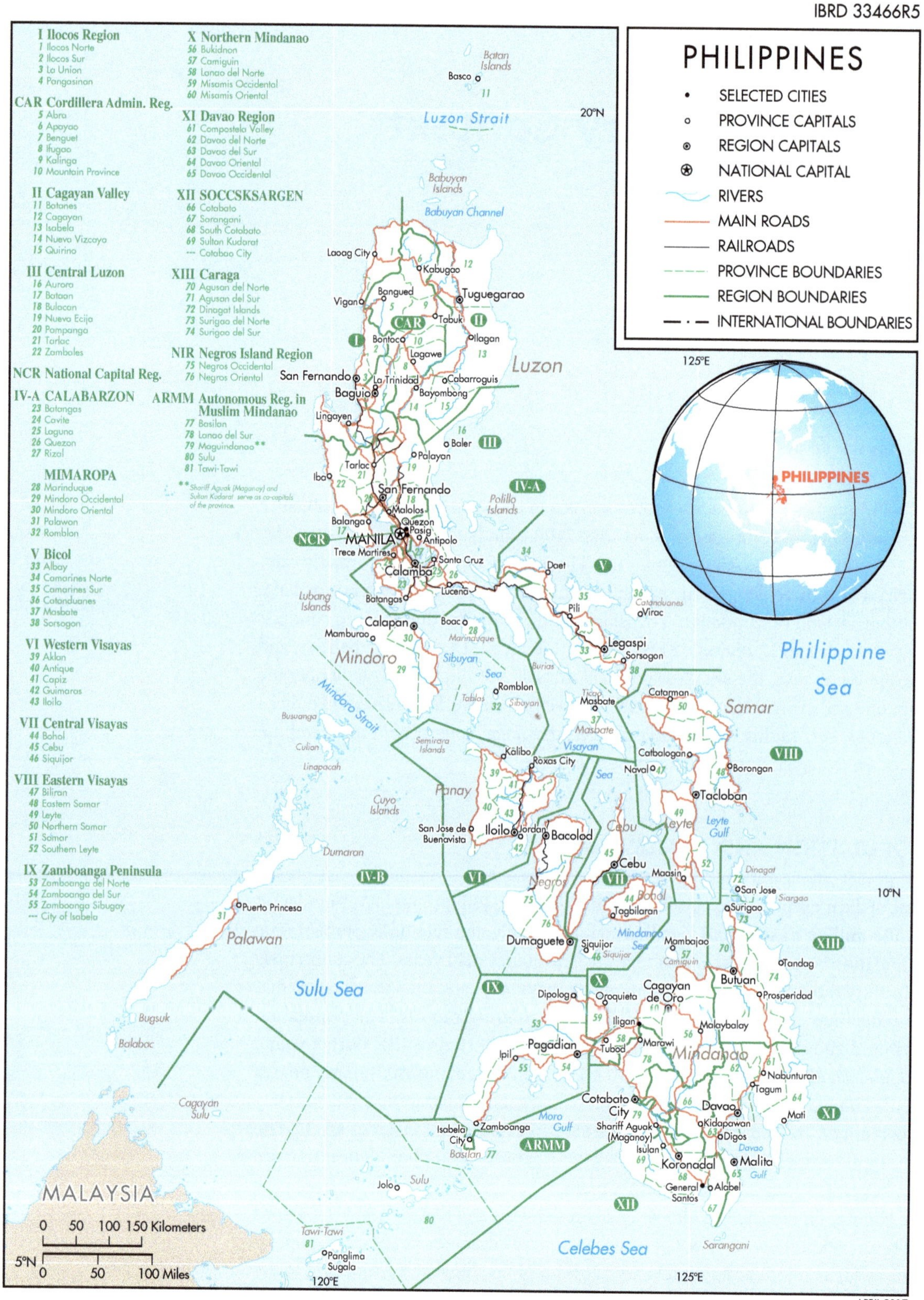

Source: World Bank.

FIGURE 1.1

Population pyramid of the Philippines, 2015

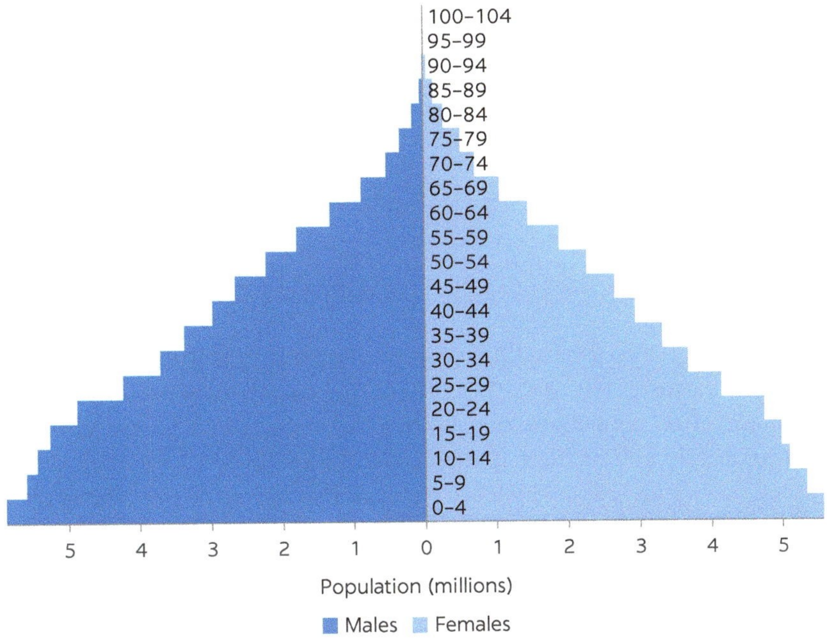

Source: UNDESA 2019.

square kilometer), directly around Metro Manila, Central Visayas (578 per square kilometer), which contains Metropolitan Cebu, and Central Luzon (512 per square kilometer). In contrast, the landlocked, mountainous Cordillera Administrative Region is the least densely populated region, at 87 persons per square kilometer. Other regions are also sparsely populated: the islands comprising MIMAROPA (100 per square kilometer), the Autonomous Region in Muslim Mindanao (ARMM) (103 per square kilometer), and Cagayan Valley (116 per square kilometer).

With rapid urbanization and migration, Filipinos are roughly evenly split between urban and rural areas. The Philippines has 33 highly urbanized cities, four of which have a population of more than 1 million. Most of these are located in Luzon: Quezon City (2.9 million), Manila (1.7 million), and Caloocan City (1.6 million). Davao City in Mindanao has a population of more than 1.6 million, while Cebu City in the Visayas has a population of about 900,000.

Ethnic minorities and cultures are found throughout the country, including Muslim ethnic groups and non-Muslim indigenous peoples. In 2010 indigenous peoples made up approximately 10–15 percent of the total population. The dominant ethnic groups include the Tagalog (28 percent), Cebuano (13 percent), Ilocano (9 percent), Bisaya (7.6 percent), Ilonggo (7.5 percent), and Bikol (6 percent). Members of Muslim groups constitute about 5 percent of the total population. Mindanao has the highest number of Muslims, at 24 million, while 90 percent of the population in the ARMM are Muslims.

For most of its history as a nation, the Philippines has been affected by internal unrest rooted partly in disputes over ancestral land, system inequities, and religion, particularly the protracted conflict in the southern region. In recent years, government efforts, with the support of the international community, have accelerated the prospects for peace and sustainable development in the region. In 2019 the ARMM was abolished, and the in Muslim Mindanao (BARMM) was formed through ratification of the Bangsamoro Organic Law. This change was the culmination of several years of peace talks between the Philippine government and several autonomist groups, which called for creating a region with more powers devolved from the national government. The Bangsamoro government is currently in transition until 2022.

CLIMATE

The Philippines has a varied topography consisting mostly of mountainous terrain and coastal lowlands. With 18,000 kilometers of shoreline, almost all major cities and more than half of all municipalities are coastal. Approximately half of the population (50 million people) reside in these coastal, low-lying areas, which are particularly vulnerable to storm surges and floods.

The country is highly exposed to natural disasters year-round, owing to its position in the Pacific and close to the equator. The islands are located within the "Ring of Fire" between the Eurasian and Pacific tectonic plates, and earthquakes and volcanoes pose serious risks to the safety of the populace. Frequent tropical storms, deadly typhoons, earthquakes, and, recently, volcanic eruptions have devastated communities and fueled poverty. The Philippines ranks third among all countries with the highest disaster risks worldwide, according to the *World Risk Report 2018*, with an index value of 25.14 percent (World Economic Forum 2018). It is also extremely vulnerable to climate change due to sensitive ecological systems (including reefs and marine fauna), large numbers of coastal populations, and exposure to frequent weather extremes (UNDRR 2019).

Over time, the Philippines has observed upward trends of maximum temperature and precipitation. In recent years, it has also recorded extreme weather events. Among countries affected by natural disasters over the past 20 years, the Philippines ranks as the fourth hardest hit, recording 304 disaster events from 2000 to 2019 that affected 149 million people (UNDRR and CRED 2020). Since 2000, more than 25,000 people have lost their lives as a result of natural disasters, and the country has suffered economic losses of more than US$14 billion (USAID 2014). In 2009 Typhoons Ketsana (known locally as Typhoon Ondoy) and Parma (Typhoon Pepeng) hit Luzon, severely affecting 9.3 million people and incurring US$4.4 billion in damages (World Bank 2011). In 2013 Typhoon Haiyan (Typhoon Yolanda), one of the most powerful tropical cyclones recorded, caused massive destruction when it made landfall in the Visayas, killing an estimated 8,000 people and displacing 4 million more (Oxfam 2014). Climate change is expected to worsen extreme weather events, depress agricultural and fishery yields, and wipe out vital ecosystems.

The economic and social impacts of climate change, such as sea-level rise, droughts, floods, and storms, are projected to be massive for the country. Changing climactic conditions may cascade to depress agricultural and fisheries production, thus limiting the availability of food and driving food prices and consumption (Duante et al. 2015). Climate change is expected to have a direct effect on agricultural productivity, livestock, and fisheries production by affecting cropping calendars, yield quality, and yield levels (OECD 2017). Extreme weather may have an indirect effect by leading to the proliferation of pests on agricultural land and driving the incidence of diseases. Rising sea levels could also negatively affect the land available for crops, increase the risk of flooding and storm damage, and lead to the salinization of coastal croplands.

The Philippines acknowledges these risks and since 2007 has prioritized climate change adaptation and mitigation policies. The National Climate Change Action Plan, 2011–2028 outlines climate change priorities related to food security, water efficiency, environmental and ecological stability, human security, climate-friendly industries and services, sustainable energy, and knowledge and capacity development. However, it does not identify pathways for each economic sector to mainstream these priorities.

ECONOMY

The Philippine economy is often described as resilient. Beset by unstable macroeconomic and political conditions over the period 1980–97, the economy grew, on average, just 2.5 percent per year, far below the average of 4.6 percent achieved by the country's structural peers and 7.6 percent by its regional peers. Structural reforms and a commitment to macroeconomic stability helped the Philippines achieve relatively high economic growth after 1998. Favorable domestic and external conditions spurred economic growth, and, since 2010, the Philippine economy has been one of the fastest-growing economies in the region, with average annual growth of gross domestic product (GDP) at 6.4 percent. Growth rates during 2010–17 were similar for all three major island groups, including Mindanao. The Gini index also dropped from 47 in 2006 to 44 in 2015, as incomes of the bottom 40 percent of the population grew at a rate of 5.1 percent from 2012 to 2015.

The country's performance on poverty reduction also has picked up in recent years. In 2018 16.6 percent of the population lived below the national poverty line, a significant drop from 23.3 percent in 2015. The most rapid declines in poverty incidence took place after 2012, while the relative magnitude of poverty and the absolute numbers of poor only started to decline in recent years. In contrast to GDP growth rates, poverty rates vary greatly across regions. In Metro Manila, as little as 2.2 percent of the population live below the poverty line. Poverty rates are below the national rate in most of Luzon. In ARMM, however, as many as 61.8 percent are poor.

A striking trend is the slow progress in eliminating poverty relative to regional comparators. Based on the international poverty line of US$1.90 per day, poverty incidence declined 2 to 2.5 percent per year in China, Indonesia, and Vietnam, while only dropping roughly 1 percent per year in the Philippines.

More significant gains have been made on human development: between 1990 and 2018, life expectancy at birth increased 4.7 years. Average years of schooling also increased 2.8 years, and expected years of schooling increased 1.9 years. In the same period, the country's gross national income increased about 140.6 percent. The United Nations human development index ranks the country at 0.712, putting it in the category of high human development (UNDP 2019). Despite these indicators, the country is still below the average ranking of 0.750 for countries in the category of high human development and below the average of 0.741 for countries in the East Asia and Pacific region.

Despite economic growth, poverty reduction, shared prosperity, and improved human development, malnutrition is still widespread in the Philippines. In 2018 the national prevalence of stunting in children under five was 30.3 percent (4 million children), a rate considered very high by the World Health Organization and the United Nations Children's Fund and above the average of 25 percent for low- and middle-income countries. Additionally, among the same group of children, the prevalence of excessive weight-for-height has increased from 3.9 percent in 2015 to 4.0 percent in 2018, an increase of 0.03 percent per year. The growth of this double burden is a serious concern that hinders the country's potential for social and economic development.

In 2020 the Philippines experienced a series of unprecedented events. Natural disasters, such as the eruption of Taal Volcano at the beginning of the year and several powerful typhoons thereafter, alongside the rise of COVID-19 infections forced the economy to a near halt due to severe disruptions in several sectors. The economy contracted 0.2 percent year-on-year in the first quarter of 2020, the first contraction in more than two decades and a sharp reversal from the 5.7 percent growth over the same period in 2019. This economic contraction in 2020 is likely to cause an increase in poverty despite government efforts to mitigate the impact of the COVID-19 outbreak.

OBJECTIVE AND ORGANIZATION OF THE REPORT

This report is intended to inform the nutrition policies and programs of the government of the Philippines through evidence-based research. To that end, it assesses and analyzes the state of maternal and child nutrition and development and identifies gaps and opportunities in the government's nutrition and nutrition-related programs and policies that are aimed at or could contribute to reducing childhood undernutrition.

This report is divided into 10 chapters. Chapter 1 describes the country context, including progress on human development outcomes. Chapter 2 analyzes nutrition in the country. Chapter 3 highlights why nutrition matters and explains why the Philippine government should prioritize nutrition as part of its development agenda. Chapter 4 assesses the determinants and causes of childhood undernutrition in the country. Chapter 5 describes the critical role of agriculture in nutrition and how the agriculture sector can contribute to improvements in nutritional outcomes. Chapter 6 analyzes the knowledge, beliefs, and practices of health workers and caregivers with reference to childhood stunting. Chapters 7 and 8 assesses the synergies and opportunities for nutrition in the health sector and the *Pantawid Pamilyang Pilipino* Program, respectively. Chapter 9 analyzes the role of local government units in tackling undernutrition. Chapter 10 then assesses the opportunities to improve data for nutrition policy and programs.

LIMITATION OF THE STUDY

A major limitation of the study is the lack of opportunity to analyze in detail the role of the water, sanitation, and hygiene (WASH) sector and opportunities that it might present for tackling undernutrition. Improved access to high-quality

WASH during pregnancy and childbirth can reduce maternal and newborn mortality and morbidity by lowering rates of infection and sepsis. Healthy WASH conditions and behaviors in a young child's feeding and play areas can prevent diarrhea and infections and are likely to reduce environmental enteric dysfunction (EED), which is associated with (and a likely cause of) chronic undernutrition (World Vision 2018). EED is a chronic infection of the small intestine caused by extended exposure to fecal pathogens. By reducing a child's ability to absorb nutrients, EED can lead to undernutrition and stunting of growth. It is greatly exacerbated by unhygienic environments in which infants and young children live and grow.

REFERENCES

Duante, Charmaine, Carmina Cuarteros, Glen Gironella, Eldridge Ferrer, Cecilia Acuin, and Mario Capanzana. 2015. "Impacts of Climate Shocks on Caloric Intake of Filipinos." Food and Nutrition Institute, Department of Science and Technology, United Nations Food and Agriculture Organization, Rome. http://www.fao.org/3/a-br337e.pdf.

OECD (Organisation for Economic Co-operation and Development). 2017. "Agricultural Policies in the Philippines." OECD Food and Agricultural Review, OECD Publishing, Paris. https://doi.org/10.1787/9789264269088-en.

Oxfam. 2014. "Rebuilding Better for Coconut Farmers, Post-Haiyan Reconstruction in the Philippines." Joint Agency Briefing Note, Oxfam and Fair Trade Alliance, Boston, MA. www.oxfam.org/sites/www.oxfam.org/files/bn-coconut-livelihoods-philippines-recovery-120214-en.pdf.

PSA (Philippine Statistics Authority). 2015. *2015 Census of Population.* Quezon City: PSA.

UNDESA (United Nations Department of Economic and Social Affairs). 2019. *World Population Prospects 2019.* Online Edition. Rev. 1. New York: United Nations, Population Division.

UNDP (United Nations Development Programme). 2019. *Human Development Report 2019: Beyond Income, Beyond Averages, Beyond Today: Inequalities in Human Development in the 21st Century.* New York: UNDP. http://hdr.undp.org/en/content/human-development-report-2019.

UNDRR (United Nations Office for Disaster Risk Reduction). 2019. *Disaster Risk Reduction in the Philippines: Status Report 2019.* Bangkok: UNDRR Regional Office for Asia and the Pacific.

UNDRR (United Nations Office for Disaster Risk Reduction) and CRED (Centre for Research on the Epidemiology of Disasters). 2020. *Human Cost of Disasters: An Overview of the Last 20 Years (2000–2019).* Bangkok: UNDRR, Regional Office for Asia and the Pacific.

USAID (United States Agency for International Development). 2014. "*Disaster Assistance and Resilience Building: Factsheet Philippines.*" USAID, Washington, DC. https://www.usaid.gov/philippines/fact-sheets/disaster-assistance-and-resilience-building.

World Bank. 2011. "*Philippines—Typhoons Ondoy and Pepeng: Post-Disaster Needs Assessment—Sector Reports.*" World Bank, Washington, DC. https://openknowledge.worldbank.org/handle/10986/2778.

World Economic Forum. 2018. *The Global Risks Report 2018,* 3d ed. Geneva: World Economic Forum.

World Vision. 2018. "Ensuring Children Survive and Thrive through Effective Integrated Action." BabyWASH Advocacy Brief, World Vision, March 19, 2018. https://www.wvi.org/babywash/publication/babywash-advocacy-brief.

2 The Face of Child Malnutrition in the Philippines

ABSTRACT In recent decades, rates of both stunting and wasting—the two principal markers of undernutrition—have fallen only slightly in the Philippines. Nearly one in three children under five years of age is stunted (30.3 percent). Rates of stunting are worse in rural areas and for boys; they are sharply higher for the poorest Filipinos. Although undernutrition rates vary substantially across municipalities, they remain high throughout the country. Micronutrient deficiencies are also frequently recorded, notably in iron as well as in vitamin A and zinc. Even the gradual (and modest) improvements in the nutritional status of Filipino children achieved in recent years are now threatened by disruptions caused by the COVID-19 pandemic. Wasting and micronutrient malnutrition rates are expected to rise, along with child morbidity and mortality. Unless immediate action is taken, millions of Filipino children who survive these deficits will suffer the consequences of poor school performance and low productivity as adults.

PATTERNS OF NUTRITION IN THE PHILIPPINES

For nearly 30 years, rates of both wasting and stunting have been nearly flat. Figure 2.1 shows undernutrition trends in the Philippines for children under age five. Wasting indicates that a child has low weight for his or her age and is a sign of acute, short-term malnutrition. The prevalence of wasting in 2019 (5.8 percent) was similar to what it was 20 years previously. Stunting, meanwhile, indicates that a child is, loosely speaking, short for his or her age. The rate of stunting fell through the early 2000s but has remained almost flat since then. The rate of stunting recorded for 2019 (28.8 percent) was only slightly lower than the 2008 level. Globally, one in five children under the age of five is stunted (21.9 percent, about 149 million children), which represents a 10 percent drop from 165.8 million children in 2012. This progress is too slow to achieve the 2025 global nutrition target on stunting (that is, around 100 million children). Globally, the prevalence of wasting was 7.3 percent in 2018, compared with 5 percent in 2012; again, the world is not on course to reach the 2025 global target: to reduce wasting and hold the level below 5 percent. Box 2.1 describes these effects of undernutrition.

FIGURE 2.1

Malnutrition trends in the Philippines for children under age five, 1989–2019

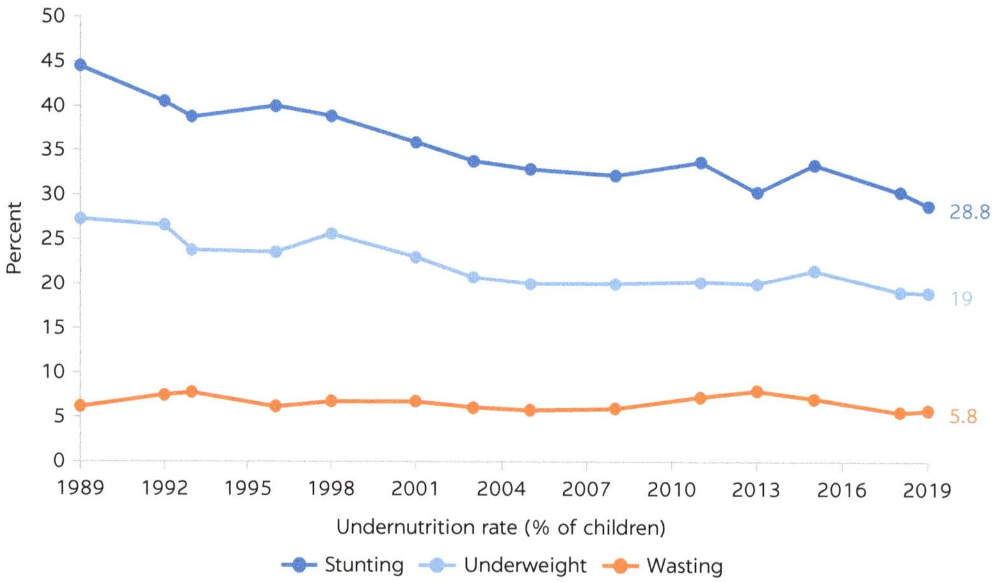

Source: National Nutrition Survey reports from the Food and Nutrition Research Institute.

BOX 2.1

What exactly is malnutrition?

The term "malnutrition" refers to a deviation from optimal nutritional status and includes both undernutrition and overnutrition.

Undernutrition, the focus of this report, refers to a state of nutritional deficiency and presents the most serious risks to health and development when experienced by young children and by women during prepregnancy, pregnancy, and lactation. There are various measures of undernutrition,[a] but stunting in young children (low height-for-age in children under five years of age) is the type of undernutrition of most concern for policy makers.

Stunting results from chronic undernutrition and indicates a failure to attain the height expected for a healthy child. Height growth and brain development not achieved during the first 1,000 days of life (from conception to two years of age) is largely irrecoverable and is associated with measurable negative consequences for health, cognition, productivity, and income across the life course (Horton and Hoddinot 2014; Victora et al. 2008).

Wasting, measured by weight-for-height, describes a recent or current severe process leading to significant weight loss, usually a consequence of acute starvation or severe diseases. It is the preferred indicator in emergency situations such as famine.

Underweight, low weight-for-age, is the least specific and most difficult indicator to interpret. A person can be underweight as the result of small body size (stunting) or small body mass (wasting).

Micronutrient deficiencies occur when there is insufficient dietary intake, insufficient absorption, or suboptimal use or excessive loss of vitamins or minerals. Globally, the most critical deficiencies for which data are available are deficiencies in vitamin A, iron, iodine, zinc, and folic acid, which are vital for immune function, organ development, and growth. Micronutrient deficiencies can lead to many health problems.

Overnutrition represents an oversupply of nutrients (usually macronutrients) relative to the body's physiological needs. Overnutrition is often measured as high body mass index (BMI), and a

continued

Box 2.1, *continued*

person is considered *overweight* if his or her BMI is equal to or greater than 25 kilograms per square meter and *obese* if his or her BMI is equal to or greater than 30.[b] Elevated BMI is a major risk factor for cardiovascular diseases, diabetes, musculoskeletal disorders, and some cancers.

a. Additional measures of undernutrition at the population level include micronutrient deficiencies among subgroups of adults and children, such as iron-deficiency anemia, iodine deficiency, and vitamin A deficiency.
b. BMI is calculated by dividing weight in kilograms by height in meters squared. BMI is a screening tool that provides the most useful population measure of increased health risks due to excess body fat. However, it is not a perfect measure at the individual level because it does not measure body composition—that is, the ratio of fat to muscle. Hence, the index can be misleading for individuals with a high proportion of muscle tissue, which pushes up their weight. Nonetheless, BMI is highly correlated with the gold standards of body composition measurement and, at the population level, is a reliable indicator of overnutrition.

BOX 2.2

Why do we focus on stunting and what does it mean?

Stunting has become the leading single measure of child malnutrition used worldwide. Stunting captures whether a child's height-for-age is more than 2 standard deviations below the median of a reference population. Linear growth retardation and stunting are *associated with* the consequences of child malnutrition: delayed child development, reduced earnings in adulthood, and increased risk of developing chronic diseases. Stunting is not, however, itself a direct *cause* of these outcomes. Rather stunting is a marker that indicates a higher probability of the underlying conditions that cause poor outcomes. This is an important distinction for two reasons. First, an individual child who is short and correctly categorized as stunted does not necessarily suffer from undernutrition. Stunting is much more suitable as a marker of undernutrition at the population level than as a definite identifier of poor nutrition at the individual level. Second, merely boosting the height of children will not improve outcomes. (Administering doses of growth hormone, for example, would probably increase height but not have an impact on long-term outcomes.)

The dramatic gradient in stunting rates by household wealth shows how undernutrition can perpetuate unequal opportunities (box 2.2). Figures 2.2, 2.3, and 2.4 identify undernutrition as moderate (underweight), chronic (stunting), or acute (wasting).[1] As shown in figure 2.2, children from poorer households are far more likely to be stunted than children from wealthier households: 11.4 percent of children in the wealthiest 20 percent are stunted compared with 42.4 percent of children in the poorest quintile. As discussed in chapter 3 of this report, children who are stunted at a young age are less likely to secure well-paid jobs as adults. Their children are also more likely to suffer from inadequate nutrition, as poverty is transmitted across generations.

The broad research on malnutrition has demonstrated that the most critical period for long-term growth starts at conception and continues through the first two years of life—often described as the first 1,000 days of life. The overall rates of stunting for all children under age five hide the fact that children fall behind during the first 1,000 days. Figure 2.3 shows stunting rates for more detailed ages. Stunting is recorded in 11 percent of infants (from birth to 5 months of age) and 14 percent of infants during the next 6–11 months of life. For children in their second year of life, the stunting rate jumps to 31 percent and remains roughly flat in the following years.

FIGURE 2.2

Rate of stunting, underweight, and wasting in children under age five in the Philippines, by wealth quintile, 2019

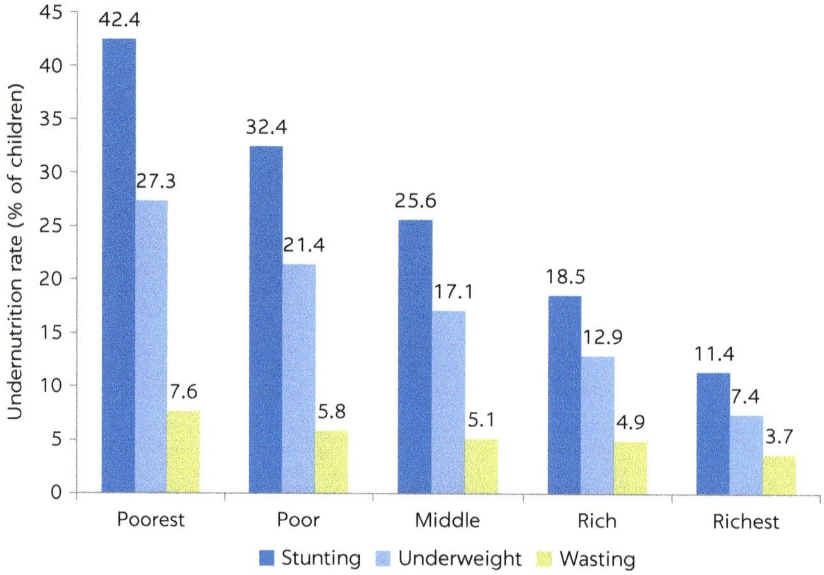

Source: FNRI 2019.

FIGURE 2.3

Rate of stunting, underweight, and wasting in children under age five in the Philippines, by age group, 2019

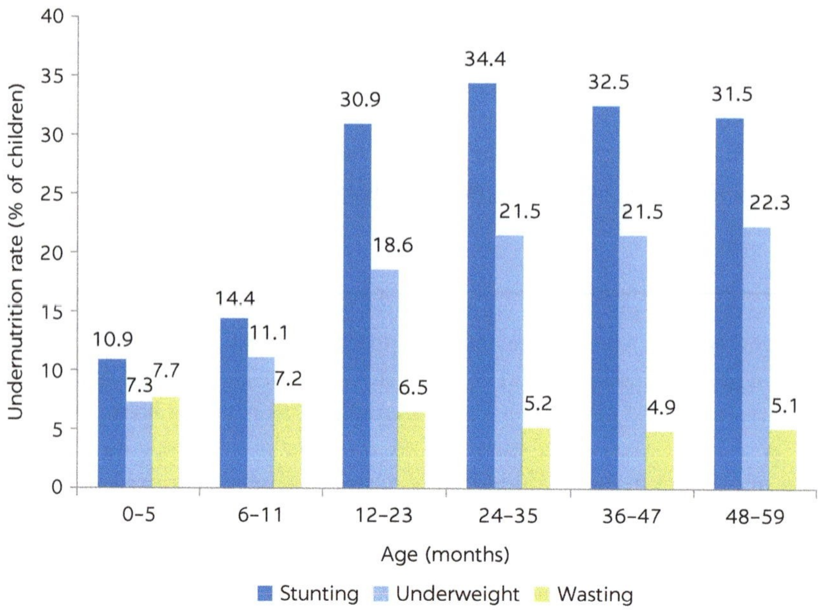

Source: FNRI 2019.

There is little difference in rates of stunting by gender. Rates of stunting are slightly higher for boys than for girls (figure 2.4). But marked geographic disparities are observed. Stunting rates are higher in rural areas (30 percent) than in urban areas (26 percent). Across regions, stunting rates are highest in the Bangsamoro Autonomous Region in Muslim Mindanao (BARMM) (45 percent) and lowest in Central Luzon (23 percent) (figure 2.5).

FIGURE 2.4

Rate of stunting, underweight, and wasting in children under age five in the Philippines, by setting (urban or rural) and gender, 2019

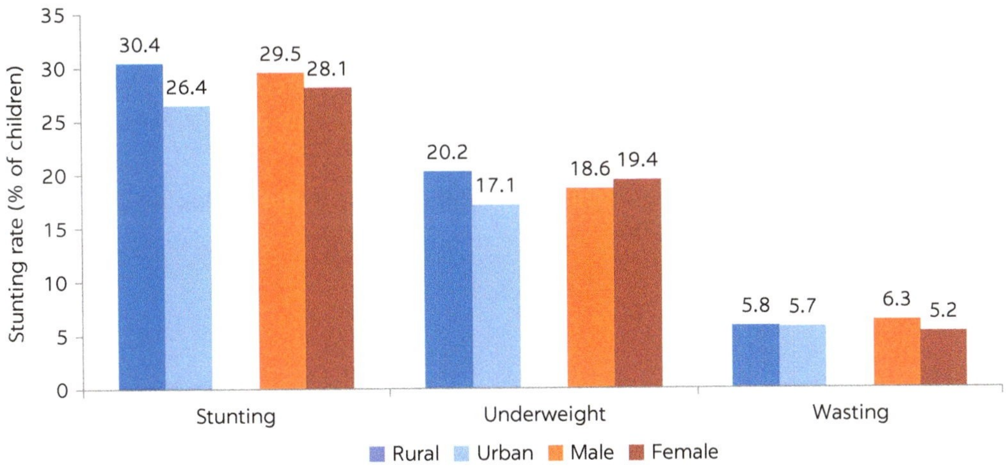

Source: FNRI 2019.

FIGURE 2.5

Rate of stunting in children under age five in the Philippines, by region, 2015

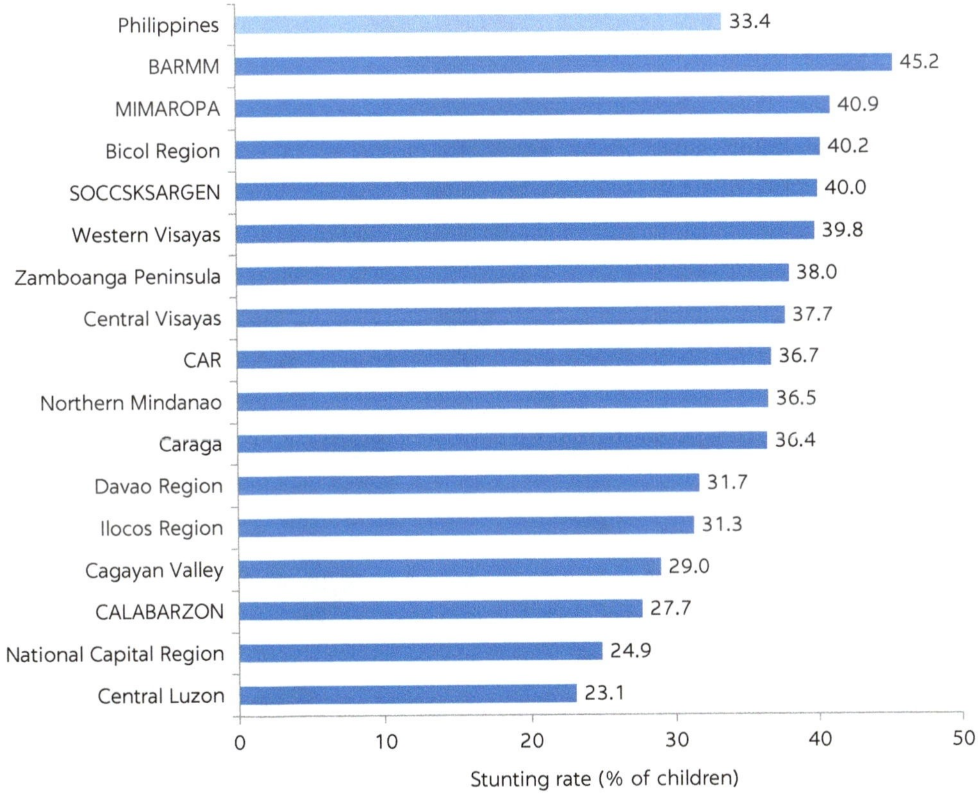

Source: FNRI 2015.
Note: BARMM = Bangsamoro Autonomous Region in Muslim Mindanao. CALABARZON = Cavite, Laguna, Batangas, Rizal, and Quezon. CAR = Cordillera Administrative Region. MIMAROPA = Occidental Mindoro, Oriental Mindoro, Marinduque, Romblon, and Palawan. SOCCSKSARGEN = South Cotabato, Cotabato, Sultan Kudarat, Sarangani, and General Santos.

Local-level estimates of stunting vary widely across the country and even within regions. The National Nutrition Survey provides the most reliable estimates of nutrition outcomes for the Philippines. The survey results can be used to produce national estimates on an annual basis and regional and provincial estimates every three years. For this report, additional estimates at the level of municipalities were produced through a statistical technique that combines data from the 2015 National Nutrition Survey and the 2015 Population Census (FNRI 2015; PSA 2015). These data are used to establish a model for predicting children's height and stunting status, based on the characteristics of the child, the household, and the community. Based on 2015 census data, the model is used to

MAP 2.1

Rate of stunting in children under age five in the Philippines, by municipality, 2015

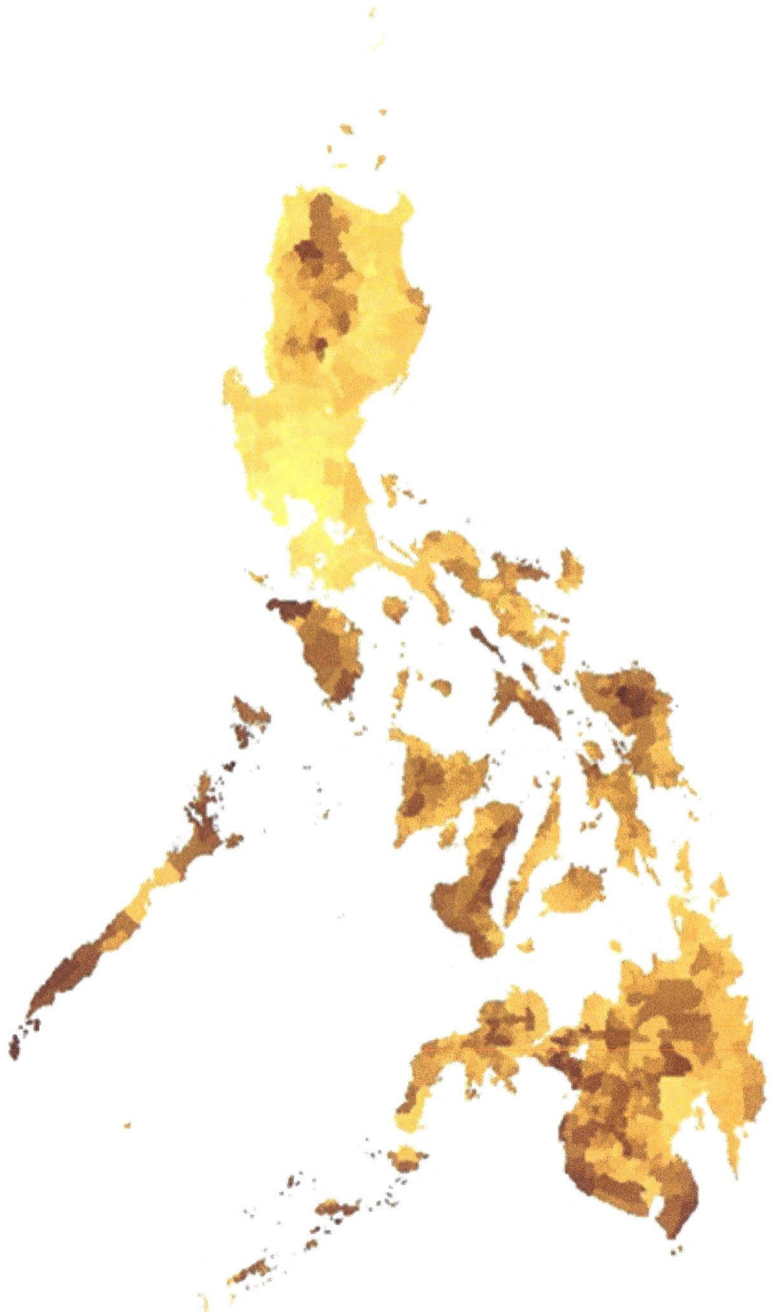

Sources: FNRI 2015; PSA 2015.
Note: The darker the color, the higher the stunting rate.

FIGURE 2.6

Rate of stunting in children under age five in the Philippines, by provincial poverty rate, 2015

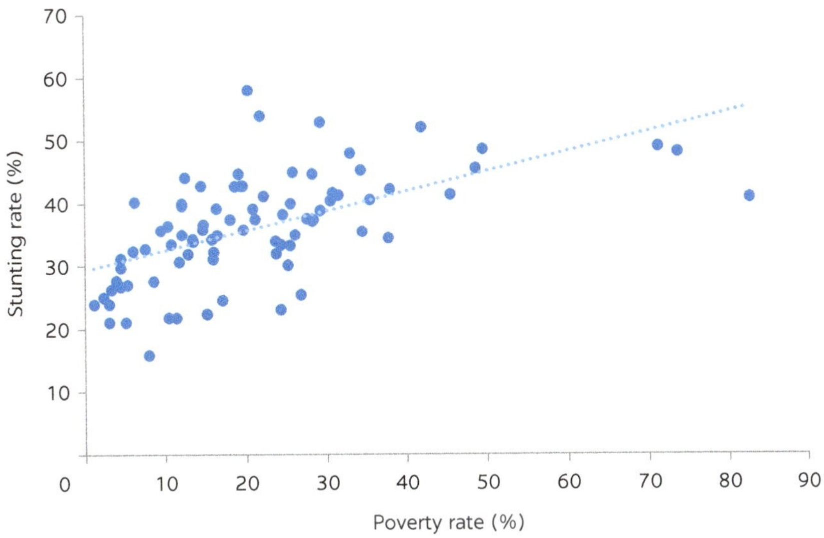

Sources: For stunting rates, FNRI 2015. For poverty rates, PSA 2019.

estimate the stunting status of all children in the Philippines. The estimates are then aggregated for provinces and municipalities using small area estimation, which is commonly used to estimate both poverty and undernutrition. While these figures involve some estimation error, they are useful in providing some basis for understanding the depth of undernutrition at the local level.[2]

High rates of stunting are found in many parts of the country (map 2.1). The lowest levels are in Metro Manila and Central Luzon. Throughout the rest of the country, there are pockets of the population with quite high levels of stunting—exceeding 40 percent of the population. The highest rates are found in parts of Western and Southern Mindanao, Mindoro, Negros, Palawan, Samar, and the far north of Luzon. Figure 2.6 shows a strong correlation ($r = 0.68$) between the poverty rate and the stunting rate at the provincial level.

Knowing the percentage of stunted children at the local level is a first step to understanding the spatial distribution of stunting. However, the percentage of stunted children does not reveal how many children might be stunted in a given location. Some locations have very small populations, and some have much larger populations. Map 2.2 shows both the percentage and the number of stunted children by municipality, indicating no correlation between the two.

NUTRITION IN THE PHILIPPINES IN INTERNATIONAL PERSPECTIVE

The country's rate of stunting is high not only for its level of income but also compared with the rates of most of its neighbors (figure 2.7). Other countries with similar levels of income have rates of stunting averaging around 20 percent. With stunting at 30 percent nationally, the Philippines is fifth among countries with the highest prevalence of stunting in the East Asia and Pacific region and among the 10 countries globally with the highest number of stunted children. In the region, China, the Republic of Korea, and Thailand all have much lower

MAP 2.2

Number and percentage of children under age five who are stunted in the Philippines, by municipality, 2015

Sources: The nutritional status of Filipino children is based on the National Nutrition Survey (FNRI 2015). The number of children is based on the 2015 Census of Population, conducted by the Philippine Statistics Authority (PSA 2015).
Note: The color indicates estimated stunting rates in municipalities; the darker the color, the higher the stunting rate. The height of the tall, shaded extruded blocks shows the number of stunted children in each municipality. The higher the block, the higher the number of stunting children.

levels of stunting. Indonesia is the only other large country in the region with a high level of stunting.

Many countries have achieved rapid declines in stunting. Globally, average stunting rates tend to decline as countries get richer, but the relationship is weak, suggesting the key role that policy decisions and other social factors play in the evolution of stunting over time. Some countries with stunting prevalence higher than 25 percent in 2000 have made remarkable progress. For example, stunting prevalence in Bolivia, Côte d'Ivoire, Ghana, Mongolia, and Peru has fallen more than 5 percent *per year* on average (figure 2.8). Within East Asia, performance has been varied. Vietnam has seen a large drop over time, while China and Thailand have built on earlier successes. Indonesia has experienced stagnation in malnutrition similar to the Philippines, while Malaysia has seen a slight increase over time and has a high level of stunting (21 percent) for its level of income.

INTRAUTERINE GROWTH RETARDATION AND LOW BIRTHWEIGHT

The prenatal equivalent of growth faltering is called intrauterine growth restriction (IUGR), which has been defined as poor fetal growth during pregnancy.

FIGURE 2.7

Prevalence of stunting worldwide, by region and country (latest available estimate)

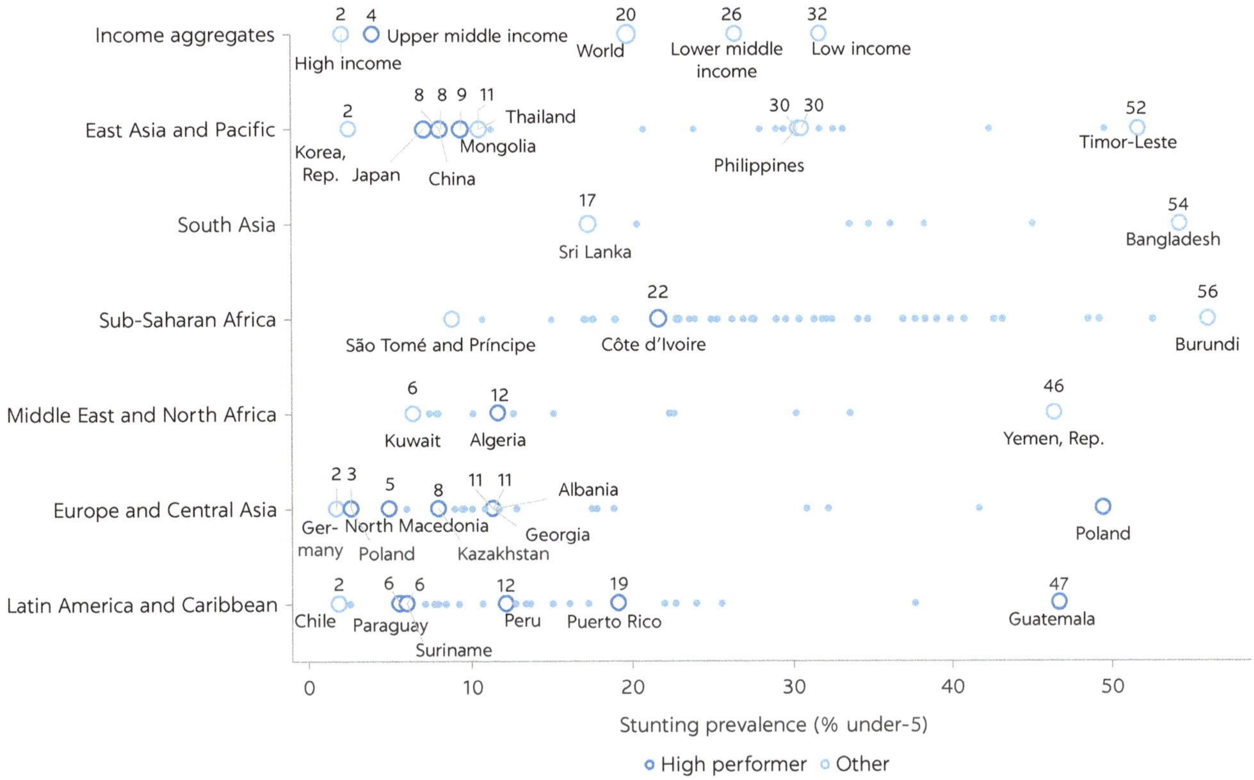

Sources: UNICEF, WHO, and World Bank Group 2020.
Note: Labeled countries have the highest and the lowest stunting rates in the region or have reduced stunting more than 6 percent per year (high performers). Data correspond to the year with the most recently available estimate for each country. The mean year for all estimates shown is 2014. The oldest estimate is for 2002, and the most recent estimates are for 2019.

IUGR is diagnosed through prenatal ultrasonic measurements or as a clinical definition applied to neonates born with attributes of malnutrition. IUGR has many causes, but it usually stems from inadequate maternal macronutrition and micronutrition before and during pregnancy. Competition for nutrients between the mother and the rapidly growing fetus (as in an adolescent pregnancy in a growing girl) is a widely known cause, as are repeated infections during pregnancy. The low birthweight that accompanies IUGR has serious consequences for immediate child survival in the neonatal and infant periods and serious consequences later in life, as it is associated with adult-onset diseases such as diabetes and coronary artery disease.

In the Philippines, the dramatic increase in institutional deliveries—from 28 percent in 1993 to 78 percent in 2017, according to the National Demographic and Health Survey (NDHS)—has enabled a better assessment of the prevalence of low birthweight among newborns (PSA 1993, 2017). From the 2017 NDHS, 84 percent of births covered by the survey had recorded birthweights, and 15 percent of these (14.5 percent of all births) had weights below 2,500 grams (the threshold for low birthweight). The prevalence of low birthweight was high among the following groups: (1) children of teenage mothers and mothers older than 35; (2) children of women who smoked during pregnancy; (3) children of women for whom this was not the first pregnancy (among firstborns) and, conversely, for whom this was the seventh or a subsequent pregnancy; and (4) children of women in the lower

FIGURE 2.8
Prevalence of stunting in selected countries, 2000–19

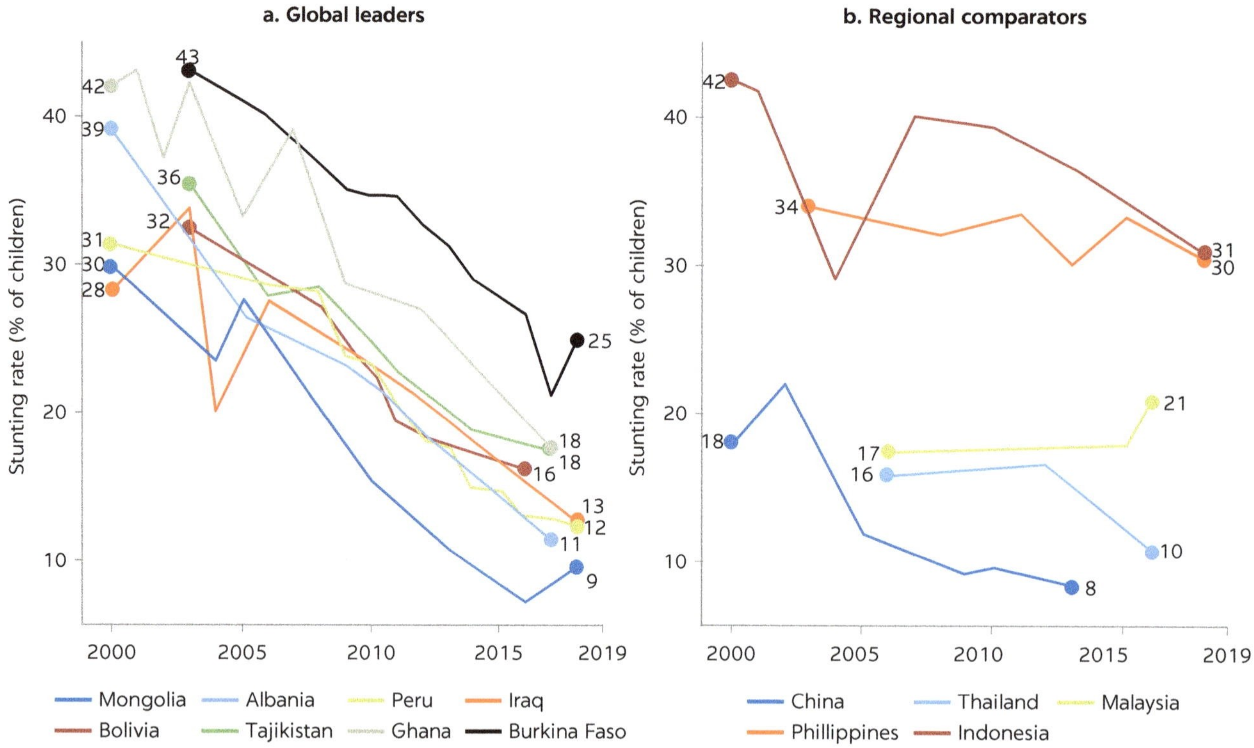

Sources: UNICEF, WHO, and World Bank Group 2020.
Note: Only countries with the following characteristics are considered "global leaders": (a) countries with stunting prevalence higher than 25% at the start of the period, (b) countries with at least three stunting estimates that cover more than a five-year interval between 2000 and 2019, and (c) countries with populations exceeding 1 million.>

wealth quintiles. There were also big differences by region, with the lowest prevalence for the National Capital Region (9.4 percent) and the Cordillera Administrative Region (8.7 percent), and the highest for Zamboanga Peninsula (20.8 percent), Davao Region (19.7 percent), and Cagayan Valley Region (19.0 percent). The NDHS, however, does not distinguish whether the low birthweight was due to small-for-gestational-age, prematurity, or other conditions not related to nutrition.

MICRONUTRIENT MALNUTRITION: THE "HIDDEN HUNGER"

"Hidden hunger" is a form of malnutrition caused by a lack of vitamins and minerals in the diet such as vitamin A, iron, zinc, folic acid, and iodine. Because these essential nutrients are required in very small amounts, they are called micronutrients. Collectively, micronutrient deficiencies are a leading cause of intellectual disability and preventable blindness in children and death of women during childbirth. They can limit a person's ability to learn, earn a living, or live a healthy life.

Anemia

Anemia is a condition in which blood has a lower-than-normal number of healthy red blood cells, which are responsible primarily for transporting oxygen from the lungs to all of the tissues in the body. During a state of anemia, the body does not receive enough of the oxygen-rich blood it needs for normal functions. The major causes of anemia include iron deficiency, hookworm infections, vitamin A deficiency, and malaria infections. Other notable causes include chronic infections, such as tuberculosis and human immunodeficiency virus, and genetic defects, including thalassemia and sickle cell disease. The most common type of anemia is iron-deficiency anemia, which results from a lack of iron in the body and is caused by blood loss, insufficient dietary intake, or poor absorption of iron from food. The consequences of iron deficiency and anemia can be dire, including impaired neurocognitive function in children, maternal mortality, and decreased work capacity in adults. Low birthweight, preterm birth, perinatal mortality, and neonatal mortality have been associated with maternal anemia.

In the Philippines, the most recent available data on anemia—the 2019 Expanded National Nutrition Survey (ENNS)—show that this marker of nutritional deficiency is still alarmingly high (FNRI 2019): 38 percent of infants 6–11 months old (down from 48 percent in 2018), 26 percent of children 12–23 months, 20 percent of pregnant women, and 12 percent of lactating women (figure 2.9). The very high rates of anemia among infants and young children probably reflect insufficient maternal stores of iron and inadequate iron content of complementary foods given to children in the first and second years of life. Throughout the first year, children depend on the iron transferred from their mothers during pregnancy and childbirth (especially immediately prior to deliberately delayed clamping of the umbilical cord) and in breast milk. A mother's inadequate supply of iron will affect the quality and quantity of that exchange.

Vitamin A deficiency

Vitamin A is an essential micronutrient that is required to maintain eye health, sustain normal cellular differentiation, develop (and maintain) the body's resistance to infections, and produce and reproduce red blood cells. Vitamin A deficiency (VAD) is usually a consequence of insufficient dietary consumption of foods rich in vitamin A (such as animal products or green leafy vegetables) and is often exacerbated by illness (for example, diarrhea, measles, and

FIGURE 2.9

Prevalence of anemia in the Philippines, by selected population groups, 2019

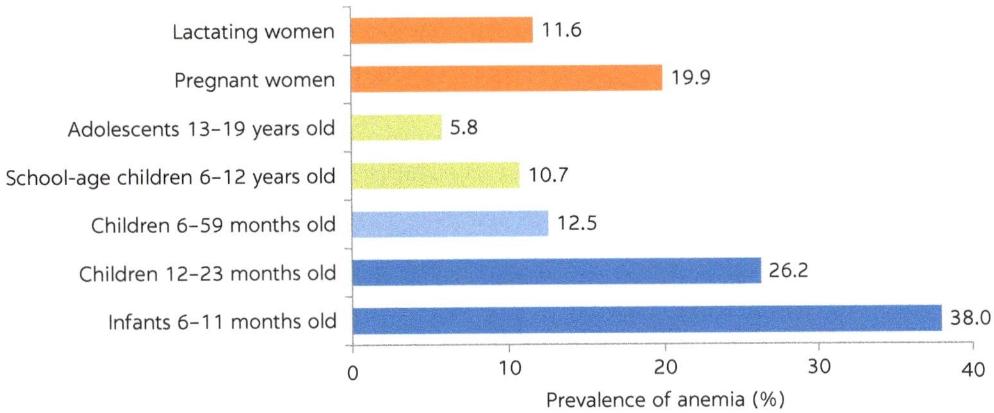

Source: FNRI 2019.

respiratory infections). VAD generally results in night blindness, severe anemia, wasting, reproductive and infectious morbidity, and increased risk of mortality.

According to the 2018 ENNS, nearly 17 percent of children ages 6–59 months were suffering from VAD; among them, children ages 12–24 months showed the highest prevalence (22 percent), followed by children ages 6–12 months (18 percent). The prevalence of VAD was 3 percent among pregnant women and 2 percent among lactating women. The survey also found that children with VAD were likely to be more stunted (and underweight), to be more anemic, and to belong to food-insecure households; they were less likely to have received their biannual vitamin A supplements than children who were vitamin A sufficient.

Zinc deficiency

Zinc is an essential micronutrient that is involved in numerous aspects of cellular metabolism. It is required for the functions of more than 100 enzymes and plays an essential role in immune functions, DNA (deoxyribonucleic acid) and protein synthesis, and cell division. Consequently, zinc also supports normal growth and development during pregnancy, childhood, and adolescence. Given its role in these critical functions, zinc deficiency is related to retarded growth in infants and young children, loss of appetite, and impaired immune function.

The most recent data on the zinc status of Filipinos are from the Eighth National Nutrition Biochemical Survey (FNRI 2013). This survey found that the prevalence of zinc deficiency was 18 percent among children 6–59 months, a level considered to be of "moderately high public health concern." Children from the poorest quintile had a prevalence more than three times that of children from the richest wealth quintile, 28 percent versus 7.5 percent. The prevalence of zinc deficiency among lactating mothers was about 25 percent (29 percent during the first six months of lactation)—a level considered to be a "high public health concern." Only 14 percent of the pregnant women surveyed were zinc deficient.

Overnutrition

The Philippines faces a double burden of malnutrition: both undernutrition and overnutrition occur simultaneously, sometimes within the same household and even within the same individual over time. Overnutrition—in particular, the loss of healthy life from a high body mass index (BMI), dietary risks, and the associated noncommunicable diseases—is a rapidly growing challenge in the country. Excess accumulation of fat is a known risk factor for cardiovascular disease (mainly heart disease and stroke), type 2 diabetes, and some cancers (endometrial, breast, and colon). Overweight rates in adults are strongly correlated with average income per capita. The link between excess weight and income hinges on the rapid income growth and economic transformation experienced by many Asian economies, accompanied by rapid urbanization, changing lifestyles, and changes in dietary patterns.

In the Philippines, overweight and obesity rates in children under five have been declining, from a peak of 5.1 percent in 2013 to 2.9 percent in 2019. The highest rates are in the richest quintile (8 percent) and in the age group 0–5 months (4.1 percent). Rates increase among older children and begin to be a public health concern among adolescents (9.8 percent in 2019, down from 11.6 percent in 2018), particularly among those from higher wealth quintiles (23 percent among the richest in 2019). Among adults, 36 percent are overweight or obese (9 percent obesity in 2019), based on BMI; rates are alarmingly high among females (23 percent with a high waist circumference and 63 percent with a high waist-to-hip ratio in 2019). These adult overweight or obesity rates have risen sharply since 2015. Of the five leading causes of death in the country, four—ischemic heart disease, cerebrovascular diseases, neoplasms, and diabetes—are associated with overweight and obesity. By contrast, pneumonia is the only remaining leading communicable cause of adult mortality (DOH 2018).

Among the health problems linked to overweight or obesity, the more disturbing trend is the rapid increase in the prevalence of impaired fasting blood glucose (9.1 percent) and high fasting blood glucose (8.2 percent); altogether almost one in five Filipino adults has abnormal sugar metabolism, a risk factor for type 2 diabetes. If we apply the more recent and stringent cutoffs for impaired fasting blood glucose (100–125 milligrams), rates would increase to 29.1 percent, resulting in more than 37 percent of Filipino adults having this problem. Rates are higher among richer quintiles, urban residents, and males.

IMPLICATIONS OF COVID-19 FOR NUTRITION IN THE PHILIPPINES

The unprecedented global social and economic crisis triggered by the COVID-19 pandemic poses grave risks to the nutritional status and survival of young children. Recent analyses suggest that among low- and middle-income countries, the prevalence of moderate or severe wasting among children younger than five could rise 14.3 percent due to COVID-19-related predicted country-specific losses in gross national income per capita. This increase would translate to an additional 6.7 million children with wasting in 2020 compared with projections for 2020 without COVID-19 (Headey et al. 2020). Malnutrition and COVID-19 are inextricably linked. Undernutrition weakens the immune system, makes individuals more susceptible to disease, increases the severity of illness, and can impede recovery. At the other extreme of the malnutrition spectrum, emerging evidence suggests that people with preexisting conditions (such as severe obesity) and diet-related noncommunicable diseases (such as diabetes) suffer more serious consequences of COVID-19, including more severe illness, including bilateral viral pneumonia, and higher health care needs, such as respirators.

The COVID-19 pandemic is expected to increase the risk of all forms of undernutrition globally (figure 2.10). Health systems, especially in low- and middle-income countries, are likely to be overwhelmed as they respond to the COVID-19 pandemic; it is inevitable that the delivery of key nutrition-specific interventions will be affected. Nutrition will be affected by the following:

- Declines in income due to the economic slowdown as a result of quarantines
- Interruption of school feeding programs due to the suspension of school attendance
- Neglect of nutrition-related health activities while the health system is focused on addressing the pandemic
- Potential decline in funding for nutrition-related programs due to government austerity measures
- Disruptions in the food supply due to restricted movement, including, initially, problems of access, particularly to animal-sourced foods, and, later, demand-side problems as incomes drop and jobs are lost or curtailed, causing sharp increases in hunger.

FIGURE 2.10
Relationship between malnutrition and other consequences of the COVID-19 pandemic

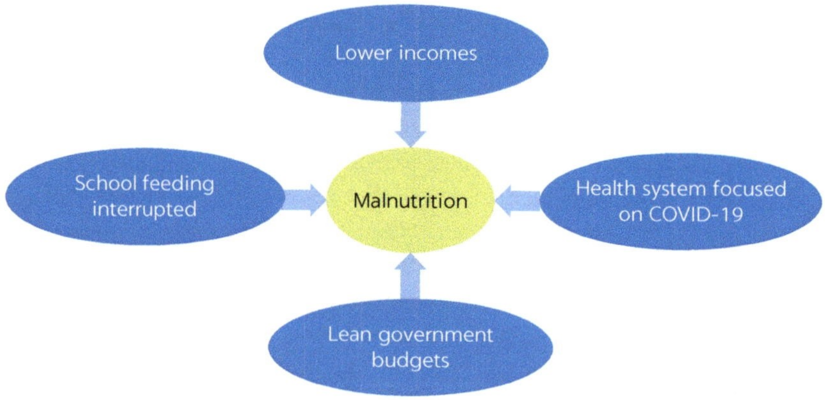

Source: World Bank.

The immediate impact of the COVID-19 pandemic was to disrupt the food supply, particularly in urban areas, as restricted movement curtailed the transport of food commodities, particularly perishables, such as fruits, vegetables, and fish. Up to 35 percent of workers in the agriculture and fisheries sector reported being unable to sell their products due to quarantines (NEDA 2020). The price of fish and vegetables rose, on average, 10 percent during the early months of the pandemic, in March and April 2020. Although food prices have since stabilized (as of the third quarter of 2020), they are still much higher than in the comparable period in 2019.

Of great concern was the 17.7 percent unemployment rate in April. Unemployment fell to 10 percent by July (compared with 5 percent for the same month in 2019). The main consequence of higher prices and higher unemployment is increasing hunger, which has risen to an unprecedented high of 30.7 percent, with 8.7 percent reported as being severe. Rapid surveys to assess nutritional status are ongoing, with great apprehension over the expected spike in acute malnutrition.

Children who were in utero during the 1918 influenza pandemic, for example, had lower educational attainment and income during adulthood (Almond 2006). The effect was even more salient among children of infected mothers. Although there is growing evidence that COVID-19 infections could negatively affect pregnant mothers and lead to premature births, much remains to be learned (Savasi et al. 2020). Currently it is expected that the most damaging erosion of the fetus's human capital will result from the disruption of health care and lower household income.

Birthweight is often interpreted as a key observable component of a child's initial endowment (Datar, Kilburn, and Loughran 2010). Children who were in utero during the 2008 recession were born with relatively lower birthweight, particularly in families at the bottom of the income distribution (Finch, Thomas, and Beck 2019). This was the case, for example, for children born in California regions that suffered unusually elevated unemployment rates during the post-2008 recession. Similarly, in Ecuador during the 1998 El Niño floods, children who were in utero, especially those in the third gestational trimester, were much more likely to be born with low birthweight, and these children were substantially shorter in stature five and seven years afterward (Rosales-Rueda 2018).

These health effects were attributed to drops in household income following the devastation of El Niño. Similar outcomes can be expected from the COVID-19 shock. As low birthweight is associated with increased likelihood of malnutrition and developmental delay, the income effects of COVID-19 may substantially affect the attainment of human capital for generations to come.

Child mortality is also likely to rise for two reasons. The first is the disruption of maternal and child health services due to COVID-19. Early simulated values project an increase in child mortality of up to 45 percent due to shortfalls in health services and reductions in access to food (Roberton et al. 2020). Second, economic downturns have been associated with significant increases in child mortality, especially in lower-income countries. A meta-analysis of studies for low- and middle-income countries suggests that a 10 percent increase in GDP per capita in purchasing power parity terms is related to a decrease in infant mortality of 4.5 percent (O'Hare et al. 2013). Recent estimates also show that this elasticity is probably higher in low-income countries. The estimates suggest that short-term aggregate income shocks translate to an increase in child mortality of 1.3 percent among low-income countries, given a 10 percent decrease in per capita GDP (Ma et al. 2020).

Stunting rates are also likely to rise due to the COVID-19 shock. Common factors related to stunting are maternal nutrition during pregnancy and nutrition during infancy, both of which will likely worsen if families have less disposable income (Galasso and Wagstaff 2019). A fall in aggregate GDP could also lead to weakened health infrastructure and less funding for nutritional interventions and services (Mary 2018). Existing estimates of elasticities suggest that a 10 percent increase in GDP leads to a decrease in stunting that may range from 2.7 to 7.3 percent.[3] Nevertheless, aggregate elasticities may obscure the fact that many of these shocks will affect the poor and disadvantaged disproportionately. Clearly it is important to ensure that these groups have access to support mechanisms that may help them mitigate or recover from such impacts.

SOME PATHWAYS FOR IMPACTS OF COVID-19 ON NUTRITION

Initial indications show that hunger in the Philippines rose sharply following the start of the pandemic. Social Weather Stations surveys have collected data on self-rated hunger going back to 1998.[4] The surveys ask how often a family has experienced hunger and had nothing to eat. Results from the September 2020 survey show that, by this measure, 30.7 percent of families were suffering hunger, and 8.7 percent were suffering severe hunger (figure 2.11)—in both cases the highest levels recorded in more than five years. These results make it likely that the level of malnutrition rose in 2020.

DISCUSSION AND CONCLUSIONS

The already "low and slow" improvements in the nutritional status of Filipino children before the COVID-19 pandemic are further threatened by the disruptions caused by the pandemic. The more proximal effects have been or are already being seen—second quarter disruptions in the food supply and escalating prevalence of hunger—and so it is likely that acute malnutrition (wasting) is already occurring. However, the full impact of the pandemic on childhood

FIGURE 2.11
Estimated rate of total and severe hunger in the Philippines, 1998–2020

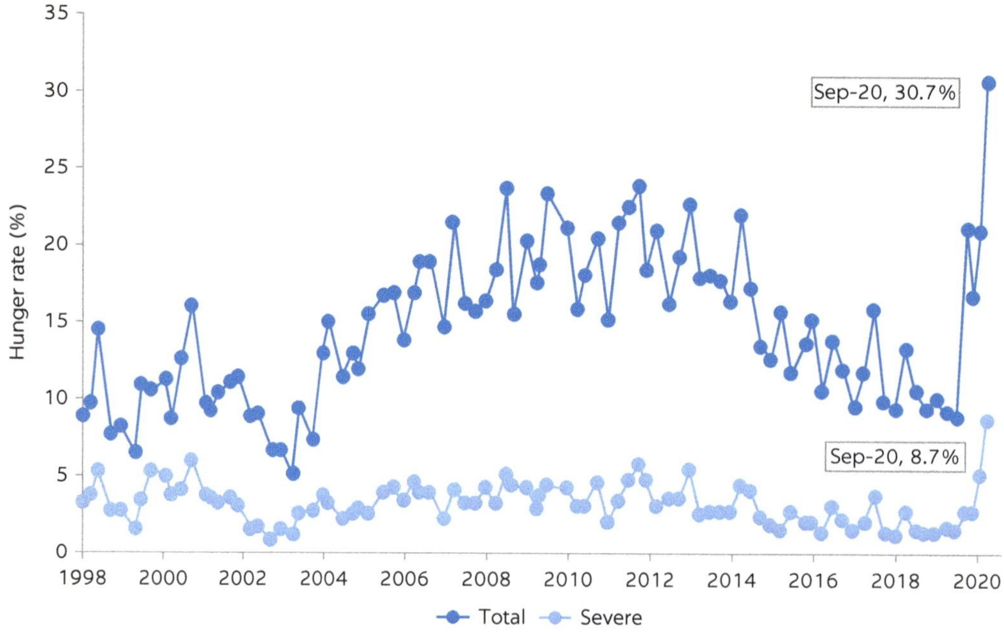

Source: Social Weather Stations Surveys, https://www.sws.org.ph/swsmain/home/.

stunting will only be observed over the next one to two years. The time to act is now if we are to identify the children with severe acute malnutrition and prevent them from getting sick and dying and keep the vast majority of children—those with moderate or mild undernutrition—from progressing to severe undernutrition and stunting.

In this COVID-19 era, government intervention will be vital, with food supplementation and social safety nets targeted at the most vulnerable households, whose children are at high risk of acute undernutrition. For food supplementation to reach those in greatest need in the most expedient way possible, it will be necessary to identify areas where households have limited access to markets to buy or cook their own food and areas where cash assistance is not efficient. The relevant logistics must be considered carefully. The procurement of food and basic supplies would ideally occur within local food systems to provide safe, nutritious food at lower transaction costs, generate jobs, and support local food producers. Selecting foods for supplementation should be based on meeting three food security and nutrition goals: (1) nutrient adequacy, (2) energy sufficiency, and (3) a healthy and nutritious diet.

The next most important step will be to reach those children at risk of chronic undernutrition (stunting), particularly during the first 1,000 days of life, when interventions are most cost-effective and more expedient to deliver. Providing food and micronutrient supplements during pregnancy and lactation, delivering essential newborn care in health facilities, and providing support for exclusive breastfeeding and continued breastfeeding are the minimum short-term investments needed. However, strengthening food systems for the equitable provision of sufficient—and sufficiently diverse—food and ensuring a clean and healthy environment are important medium-term needs.

The impact of COVID-19 compounds a regrettable scenario of already high rates of food insecurity and stunting. With declines in stunting (from 33.4 percent in 2015 to 28.8 percent in 2019) already deemed too slow to meet Sustainable Development Goal targets, the current pandemic could prove catastrophic for child malnutrition. Wasting and micronutrient malnutrition rates are expected to rise, along with child morbidity and mortality. Without immediate action, millions of Filipino children who survive these deficits will suffer the consequences of poor performance in school and low productivity in jobs once they become adults. The magnitude and urgency of the problem require an all-of-government response alongside a multisectoral all-of-society response.

The Philippines has the basic infrastructure to deliver essential nutritional investments to its people. But the delivery mechanisms are fragmented, and gaps may have widened as a consequence of the COVID-19 pandemic. A focus on the most vulnerable—infants and young children as well as pregnant and lactating women—would not only be a benefit today, but also be as an investment for tomorrow.

NOTES

1. Children who are moderately stunted are between 2 and 3 standard deviations below the median from the reference population used by the World Health Organization, and children who are severely stunted are more than 3 standard deviations below the median.
2. The maps in this chapter show estimates, which necessarily involve uncertainty. The uncertainty is measured as standard errors, which tend to be larger for municipalities with small populations.
3. Mary (2018) suggests that the decrease may be 2.7 percent, while Mary, Shaw, and Gomez y Paloma (2017) estimate a decrease of 7.3 percent, and Ruel, Alderman, and the Maternal and Child Nutrition Study Group (2013) estimate a decrease of 6 percent.
4. For Social Weather Stations surveys, see www.sws.org.ph/sws.

REFERENCES

Almond, Douglas. 2006. "Is the 1918 Influenza Pandemic Over? Long-Term Effects of In Utero Influenza Exposure in the Post-1940 U.S. Population." *Journal of Political Economy* 114 (4): 672–712.

Datar, Ashlesha, M. Rebecca Kilburn, and David S. Loughran. 2010. "Endowments and Parental Investments in Infancy and Early Childhood." *Demography* 47 (February): 145–62.

DOH (Department of Health). 2018. "The 2018 Philippine Health Statistics." Epidemiology Bureau, DOH, Manila.

Finch, Brian K., Kyla Thomas, and Audrey N. Beck. 2019. "The Great Recession and Adverse Birth Outcomes: Evidence from California, USA." *Population Health* 9 (December): Art. 100470.

FNRI (Food Nutrition and Research Institute). 2013. *Eighth National Nutrition Biochemical Survey*. Taguig City: Department of Science and Technology, FNRI.

FNRI (Food Nutrition and Research Institute). 2015. *2015 Updating Survey Results*. Taguig City: Department of Science and Technology, FNRI.

FNRI (Food Nutrition and Research Institute). 2019. *2019 Expanded National Nutrition Survey*. Taguig City: Department of Science and Technology, FNRI.

Galasso, Emanuela, and Adam Wagstaff. 2019. "The Aggregate Income Losses from Childhood Stunting and the Returns to a Nutrition Intervention Aimed at Reducing Stunting." *Economics & Human Biology* 34 (August): 225–38.

Headey, Derek, Rebecca Heidkamp, Saskia Osendarp, Marie Ruel, Nick Scott, Robert Black, Meera Shekar, et al. 2020. "Impacts of COVID-19 on Childhood Malnutrition and Nutrition-Related Mortality." *The Lancet* 396 (10250): 519–21. http://dx.doi.org/10.1016/S0140-6736(20)31647-0.

Horton, Susan, and John Hoddinott. 2014. "Benefits and Costs of the Food and Nutrition Targets for the Post-2015 Development Agenda: Post-2015 Consensus." Copenhagen Consensus Center Working Paper, Copenhagen Consensus Center, Tewksbury, MA.

Ma, Yueling, Yadong Zhao, Jiangtao Liu, Xiaotao He, Bo Wang, Shihua Fu, Jun Yan, Jingping Niu, Ji Zhou, and Bin Luo. 2020. "Effects of Temperature Variation and Humidity on the Death of COVID-19 in Wuhan, China." *Science of the Total Environment* 724 (July): Art. 138226.

Mary, Sébastien. 2018. "How Much Does Economic Growth Contribute to Child Stunting Reductions?" *Economies* 6 (4): 1–18.

Mary, Sébastien, Kelsey Shaw, and Sergio Gomez y Paloma. 2017. "Does the Sectoral Composition of Growth Affect Child Stunting Reductions?" *Development Policy Review* 37 (2): 225–44.

NEDA (National Economic Development Authority). 2020. "Weekly Economic Updates—29 April 2020." NEDA, Pasig City.

O'Hare, Bernadette, Innocent Makuta, Levison Chiwaula, and Naor Bar-Zeev. 2013. "Income and Child Mortality in Developing Countries: A Systematic Review and Meta-Analysis." *Journal of the Royal Society of Medicine* 106 (10): 408–14. doi:10.1177/0141076813489680.

PSA (Philippine Statistics Authority). 1993. *1993 National Demographic and Health Survey.* Quezon City: PSA.

PSA (Philippine Statistics Authority). 2015. *2015 Census of Population.* Quezon City: PSA. http://psa.gov.ph/statistics/census/2015-census-of-population.

PSA (Philippine Statistics Authority). 2017. *2017 National Demographic and Health Survey.* Quezon City: PSA.

PSA (Philippine Statistics Authority). 2019. "2018 Full Year Official Poverty Statistics." Press Release, PSA, December 6, 2019. https://psa.gov.ph/content/proportion-poor-filipinos-was-estimated-166-percent-2018.

Roberton, Timothy, Emily D. Carter, Victoria B. Chou, Angela R. Stegmuller, Bianca D. Jackson, Yvonne Tam, Talata Sawadogo-Lewis, and Neff Walke. 2020. "Early Estimates of the Indirect Effects of the COVID-19 Pandemic on Maternal and Child Mortality in Low-Income and Middle-Income Countries: A Modelling Study." *The Lancet Global Health* 8 (7): e901–e08.

Rosales-Rueda, Maria. 2018. "The Impact of Early Life Shocks on Human Capital Formation: Evidence from El Niño Floods in Ecuador." *Journal of Health Economics* 62 (November): 13–44.

Ruel, Marie, Harold Alderman, and the Maternal and Child Nutrition Study Group. 2013. "Nutrition Sensitive Interventions and Programmes: How Can They Help to Accelerate Progress in Improving Maternal and Child Nutrition?" *The Lancet* 382 (9891): 536–51.

Savasi, Valeria M., Francesca Parisi, Luisa Patanè, Enrico Ferrazzi, Luigi Frigerio, Antonio Pellegrino, Arsenio Spinillo, et al. 2020. "Clinical Findings and Disease Severity in Hospitalized Pregnant Women with Coronavirus Disease 2019 (COVID-19)." *Obstetrics & Gynecology* 136 (2): 252–58.

UNICEF (United Nations Children's Fund), WHO (World Health Organization), and World Bank Group. 2020. *Levels and Trends in Child Malnutrition: UNICEF/WHO/World Bank Group Joint Child Malnutrition Estimates.* Geneva: WHO.

Victora, Cesar, Linda Adair, Caroline Fall, Pedro Hallal, Reynaldo Martorell, Linda Richter, and Harshpal Singh Sachdev. 2008. "Maternal and Child Undernutrition: Consequences for Adult Health and Human Capital." *The Lancet* 371 (9609): 340–57.

3 Why Nutrition Matters

ABSTRACT The persistence of very high levels of childhood undernutrition, despite decades of economic growth and poverty reduction, could lead to a staggering loss of the country's human and economic potential. A Filipino child with optimal nutrition will have greater cognitive development, stay in school longer, learn more in school, and have a brighter future as an adult, while undernutrition robs other children of their chance to succeed. Eliminating malnutrition and boosting child development overall could increase the country's gross domestic product (GDP) growth by a significant percentage. Investments in nutrition have a very high return for the Philippines.

CONSIDER THE LIVES OF TWO FILIPINOS

Joshua was born outside Cebu City in 1983 as one of eight siblings. His parents had moved to the city from the countryside a few years earlier. His father worked as a stevedore, and his mother ran a *sari-sari* store, selling sundries from the front of their home. While Joshua was in his mother's belly, his father lost his job, and the family struggled to make ends meet. They had to cut back on meals, eating little besides rice, and could not afford to see a doctor during the pregnancy. Joshua was born prematurely and weighed just 2 kilograms at birth. His mother was too malnourished to breastfeed, and the family could not afford formula, so baby Joshua drank powdered cow's milk mixed with water from a nearby river. His diet as a toddler consisted mostly of rice. At age two, Joshua was the shortest among his peer group, measuring just 80 centimeters tall. Joshua started first grade at age seven and never showed much interest in school. His classmates teased him because of his small size, and he struggled to learn to read and grasp basic arithmetic. He dropped out of school after completing primary school and then worked full time helping his mother in the store and taking odd jobs in the barangay (district) when he could find them. At age 25, he was still living with his parents, with no prospects.

Daniel was born down the street from Joshua one month later and was one of only three children. Daniel's father sold *bananacue* (banana barbecue) from a stand outside the barangay hall, while his mother washed laundry for a hotel. They did not have much money but received small wire transfers at the beginning of most months from Daniel's aunt, who was working as a nurse in Australia. His parents spent their meager income carefully, using it to ensure that his mother was well nourished and had several prenatal visits during her pregnancy. Daniel weighed more than 3 kilograms when he was born. His mother fed him only breast milk until he was six months old and then introduced other foods, following the advice of his aunt and the local Barangay Health Worker. Daniel grew quickly, and on his second birthday he was 10 centimeters taller than Joshua. He started first grade at age six and was a quick and energetic student. He finished secondary school at age 16 and enrolled in a vocational college course to learn the basics of computers. When a business process outsourcing firm opened its doors in Cebu, he applied for a job and was one of its first hires. Income from the job enabled him to rent a modest apartment, where he lives with his wife and two daughters.

These stories illustrate how good nutrition can determine the future prospects of children born in the Philippines. The persistence of high levels of undernutrition, despite decades of economic growth and poverty reduction, contributes to a huge loss of human capital and economic potential. A wide variety of evidence drawn from global experience and from following children in the Philippines over time has shown how much the nutrition of mothers and their children matters for the future of the country.

NUTRITION AND ECONOMIC GROWTH

Undernutrition affects health and economic growth through three key channels:

- First, undernutrition elevates the risk of morbidity and mortality, with the potential for transmission across generations. Undernutrition is the underlying cause of about 20 percent of maternal deaths and more than 45 percent of child deaths globally each year (Black et al. 2008; Black et al. 2013). In many countries with high levels of stunting, child and maternal undernutrition remains among the top three risk factors for disability, morbidity, and premature mortality. Undernourished children are more likely to suffer serious infections and are at increased risk of death from common childhood illnesses such as diarrhea, measles, pneumonia, and malaria.
- Second, undernutrition is associated with decreased lifelong earning potential and labor force productivity. Stunting has been associated with cognitive delays (Grantham-McGregor et al. 2007) and lower educational attainment.[1] Stunting in childhood is associated with reduced height and productivity as an adult.[2] Conversely, children who are well nourished during their early years have 5–50 percent higher incomes as adults and are 33 percent more likely to escape poverty (Hoddinott et al. 2011). Many of the countries with a high burden of stunting also experience a high burden of anemia among adults. Anemia directly reduces work capacity and has a significant impact on agricultural labor capacity and output (Horton and Ross 2003).[3]

Drawing on national sources alongside the Cebu Longitudinal Health and Nutrition Survey (CLHNS), which tracked children born in 1983–84 into adulthood in 2009, Glewwe, Jacoby, and King (2001) found that children who were better nourished in the early years performed significantly better in school. Those children not only entered school earlier and thus had more schooling, but also had higher learning productivity per year of schooling. A 1 standard deviation increase in height-for-age in the first two years of life translates into a total effect of 11.9 points on an achievement test, which is equivalent to 1.1 years of school attendance. For the most malnourished children, the total estimated effect of a 1 standard deviation increase in height-for-age is 22.6 points, which is equivalent to 2.1 years of school attendance.

Another study using the CLHNS data found that low height-for-age at young ages was associated with a reduced likelihood of working in a formal wage job as an adult. This follow-up study was conducted in 2005, when participants were approximately 21 years of age, and the effect persisted in 2009 (Carba, Tan, and Adair 2009).

Children who are better nourished grow up to be wealthier adults. Wealth in 2009 was estimated for individuals from the CLHNS using a composite index of their assets (based on analyses conducted by Gabriel Demombynes and Ann Jillian Villanueva Adona for this book). Figure 3.1 shows the distribution of those individuals in three categories: not stunted, moderately stunted, or severely stunted. Children who were not stunted at age two were materially better off 25 years later. This finding holds even after controlling for the child's circumstances at age two, including wealth, mother's education, mother's age and height, and whether the child grew up in an urban or a rural area.

In an earlier study, Haddad and Bouis (1991) found that the productivity of sugarcane workers in the Philippines increased 1.38 percent for every 1 percent increase in height. Conversely, productivity declined 8.6 percent for severely stunted and 6 percent for moderately stunted individuals.

Third, undernutrition increases the costs of health care and social safety nets—costs that are borne largely by the public sector—and lowers the efficacy of investments in education, reflecting the impact of malnutrition on morbidity, mortality, and poverty. Well-nourished populations are healthier and spend less on health care. In countries with a heavy burden of stunting, maternal and child undernutrition translates into more frequent and severe illness and therefore higher health care costs. High levels of childhood stunting make spending on

FIGURE 3.1

Rate of stunting in children at 24 months of age in the Philippines, by wealth quintile, 2009

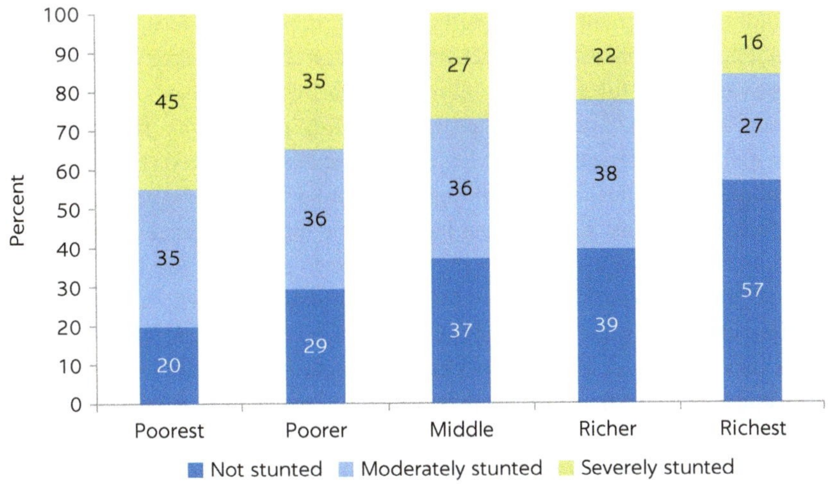

Source: Based on analyses conducted by Gabriel Demombynes and Ann Jillian Villanueva Adona for this book.

education less efficient, because malnourished children are likely to suffer from cognitive delays, time away from school, and poorer learning outcomes. In countries with a high burden of stunting, up to half of children are unable to realize the full benefit of public investments in education.

Globally, productivity losses due to childhood undernutrition represent more than 10 percent of an individual's lifetime earnings, and the GDP lost to undernutrition could be as high as 2–10 percent. Two studies have sought to assess the total cost of undernutrition for the Philippines. The first study, by Save the Children (2016), estimated the costs of undernutrition in terms of both the income forgone due to the lives lost as a consequence of stunting and the lost productivity of stunted children who survive to adulthood. Approximately 838,000 lives were lost to stunting before the age of five years among children who would have reached working age in 2013. Excluding this group from the workforce implies a loss in income to the country of ₱160 billion (US$8.9 billion). For those children under five who were stunted but survived, the cost of lost productivity resulting in lower earnings was estimated to be equivalent to 2.83 percent of GDP. The study also estimated that school grade repetitions were equivalent to 0.01 percent of GDP. Morbidity attributed to undernutrition (stunting and low birthweight due to intrauterine growth restriction, diarrhea, acute respiratory infection, and anemia) was estimated at 3.7 million episodes, resulting in private and social health costs equivalent to 0.05 percent of GDP.

The second study, by UNICEF (2017b), estimated the cumulative economic loss from undernutrition due to various nutritional indicators. The study considered the following consequences of malnutrition: (1) lost earnings due to child mortality attributed to undernutrition marked by poor maternal nutrition, low weight-for-age, suboptimal breastfeeding, and zinc and vitamin A deficiencies; (2) lost productivity due to poor cognition as a consequence of undernutrition; (3) lost productivity due to anemia among the working adult population; and (4) spending on health care to address zinc deficiencies, suboptimal breastfeeding, and low birthweight. The total cost to the economy through all of these channels amounted to US$4.4 billion or 1.5 percent of the Philippine GDP in 2015. Earnings forgone due to lost productivity associated with undernutrition constituted two-thirds (71 percent) of this burden, while stunting alone constituted half.

An additional approach is to consider the long-term impacts of nutrition on the overall economy through the lens of the World Bank's Human Capital Index (HCI), described in box 3.1. The index was developed to link the human capital of children today quantitatively with future economic outcomes (World Bank 2018). The HCI captures the impact of human capital on future growth prospects and serves as a useful starting point for considering human capital challenges. The country's HCI of 0.52 indicates that the future productivity of a child born today will be 48 percent below what could have been achieved with complete education and full health. The Philippines ranks 84 in the world and 14 (among 24 countries) in East Asia and the Pacific. How big a difference could better nutrition make for future GDP? It is possible to simulate the HCI under a "better future" scenario, whereby the fraction of children who are stunted is reduced to 5 percent, the adult survival rate increases modestly to 90 percent, the child survival rate increases to 99 percent, years of schooling increase by one year, and harmonized test scores increase by 10 percent. These parameters for the simulation correspond roughly to the estimated impacts from a micro study conducted for this book. These parameters imply an increase of 22 percent in the HCI or a roughly 1 percent increase in GDP growth over 20 years (table 3.1).

BOX 3.1

The Human Capital Index

The Human Capital Index (HCI) quantifies the level of human capital that a child can expect to attain by age 18. The HCI consists of three components:

- *Survival.* The proportion of children who survive from birth to school age
- *Schooling.* The number of "learning-adjusted" years of schooling that a child born today is expected to complete
- *Health.* A combination of the child stunting rate and the adult survival rate.

HCI uses techniques from the literature on development accounting to convert measures of health and education into contributors to worker productivity, relative to a benchmark of complete education and full health. The resulting index ranges between 0 and 1. A country in which a child born today can expect to achieve full health (no stunting and 100 percent adult survival) and full education potential would score a value of 1. Therefore, a score of 0.70 signals that the future productivity of a child born today is 30 percent below what could have been achieved with complete education and full health. Because the theoretical underpinnings of the HCI are in the development accounting literature, the HCI offers a realistic view of the income a country is likely to gain or sacrifice in the long run. If a country has a score of 0.50, then the GDP per worker could be twice as high if the country reached the benchmark of complete education and full health.

TABLE 3.1 **Human Capital Index for the Philippines under the actual and a "better future" scenario**

INDICATOR	ACTUAL SCENARIO, 2020	BETTER FUTURE SCENARIO
Index component 1: Survival		
Probability of survival to age five (%)	97	99
Index component 2: School		
Expected years of school	12.9	13.9
Harmonized test scores	362	398
Index component 3: Health		
Survival rate from age 15 to 60 (%)	82	90
Share of children under five not stunted (%)	70	95
Overall Human Capital Index score	0.52	0.63
Projected boost in GDP from better future scenario (%)		22

Source: Based on authors' microsimulation.

THE ECONOMIC RETURNS FROM INVESTING IN NUTRITION

Investments in nutrition are highly cost-effective. Unlike investments in physical infrastructure, investments intended to reduce malnutrition generate benefits that are durable, inalienable, and portable. These investments also fuel progress on all of the 17 goals enshrined in the Social Development Goals (SDGs), including education and alleviating poverty. The benefits of scaling up key nutrition-specific interventions have been quantified (Shekar et al. 2017).

FIGURE 3.2

Rate of return to investments to reduce stunting, by country, 2013

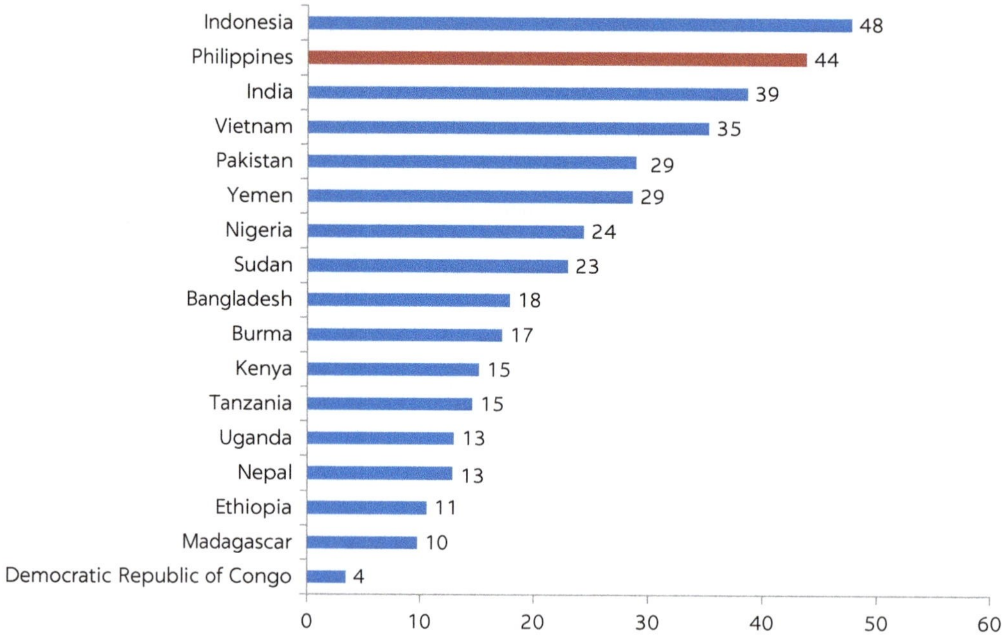

Source: Hoddinott et al. 2013.

The bulk of the benefits (about 98 percent) would be the consequence of cognitive losses avoided in children under age five and the resulting improvements in their economic productivity. The remaining 2 percent would result from premature mortality averted.

Scaling up evidence-based, high-impact nutrition interventions, especially during the critical 1,000-day window of opportunity from conception to two years of age, would pay lifelong dividends, translating to a healthier society and a more robust economy. Hoddinott et al. (2013) estimate the benefit-cost ratio for nutrition investments in the Philippines at 44 (figure 3.2). In other words, every dollar invested in nutrition has the potential to yield a US$44 return. This rate of return is among the highest for countries examined in the analysis. UNICEF (2017a) obtains a lower estimate, projecting the benefits accruing from a nutrition intervention scenario at the national level through key nutrition-specific interventions rolled out over 10 years at full coverage. The study estimates the cumulative benefits to be US$12.8 billion over a 10-year period, with a corresponding cost of US$1,062 million, yielding a benefit-cost ratio of 12:1.

As the Philippines stands on the cusp of the new SDGs, the country has an unprecedented opportunity to save children's lives, build future human capital, and drive faster economic growth. Undertaking nutrition-sensitive interventions, such as conditional cash transfers and agricultural interventions for food security, while addressing water, sanitation, and hygiene, would dovetail with medical and alimentary initiatives and enable the Philippines to meet its nutrition-related SDGs.

The country recognizes that nutrition matters, as articulated in its goals for its people to be free of hunger (Ambisyon Natin 2040, the Philippine long-term development plan NEDA 2017a) and enjoy good nutrition and health (the medium-term Philippine development plan 2017–22; NEDA 2017b). The Philippine Plan of Action for Nutrition 2017–2022 lays out a blueprint for how this may be achieved (NNC 2017). Every administration has made efforts to eradicate hunger, the most current being those of the Inter-Agency Task Force on Zero Hunger. However, these efforts have performed poorly, attributed partly to the weak multisectoral and multilevel approach taken to address malnutrition and partly to the inadequate resources allocated to nutrition, particularly at the local level.

In sum, the financing needed to reach the country's nutrition targets will require coordinated efforts by all stakeholders and a supportive policy environment. Accelerating the reduction of childhood stunting in the Philippines will be essential for maximizing the return on investments in early childhood development, in education, and more broadly in policies aimed at fostering and enhancing human capital accumulation and job creation. The scale-up of key nutrition-specific and nutrition-sensitive interventions to reduce stunting could generate considerable returns in economic benefits over the productive lives of beneficiaries; such scale-up is needed to build human capital through investment in the early years and harness the potential benefits of the country's demographic dividend.

NOTES

1. On average, stunting and associated nutrient deficiencies can result in delays in starting school, loss of attained schooling (Hoddinott et al. 2013), and a higher likelihood of dropping out of school. Additionally, children suffering from iodine deficiency lose on average 13 IQ (intelligent quotient) points, and iron deficiency anemia reduces performance on tests by 8 IQ points (World Bank 2006).
2. Several studies document associations between height and labor market outcomes (Hoddinott et al. 2013). For example, a 1 percent increase in adult height is associated with a 2.4 percent increase in productivity (Thomas and Strauss 1997). The effect may arise because adult height is a proxy for general health, social skills, and social class.
3. Anemia (low number, size, or hemoglobin concentration of red blood cells) has multiple causes (including bacterial and parasitic infections, other nutritional deficiencies, genetic conditions, and blood loss), but the most common cause globally is iron deficiency.

REFERENCES

Black, Robert, Lindsay Allen, Zulfiqar Bhutta, Laura Caulfield, Mercedes De Onis, Majid Ezzati, Colin Mathers, and Juan Rivera for the Maternal and Child Undernutrition Study Group. 2008. "Maternal and Child Undernutrition: Global and Regional Exposures and Health Consequences." Maternal and Child Undernutrition Series. *The Lancet* 371 (9608): 243–60.

Black, Robert, Cesar Victora, Susan Walker, Zulfiqar Bhutta, Parul Christian, Mercedes De Onis, Majid Ezzati, et al. 2013. "Maternal and Child Undernutrition and Overweight in Low-Income and Middle-Income Countries." *The Lancet* 382 (9890): 427–51. https://doi.org/10.1016/S0140-6736(13)60937-X.

Carba, Delia, Vivencia Tan, and Linda Adair. 2009. "Early Childhood Length-for-Age Is Associated with the Work Status of Filipino Young Adults." *Economics and Human Biology* 7 (1): 7–17.

Glewwe, Paul, Hannah Jacoby, and Elizabeth King. 2001. "Early Childhood Nutrition and Academic Achievement: A Longitudinal Analysis." *Journal of Public Economics* 81 (3): 345–68.

Grantham-McGregor, Sally, Yin B. Cheung, Santiago Cueto, Paul Glewwe, Linda Richter, Barbara Strupp, and International Child Development Steering Group. 2007. "Developmental Potential in the First 5 Years for Children in Developing Countries." *The Lancet* 369 (9555): 60–70.

Haddad, Lawrence J., and Howarth E. Bouis. 1991. "The Impact of Nutritional Status on Agricultural Productivity: Wage Evidence from the Philippines." *Oxford Bulletin of Economics and Statistics* 53 (1): 45–68.

Hoddinott, John, Harold Alderman, Jere Behrman, Lawrence Haddad, and Susan Horton. 2013. "The Economic Rationale for Investing in Stunting Reduction." *Maternal and Child Nutrition* 9 (Suppl. 2): 69–82.

Hoddinott, John, John Maluccio, Jere Behrman, Reynaldo Martorell, Paul Melgar, Agnes R. Quisumbing, Manuel Ramirez-Zea, Aryeh D. Stein, and Kathryn M. Yount. 2011. "The Consequences of Early Childhood Growth Failure over the Life Course." IFPRI Discussion Paper 01073, International Food Policy Research Institute, Washington, DC. https://core.ac.uk/download/files/153/6314946.pdf.

Horton, Susan, and J. Ross. 2003. "The Economics of Iron Deficiency." *Food Policy* 28 (1): 51–75.

NEDA (National Economic and Development Authority). 2017a. "Ambisyon Natin 2040, a Long-Term Vision for the Philippines." NEDA, Pasig City.

NEDA (National Economic and Development Authority). 2017b. "Philippine Development Plan 2017–2022." NEDA, Pasig City.

NNC (National Nutrition Council). 2017. "Philippine Plan of Action for Nutrition 2017–2022: Executive Summary." NCC, Manila.

Save the Children. 2016. "Cost of Hunger: Philippines; The Economic Impact of Child Undernutrition on Education and Productivity in the Philippines." Save the Children Philippines, Makati City.

Shekar, Meera, Jakub Kakietek, Julia Dayton Eberwein, and Dylan Walters. 2017. *An Investment Framework for Nutrition: Reaching the Global Targets for Stunting, Anemia, Breastfeeding, and Wasting.* Directions in Development—Human Development. Washington, DC: World Bank. doi:10.1596/978-1-4648-1010-7.

Thomas, Duncan, and John Strauss. 1997. "Health and Wages: Evidence on Men and Women in Urban Brazil." *Journal of Econometrics* 77 (1): 159–85.

UNICEF (United Nations Children's Fund). 2017a. "Business Case for Nutrition Investment in the Philippines." UNICEF, New York.

UNICEF (United Nations Children's Fund). 2017b. "The Economic Consequences of Undernutrition in the Philippines: A Damage Assessment Report (DAR)." UNICEF, New York.

World Bank. 2006. "Why Invest in Nutrition?" In *Repositioning Nutrition as Central to Development: A Strategy for Large-Scale Action.* Washington, DC: World Bank.

World Bank. 2018. "Human Capital Index and Components." World Bank, Washington, DC. https://www.worldbank.org/en/data/interactive/2018/10/18/human-capital-index-and-components-2018.

4 Why Are So Many Children Undernourished in the Philippines?

ABSTRACT This chapter provides a detailed multivariate analysis of potential drivers of childhood undernutrition in the Philippines. Using data from the 2015 National Nutrition Survey, the analysis finds that stunting at ages 24–60 months is associated principally with suboptimal prenatal conditions and inadequate security and diversity of food. If the results are given a causal interpretation, they imply that if all Filipino newborns had adequate prenatal conditions, the fraction who are stunted at age 24–60 months would fall 20 percent. Similarly, providing adequate food security and diversity to all Filipino children would reduce stunting 22 percent. Additional factors include access to clean water and sanitation, adolescent pregnancy, and child health care. These results point to a series of policy priorities to reduce stunting: supporting the nutrition and health of expectant mothers, providing access to contraception to reduce adolescent pregnancy, and ensuring that children consume a variety of healthy foods, including protein-dense foods, such as milk, meat, and eggs.

INTRODUCTION

International evidence has shown that malnutrition has no single cause and can be driven by a wide variety of factors acting together. For example, the conceptual framework of the United Nations Children's Fund (UNICEF) posits that childhood malnutrition is an outcome of immediate, underlying, and basic causes (UNICEF 1990). At the immediate level, nutritional status is determined by the availability of nutrients to meet the body's requirements; the underlying causes are related to food security (access, availability, and use of food), maternal and childcare practices, water and sanitation, and personal hygiene. These determinants are heavily influenced by the social status of women and an array of constraints: institutional (structural), political, ideological, economic, and environmental. In addition, man-made disasters, such as conflicts and wars, exacerbate the situation, as do natural disasters, such as recurrent floods and droughts. Therefore, achieving sustainable nutrition security entails a fundamental challenge that demands not only direct intervention, but also a cogent approach to the critical determinants of nutrition, which span multiple sectors.

This chapter considers empirical evidence on the principal drivers of undernutrition in the Philippines, including the first detailed multivariate study of the drivers of stunting in that country. The analysis relies on the nationally representative 2015 National Nutrition Survey (NNS) conducted by the Food and Nutrition Research Institute (FNRI) of the Department of Science and Technology (DOST). It also uses data on household income and consumption from the 2015 Family Income and Expenditure Survey (FIES), given that households in the 2015 FIES can be matched to the 2015 NNS.

CONCEPTUAL FRAMEWORK

The underlying environmental conditions and risk factors that influence stunting in the antenatal and postnatal period can be grouped into five categories: (a) prenatal health and nutrition (such as whether a pregnant women is stunted or has anemia) and birth outcomes; (b) care and feeding practices that a child receives at home (such as breastfeeding and timely transition to complementary foods); (c) degree of household food security and access to diverse foods; (d) ability of the household to prevent the transmission of infectious disease with adequate water, sanitation, and hygiene (WASH) infrastructure; and (e) use of maternal and child health care services, technologies, and interventions to prevent disease and boost nutrition. This categorization builds on UNICEF's original conceptual framework. It follows the CHEF (care, health, environment, and food) approach used in recent World Bank reports examining the drivers of stunting in Indonesia (for example, World Bank 2018b) and across Sub-Saharan Africa and adds a category (the "plus" element of CHEF+) for maternal health and nutrition to highlight the importance of prenatal conditions (Skoufias, Vinha, and Sato 2019, forthcoming).

Three implications arise from the interlinked nature of the causal pathways that lead to stunting. The first is that the specific factors most heavily influencing the failure of children to grow in one context may not prevail in another. For example, stunting among children in poor, low-lying coastal neighborhoods affected by floodwater may be caused largely by increased exposure to infectious disease in a setting without adequate WASH infrastructure. By contrast, stunting among children in neighborhoods with no flood risk and with good WASH infrastructure may be caused largely by inadequate dietary diversity due to high prices or limited supply of nutritious foods. The second implication is that the presence of one driver (such as exclusive breastfeeding) may not necessarily prevent stunting without the presence of another driver (such as when the mix of complementary foods introduced at six months fails to meets the calorific needs of the child). In other words, a subset of drivers may be necessary for healthy growth such that they cannot be substituted by the presence of other drivers. The third implication is that stunting is cyclical (figure 4.1). Several studies have established a link between maternal anthropometry, such as small-for-gestational-age status and height of the mother, and offspring outcomes, including low birthweight and stunting. Some frameworks make the cyclical nature of stunting explicit and suggest that any sustained progress to combat stunting will involve interrupting its intergenerational causal pathways (Prendergast and Humphrey 2014).

FIGURE 4.1

A framework emphasizing the cyclical nature of stunting

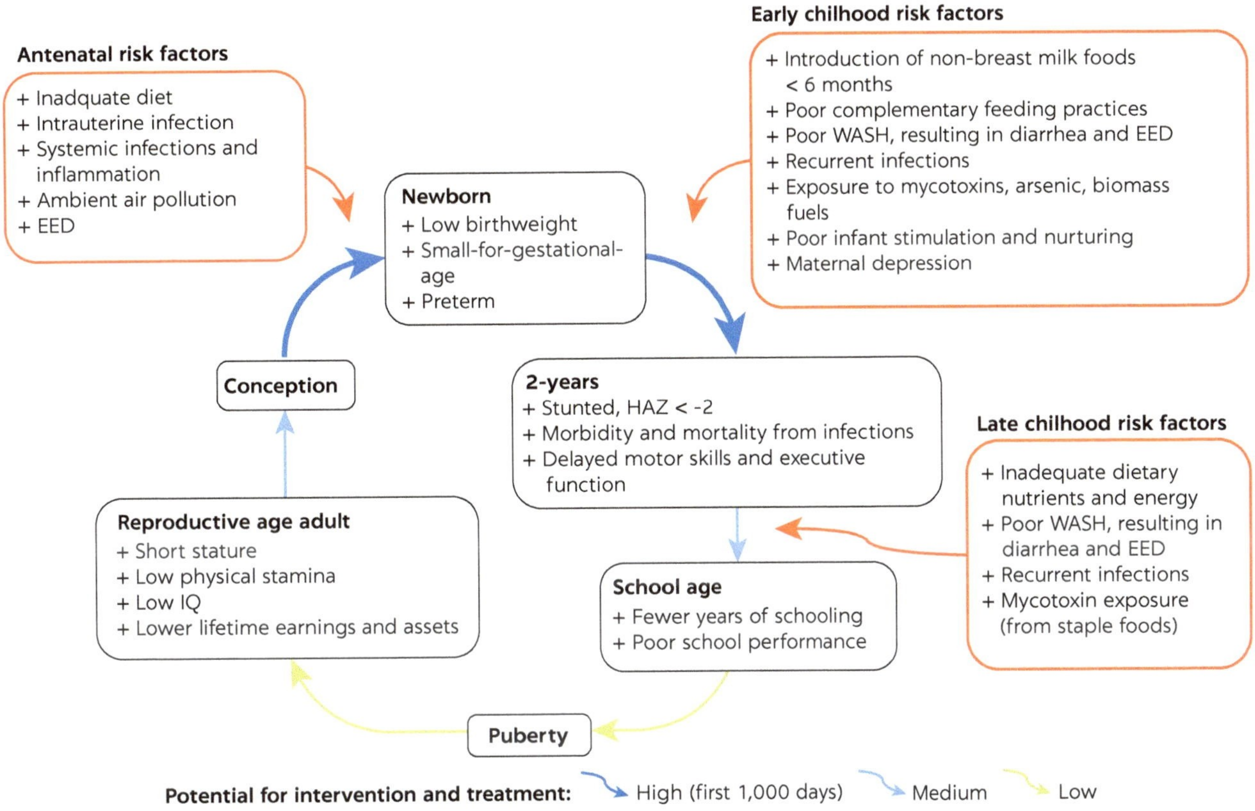

Source: World Bank.
Note: EED = environmental enteric dysfunction. HAZ = height-for-age Z score. IQ = intelligence quotient. WASH = water, sanitation, and hygiene.

"PLUS": PRENATAL HEALTH AND NUTRITION

In the prenatal period, fetal growth is governed by the mother's nutrition, endocrine and metabolic signals, and placental development. Newborn birthweight and gestational age reflect the intrauterine environment. *Low birthweight* is defined as a child weighing less than 2.5 kilograms at birth and is often used as a proxy for undernutrition in utero. It reflects two related phenomena: preterm delivery and a child who is considered small-for-gestational-age. *Preterm* denotes live births that occur before 37 weeks of completed gestation. *Small-for-gestational-age* is defined as being smaller than the 10th percentile for fetal growth of the 1991 reference population in the United States.

Filipino newborns are among the world's most likely to be born too small or too soon. An estimated 15 percent of live births in low- and middle-income countries are low birthweight. In the Philippines, the 2017 National Demographic and Health Survey (NDHS) estimated that 14.5 percent of live births were low birthweight, reflecting a substantial improvement from 21.4 percent in 2011 (Lee et al. 2013). Using data from the INTERGROWTH-21st project, a recent study examined the global prevalence and burden of small-for-gestational-age and estimated that in 2012, 25.6 percent of Filipino newborns were small-for-gestational-age and that 22.7 percent of neonatal deaths were attributable to this (either at term or preterm), placing the Philippines among the 10 countries globally with the highest burden of babies who are born small for their gestational age (PSA 2017).[1] Recent global and national estimates suggest that the prevalence of preterm births in the Philippines was 13 percent in 2014 and has more than doubled since 2000 (Lee et al. 2017).

Both globally and in the Philippines, small-for-gestational-age is strongly associated with maternal height and low body mass index (BMI), which are, in turn, associated with adolescent health and teenage pregnancy. One study using global data found that children of mothers measuring 145 centimeters or less had an 80.5 percent probability of being stunted, compared with 18.9 percent of children of mothers measuring 160 centimeters or more (Christian et al. 2013). Other studies have established links between maternal birth outcomes and offspring outcomes including stunting. A study using the Cebu Longitudinal Health and Nutrition Survey (CLHNS) found that the likelihood of stunting is inversely related to the mother's height and birthweight (Özaltin, Hill, and Subramanian 2010).

POSTNATAL RISK FACTORS

Care and feeding practices

During infancy and childhood, epidemiological studies point to suboptimal complementary feeding and micronutrient deficiencies as important proximal determinants of stunting. Findings from a study using the Cebu data show that the likelihood of stunting is increased by diarrhea, respiratory infections, and early stoppage of breastfeeding (Black et al. 2013). Notably, the study found a clear risk in early weaning (off breast milk) and noted that the protective effects of breastfeeding and negative effects of inappropriate complementary feeding were strongest in the first year of life. The study described the weaning of breastfed infants as typically the time when "high-quality nutrients from breast milk are replaced with lower-quality nutrients from weaning diets based on corn or rice."

Some evidence points to the role of animal-sourced foods in the promotion of early childhood growth (Headey, Hirvonen, and Hoddinott 2018). Randomized control studies in China, Ecuador, and Jamaica, for example, supplemented children's usual diets with high-protein milk, minced pork, and eggs; in all cases, children receiving these supplements grew taller than their counterparts in the control group. In the Ecuador study, stunting prevalence declined 47 percent among randomly assigned preschool children 6–9 months who were provided one egg per day over a six-month period relative to the control group of children who followed their usual diet (Iannotti et al. 2017). A recent study by Denney et al. (2018), together with FNRI scientists, used NDHS data to examine the relationship between consumption of animal-sourced foods and stunting globally. It found that children ages 18–23 months who consumed two or three types of animal-sourced foods per day were roughly 6 percentage points less likely to be stunted than their peers who did not consume any animal-sourced foods.

Early childhood nutritional intake is directly dependent on the feeding practices adopted by caregivers in the home, including, for infants, whether mothers decide to breastfeed and for how long, and, for older children, what kinds of solid foods are given, how frequently, and how diverse the foods are. The World Health Organization (WHO) recommends exclusive breastfeeding for children from birth to six months of age, with the introduction of solid or semisolid foods over the next two months, such that breastfeeding continues alongside complementary foods until two years of age. The WHO also has guidelines on dietary frequency and diversity for children above the age of six months. Other important and related aspects of child care in the home include the hygienic preparation of food and whether the child receives cognitive stimulation. Six indicators in the NNS data were identified as indicators of child care and feeding practices at home. Of these, two are considered necessary evidence of an adequate child care and feeding environment at home: the child is age-appropriately fed (breastfed), and the mother always washes her hands before preparing food and feeding her children, before and after eating, and after using the toilet. Unfortunately, three other essential indicators of optimum child-feeding practices were not made available for this study: minimum meal frequency, minimum dietary diversity, and minimum acceptable diet for children six months of age and older.

Health care of mother and child

The postnatal health and well-being of the mother and child are important factors that enable childhood nutrition. Eight indicators from the NNS survey were identified as measures of postnatal maternal and child health care, of which three are considered necessary evidence of adequate health care: the mother received a postnatal checkup by a skilled practitioner, the child underwent neonatal screening, and the child received vaccinations according to the recommended WHO age schedule: BCG (Bacillus Calmette–Guérin), oral polio, DTP (diphtheria, tetanus, pertussis) or pentavalent, and measles.[2]

Food security and access to diverse foods

Another key factor shaping the nutritional environment is the degree to which the household experiences food insecurity and the range of foods regularly consumed. The NNS and FIES identified 12 indicators of household food security and diversity. Of these, two are considered necessary evidence of adequate household food security and access to diverse foods: the household is food secure based on its household food insecurity access status (HFIAS), and the household consumed protein-rich foods (meat, eggs, and milk) at least once in the past seven days. Based on the HFIAS methodology (Coates, Swindale, and Bilinsky 2007), food-secure status means that the household does not frequently worry about having enough food, does not give up preferred foods or reduce the size or number of meals, and does not run out of food, go to bed hungry, or go a whole day without eating.

Environment: Water, sanitation, and hygiene infrastructure

Access to clean water and appropriate sanitation is thought to be a significant determinant of good childhood nutrition. Specifically, environmental enteric dysfunction—a condition of the gut caused by fecal contamination that impairs nutrient absorption—may be a key bottleneck for childhood growth. However, recent studies in Bangladesh and Kenya tested to see whether WASH interventions improved nutrition and did not find any substantial effects on growth (Black et al. 2013).[3]

Whether a child comes into contact with infectious diseases or other environmental pathogens is determined partly by the conditions of the dwelling and the surrounding community. Six indicators from the NNS were identified as measures of the sanitary and hygienic conditions of the household. Of these, three are considered necessary evidence of adequate WASH conditions for the child: the household uses drinking water from an improved source, the household uses a toilet facility that is water sealed, and at least 75 percent of households in the municipality have improved sanitation.

STUNTING RISK FACTOR TRENDS IN THE PHILIPPINES

Average living standards in the Philippines have improved markedly since 2000. Gross domestic product per person (adjusted for inflation) rose by more than 4 percent per year in 9 of the 18 years between 2000 and 2017, contributing to an overall increase in real income per capita of close to US$1,300 over this period. Overall, the distribution of income growth since 2006 has been inclusive and pro-poor, especially between 2012 and 2015, when income per capita among the poorest 20 percent of households increased 16 percent (World Bank 2018a). As a result, between 2006 and 2015, poverty rates using the national poverty line fell from 26.6 percent to 21.6 percent (and from 14.5 percent to 6.6 percent using the international or "extreme" poverty line of US$1.90 per day).

Other risk factors or interventions closely associated with stunting also improved between 2000 and 2017 and now affect less than 25 percent (or cover at least 75 percent) of the population, including anemia prevalence among women (pregnant or lactating), anemia prevalence among children between the ages of one and five years, diarrhea prevalence among children under the age of three, breastfeeding prevalence, share of births assisted by a skilled health practitioner, and share of the population with access to an improved, nonshared sanitation facility. Other risk factors or interventions improved, but still affect more than 25 percent (or cover less than 75 percent) of the population: anemia prevalence in children between six months and one year of age, exclusive breastfeeding prevalence among infants 0–5 months of age and children 6–23 months of age, and evidence of a diverse or acceptable diet.[4]

Amid these positive trends are a few key areas of concern. Adolescent fertility and childbearing are on the rise. Preterm births have more than doubled since 2000 (Chawanpaiboon et al. 2019), and NDHSs conducted between 1993 and 2015 found that low birthweight prevalence (among all live births in the five years preceding the survey) increased from 14.7 to 21.4 percent. However, the most recent NDHS estimate from 2017 found low birthweight prevalence to have fallen significantly to 14.5 percent. According to estimates based on NNS data, the share of children under the age of four whose mother reported a low birthweight (with or without a written record) was 15.9 percent in 2011, 11.1 percent in 2013, and 14.5 percent in 2015.[5] According to estimates based on recent NNS reports (FNRI 2011, 2013, 2015), the proportion of pregnant women "nutritionally at risk" has flatlined at roughly one in four. Furthermore, in 2019 pregnant women under the age of 20 were more likely to be nutritionally at risk as women above the age of 20 (28.5 versus 22.3 percent, respectively). The relative risk of having deficient nutrition during a pregnancy associated with adolescence is greater than the risk associated with wealth.

According to the government's vaccination schedule, coverage of all eight basic vaccinations slipped from 79 to 71 percent between 2000 and 2003 and has remained around that level since.

The overall picture of child nutrition in the Philippines presents a puzzle. Why did the country's stunting rates stagnate between 2000 and 2015 amid improving living standards, improved child survival, expanding coverage of key health interventions, implementation of a targeted cash transfer scheme, and sustained progress in efforts to combat stunting elsewhere in the region? Examination of the trends in key risk factors provides some clues. For example, against a background of increasing adolescent fertility, lower nutritional status among pregnant adolescents presents a major headwind for infant and child nutrition even as economic conditions improve. Closely associated are the rise of preterm births and the prevalence of low birthweight, which signal broader challenge for maternal health and nutrition. In addition, given that preterm births also face a significantly higher risk of neonatal mortality (Katz et al. 2013), one implication of rising preterm birth rates in a context of improving care for vulnerable neonates—which appears to be the case in the Philippines—is that, as more preterm newborns survive past the first 30 days of life, future cohorts of older children will include comparatively more individuals who are at a greater risk of stunting.

It is not clear how important these factors are in the overall evolution of stunting in the Philippines. The sections that follow seek to identify more precisely which pathways seem to drive stunting through an empirical assessment of the relationship between stunting and its known risk factors (figure 4.2).

FIGURE 4.2

Trends in key risk factors for stunting in the Philippines, 2000–17

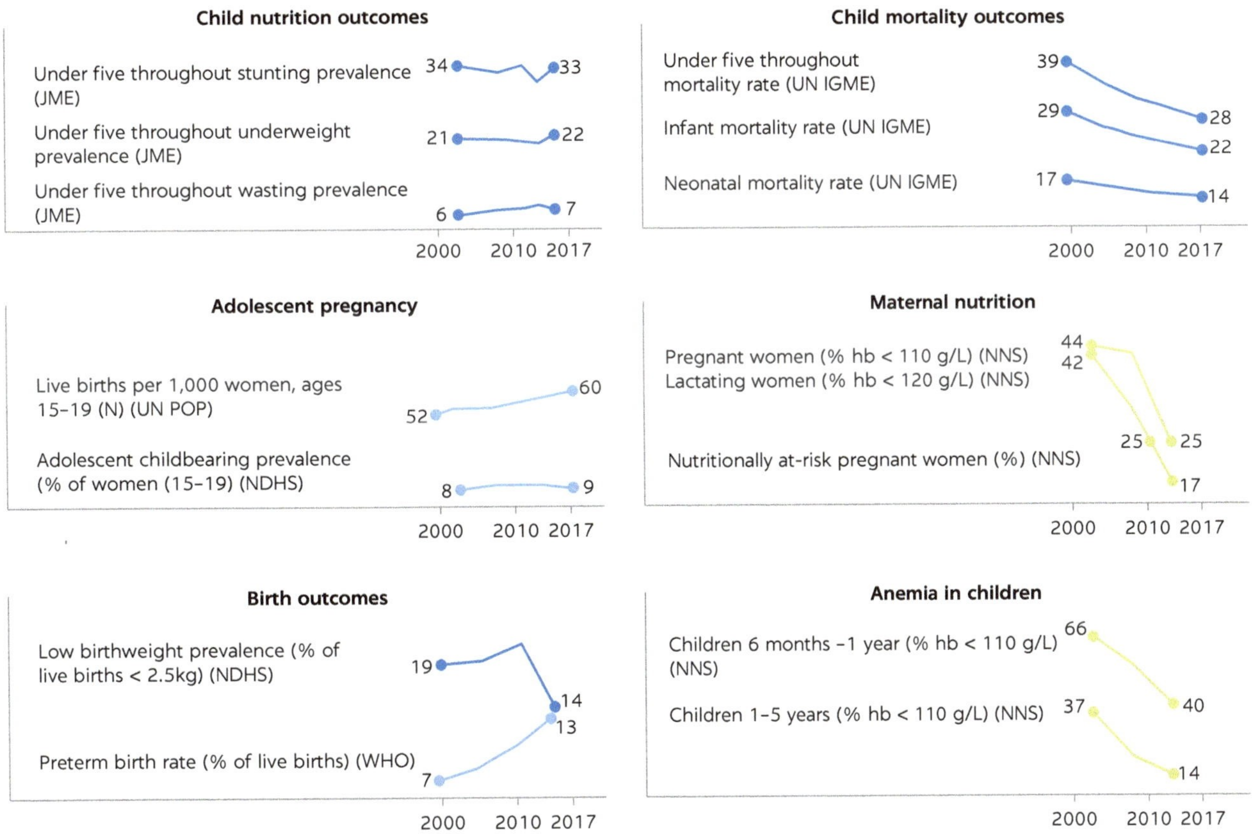

continued

FIGURE 4.2, *continued*

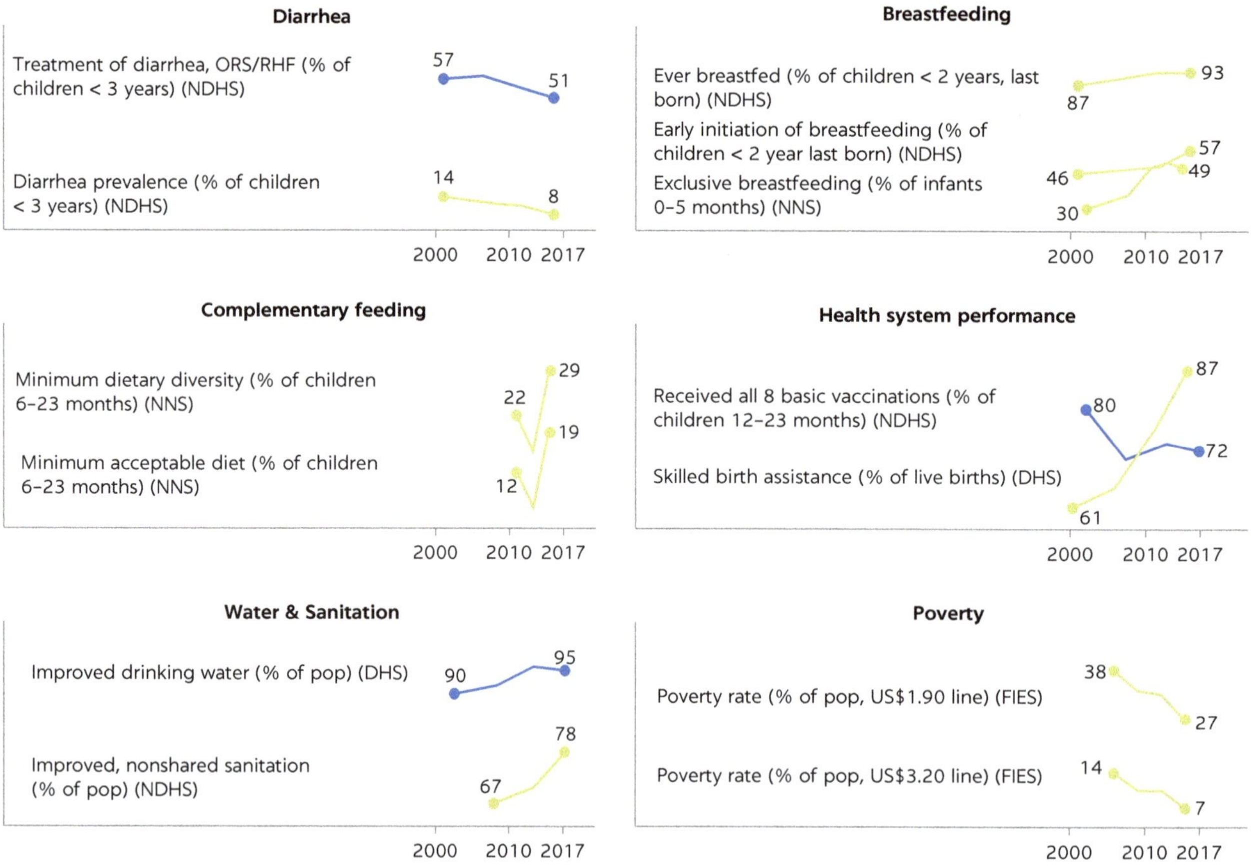

Source: The source for each indicator is indicated in parentheses.
Note: Risk factors with average rates of change greater than 0.5% per year or less than −0.5% per year, depending on the indicator, are labeled as showing a clear improvement or a clear worsening. FIES = Family Income and Expenditure Survey. g/L = grams per liter. hb = hemoglobin. JME = United Nations Children's Fund, World Health Organization, and World Bank Joint Child Malnutrition Estimates. NDHS = National Demographic and Health Survey. NNS = National Nutrition Survey. ORS = oral rehydration solution. Pop = population. RHF = recommended home fluids. UN IGME = United Nations Interagency Group for Child Mortality Estimation. UN POP = United Nations Population Division. WHO = World Health Organization.

MULTIVARIATE ANALYSIS

Three sets of analyses were conducted to model the association of nutrition drivers with stunting. The first set used a wide set of risk factors and interventions for three age groups: newborns, infants ages 0–5 completed months, and older children ages 24–60 months. The second set assessed the association of stunting with five aggregate indicators that measure adequate access to the five categories of nutrition drivers, while the third set explored whether synergies are evident between these broad categories in their association with stunting. While all analyses control for biological factors of the child (age, sex, and twin status), the results are presented separately for regressions that adjust for additional socioeconomic and demographic characteristics (household size, number of children, household income, mother's education, occupational status, marital status, and mother's age when the child was born) and those that do not.

Variables associated with stunting of infants are shown in figure 4.3. Infants with low birthweight have 3.3 times the risk of stunting compared with infants with normal birthweight (predicted probability of stunting of 21.3 and

FIGURE 4.3

Relative risk of stunting in children ages 0–5 months in the Philippines, by risk factor

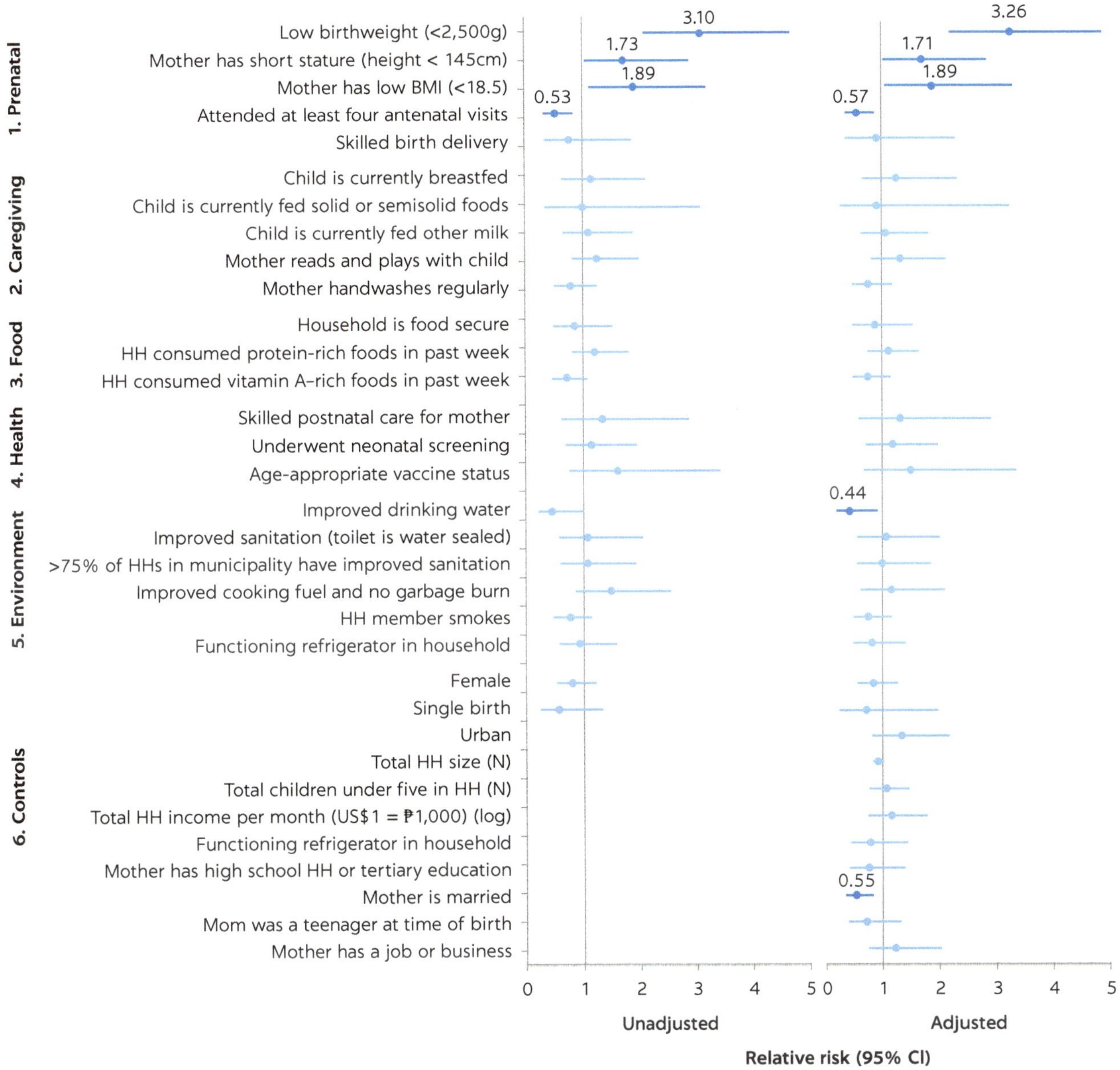

Source: Calculations based on the 2015 National Nutrition Survey (FNRI 2015).
Note: Only the relative risk estimates for significant risk factors are labeled. Age, age squared, and age cubed (in months) are also used as controls, but are not shown in the figure. Unadjusted regression models do not control for socioeconomic factors. 95% confidence intervals are shown. BMI = body mass index. CI = confidence interval. HH = household.

6.6 percent, respectively). To a lesser degree, short stature and low BMI of the mother are also associated with an increased risk of stunting. Infants whose mothers attended at least four antenatal care visits are almost half as likely to be stunted as infants whose mothers did not attend at least four visits (adjusted predicted probability of stunting of 7.3 and 12.8 percent, respectively). Only one postnatal factor is associated with stunting: infants from households with access to improved drinking water are 0.44 times less likely to be stunted as infants without access to improved drinking water (adjusted predicted probability of stunting of 7.5 and 17.2 percent, respectively). Only one socioeconomic predictor—whether the mother is married—is significantly associated with stunting. Married women are almost half as likely to have infants who are stunted as single women, all other factors being equal.

Variables associated with stunting in older children, two and five years of age, are shown in figure 4.4. The set of variables is smaller for this group due to limitations of the survey data (namely, the lack of data for this group on access to prenatal care, access to skilled postnatal care, and handwashing and feeding practices). While the association between maternal short stature and stunting persists for this older age group, the association between low birthweight and low maternal BMI diminishes. Several postnatal factors are associated with a reduced risk of stunting. Children in households that are food secure and have

FIGURE 4.4

Relative risk of stunting in children ages 24–60 months in the Philippines, by risk factor

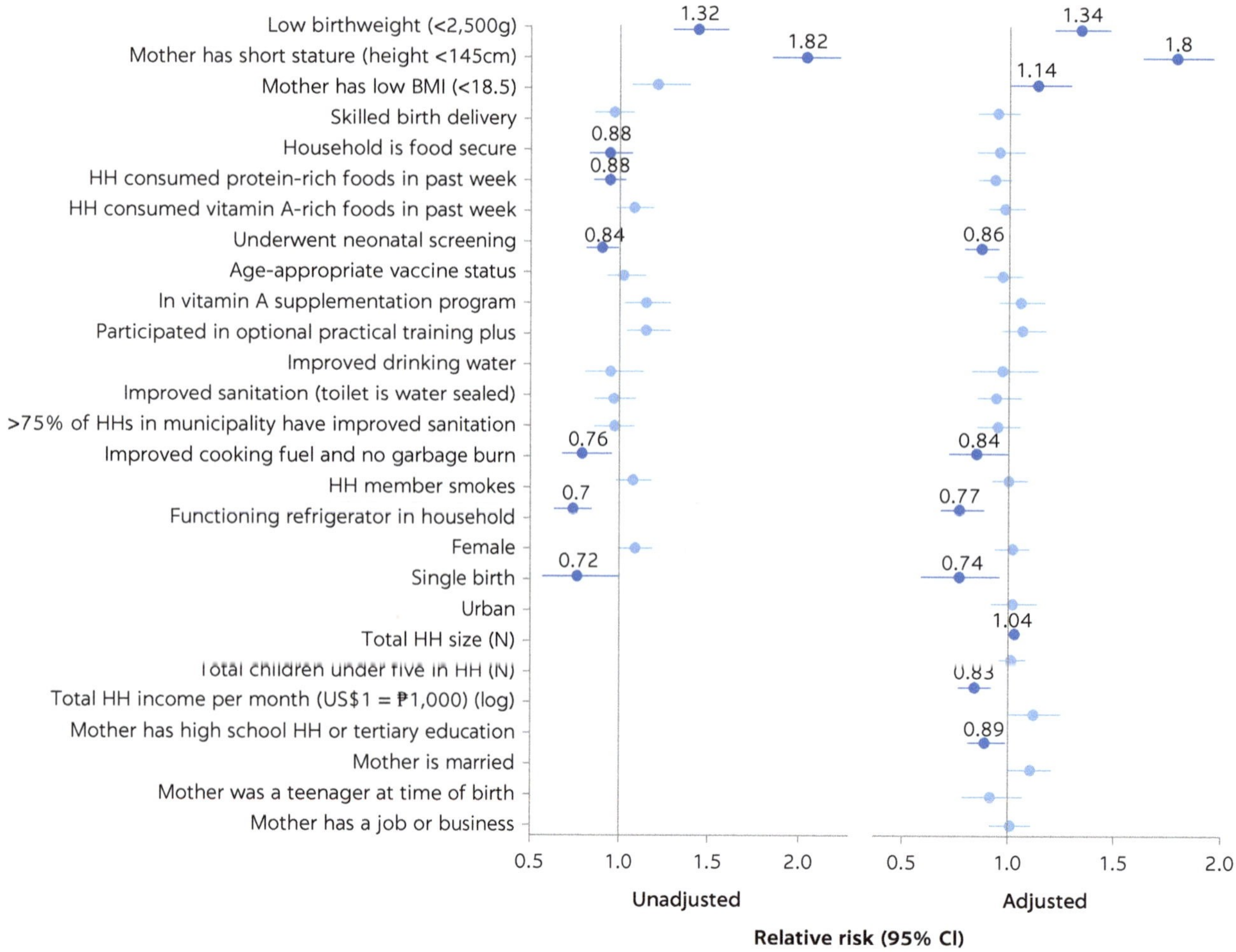

Source: Calculations based on the 2015 National Nutrition Survey (FNRI 2015).
Note: Only the relative risk estimates for significant risk factors are labeled. Age, age squared, and age cubed (in months) are also used as controls, but are not shown in the figure. The unadjusted regression model does not control for socioeconomic factors. 95% confidence intervals are shown. BMI = body mass index. CI = confidence interval. HH = household.

access to animal-sourced foods are around 10 percent less likely to be stunted than children in households that are less food secure and have less access to animal-sourced foods. However, the inclusion of socioeconomic factors in the adjusted model attenuates these associations, likely reflecting the role of income in mediating access to food. Neonatal screening is associated with a 14 percent reduction in the risk of stunting, while the use of improved cooking fuel and access to a functional refrigerator are associated with reductions in stunting of roughly 15 and 25 percent, respectively. Children whose mothers have a high school or tertiary education are 11 percent less likely to be stunted than those whose mothers have less educational attainment.

Aggregating the risk factors for stunting into the five CHEF+ categories shows that an adequate prenatal environment is associated with a 63 percent reduction in stunting risk and that access to adequate water, sanitation, and hygiene is associated with a 37 percent reduction in stunting risk (figure 4.5).

Results for children over the age of 24 completed months show comparable reductions in stunting risk associated with prenatal conditions and food security as well as reductions in stunting risk associated with water and sanitation infrastructure and postnatal child health care. To the extent that linear growth retardation by the age of two (and extending beyond that age) reflects the accumulated impact of adverse environmental effects during the child's first 1,000 days, this model may provide the most comprehensive general description of the relative importance of the drivers of stunting in the Philippines. The relatively large attenuation of the relative risks of stunting associated with food security, water and sanitation, and health care in the unadjusted versus the adjusted model also points to the importance of current income as a key mediating factor enabling households to secure favorable environments in those domains.

FIGURE 4.5

Predicted probability of stunting in children ages 0–6 months in the Philippines, by aggregate risk factors

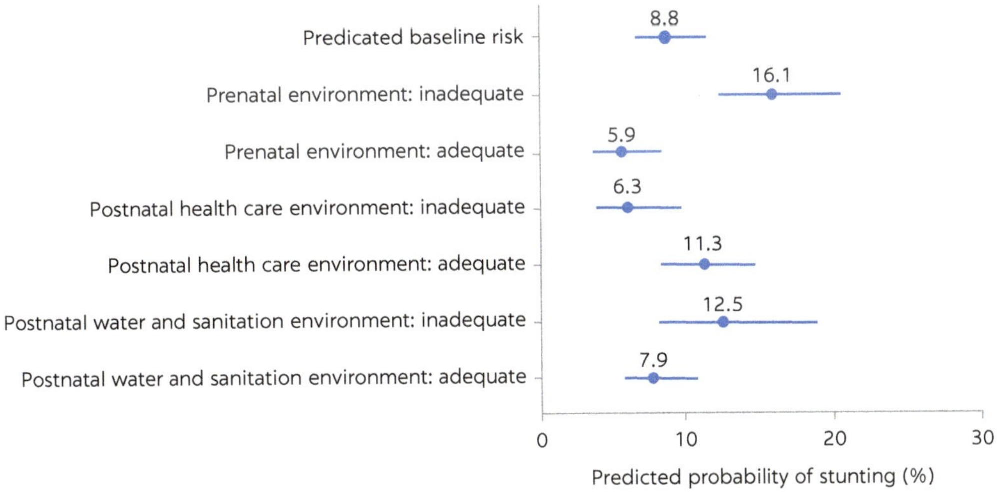

Source: Calculations based on the 2015 National Nutrition Survey (FNRI 2015).
Note: The predicted probabilities are based on model 2a (adjusted) and are calculated at the means for all other predictors. 95% confidence intervals are shown.

Further analyses were conducted to compare the relationship between having simultaneous access to one or more of the five domains (categories) of nutrition drivers and stunting for children under the age of two years (n = 2,927) and not having adequate access to any of them (figures 4.6 and 4.7). Large and statistically significant marginal reductions in stunting risk are associated with moving from having adequate access to no (zero) domains to having adequate access to any three (the predicted probability of stunting declines from 29 to 19 percent, respectively). The same reductions are true for moving from having adequate access to any three domains to having adequate access to any four or five domains (the predicted probability of stunting declines from 19 to 13 percent, respectively).

For children between the ages of two and five years, by contrast, the maximum total number of domains to which a child can have simultaneous access is four (since caretaking and feeding indicators were not available in the NNS for this age group). Unlike for children under two, there is a clear relationship between having access to more driver domains and the risk of stunting. The presence of one additional favorable environmental domain reduces the risk of stunting between 5 and 8 percentage points (figure 4.8). The cumulative

FIGURE 4.6

Relative risk of stunting in children ages 0–24 months in the Philippines for different degrees of simultaneous access to stunting driver domains

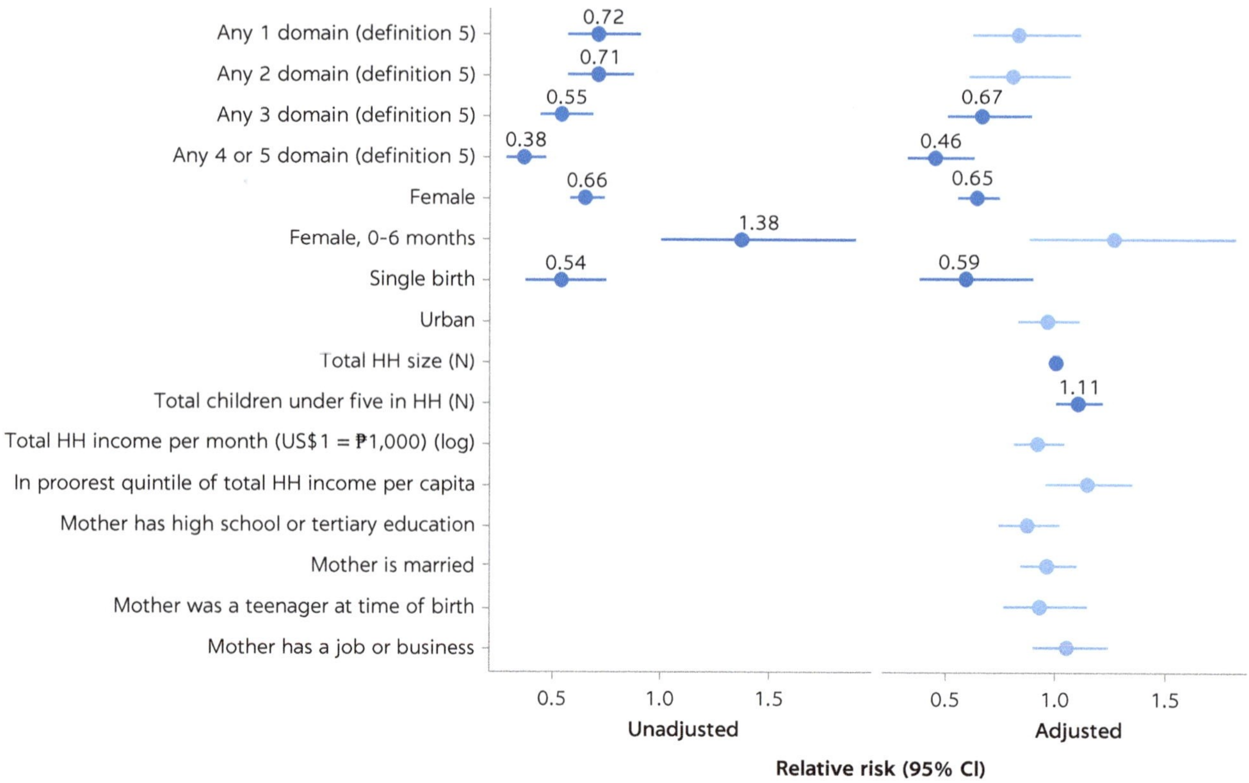

Source: Calculations based on the 2015 National Nutrition Survey (FNRI 2015).
Note: Only the relative risk estimates for statistically significant predictors are labeled. 95% confidence intervals are shown. HH = household.

FIGURE 4.7

Predicted probability at sample means in children ages 0–24 months in the Philippines for different degrees of simultaneous access to the domains driving stunting

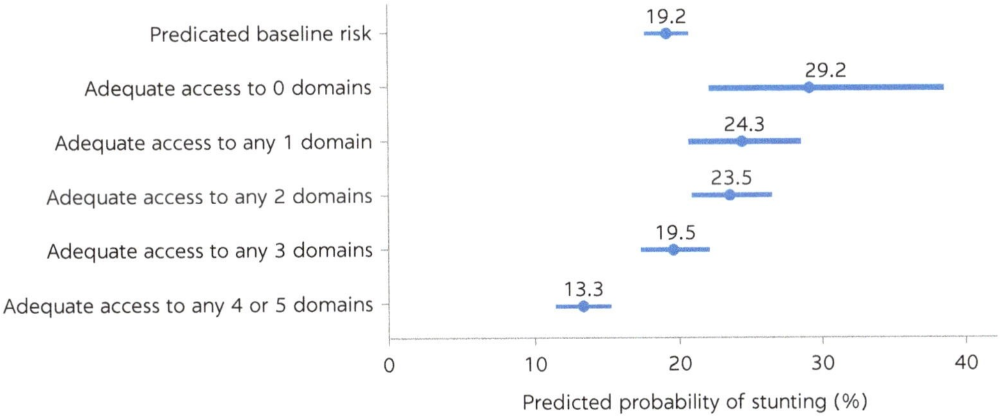

Source: Calculations based on the 2015 National Nutrition Survey (FNRI 2015).
Note: The predicted probabilities are based on model 3a (adjusted) and calculated at the means for all other predictors. 95% confidence intervals are shown.

FIGURE 4.8

Relative risk of stunting in children ages 25–60 months in the Philippines for different degrees of simultaneous access to the domains driving stunting

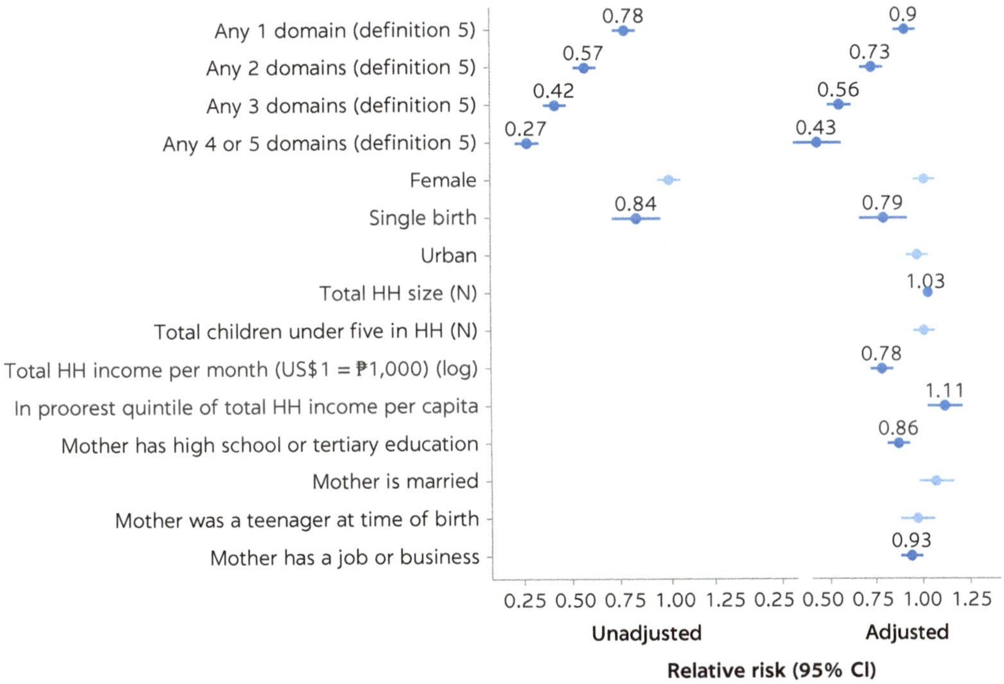

Source: Calculations based on the 2015 National Nutrition Survey (FNRI 2015).
Note: Only the relative risk estimates for statistically significant predictors are labeled. 95% confidence intervals are shown. HH = household.

difference in the predicted probability of stunting for children without access to any domain is 46.2 percent, compared with 19.7 percent for children with access to all four. This finding lends support to the conceptual framework.

DISCUSSION

The findings from these analyses for the Philippines suggest that a significant fraction of stunting that manifests in infancy and early childhood has its origins in utero. Among children under two, 43 percent lack strong evidence of having had an adequate prenatal environment leading up to their birth. Such an environment is measured by having normal birthweight and a mother with normal BMI and stature (height greater than 145 centimeters) as well as access to appropriate antenatal care and support during labor. Children under two who lack an adequate prenatal environment have 1.75 times the risk of stunting as children with evidence of a more optimal antenatal environment.[6] An estimated 24 percent of cases of stunting among children under two in the Philippines are attributable to exposure to a suboptimal prenatal environment.[7] For children between the ages of two and five years, suboptimal prenatal exposures increase the risk of stunting 1.38 times, and an estimated 20 percent of cases of stunting among this age group are attributable to exposures in the prenatal environment (table 4.1).

Unlike the stunting risk associated with low birthweight and low maternal BMI, which diminishes as the child gets older, the risk of stunting associated with maternal short stature persists from infancy through childhood. This finding could suggest that different mechanisms link stunting with two nutritional shocks: (1) nutritional shocks faced during pregnancy (those that contribute to low birthweight and low maternal BMI) and (2) intergenerational or chronic nutritional shocks (those that contribute to the stunted growth of mothers during their own childhood and adolescence). The fact that maternal short stature is associated with child nutrition outcomes independent of an association with low birthweight suggests that adolescent and reproductive health for girls, not just nutrition during pregnancy, is important.

TABLE 4.1 Suboptimal environments and stunting in late childhood (ages 24–60 months) in the Philippines

ENVIRONMENT	PREVALENCE (% OF CHILDREN EXPOSED)	RELATIVE RISK OF STUNTING (ADJUSTED)	PREDICTED INCREASE IN ABSOLUTE PROBABILITY OF STUNTING ASSOCIATED WITH SUBOPTIMAL CONDITIONS IN A DOMAIN (PERCENTAGE POINTS)	POPULATION-ATTRIBUTABLE FRACTION
Suboptimal prenatal environment[a]	67.4	1.38	11.10	20
Suboptimal home care and feeding practices	—	—	—	—
Suboptimal household food security and diversity	84.1	1.34	11.20	22
Suboptimal postnatal maternal and child health care[b]	64.8	1.10	3.80	6
Suboptimal household water, sanitation infrastructure, and environment	27.9	1.12	3.50	3

Source: Authors' calculations based on the 2015 National Nutrition Survey.
Note: 2015 stunting prevalence = 37.6%. — = not available.
a. Excludes recommended use of at least four antenatal care visits (not asked in relation to the pregnancies of children above the age of two).
b. Excludes access by mother to skilled postnatal checkup (not asked in relation to the pregnancies of children above the age of two).

As the stunting risk associated with the nutritional status of the mother and child during pregnancy diminishes for older children, there is an increase in the stunting risk associated with the family's ability to supply adequate nutrition to the child after he or she is born. Children are less likely to be stunted in households that consume eggs, meat, and milk or have the means or appliances to improve their ability to consume such foods safely. The presence of a refrigerator and use of improved cooking fuels are both associated with lower stunting risk. Several possibilities might explain this association. Both of these factors protect against illness (by lowering the degree of indoor air pollution and preventing food spoilage and food-borne illness) and facilitate care and feeding at home (a refrigerator enables households to purchase nutrient-rich perishable foods; a cook stove that uses cleaner fuel can ease meal preparation and reduce cooking times).

Nearly 85 percent of children under five years of age in the Philippines reside in moderately or severely food-insecure households that do not regularly consume protein-rich foods. These children have 1.35 times the risk of stunting compared with children with access to more secure and more diverse food, controlling for socioeconomic factors and other determinants of prenatal and postnatal stunting. Around 23 percent of cases of stunting among children under five are attributable to inadequate household food security and diversity. Without measures of the actual frequency, quantity, and quality of children's diets in the NNS data used for this study, it is unclear to what degree food security and diversity at the household level translate to child-level food consumption. It is plausible that this relationship reflects in part the benefits of a higher-quality diet enabled by food security and access to animal-sourced foods high in protein. More research would help shed light on both the supply-side constraints (such as the availability and price of animal-sourced foods in markets) and the demand-side constraints (such as knowledge, traditions, and preferences) to diversity in children's diets.

Energy intake from milk by children between 6 and 24 months of age is associated with a reduction in stunting risk even after controlling for income and mother's education. Use of breast milk substitutes is strongly associated with family income and mother's education, reflecting a preference among mothers with more financial resources and education not to breastfeed. More research and data are needed to untangle the behaviors and factors associated with milk feeding that might help explain why it is associated with better nutrition.

There is some evidence that factors associated with children's postnatal health reduce stunting risk. Among infants, access to improved drinking water is associated with a reduction in the risk of stunting. This effect could be linked to the low prevalence of exclusive breastfeeding in the Philippines and the potential prevention of illness among infants whose formula is prepared with clean water. Assistance during birth by a skilled practitioner is negatively associated with stunting for children between the ages of two and five years. Given that other measures of the use of child health care were not available in the NNS data for children in this age group, this predictor may be capturing the benefits of health-seeking behaviors more broadly (for example, mothers who delivered in hospital may be more likely to vaccinate their children or seek professional health care in other situations, such as when their child is ill).

Two socioeconomic factors also emerge as important independent drivers of child nutrition in this analysis. Infants under the age of six months in single-mother households have an elevated risk of stunting relative to children in two-parent households, possibly reflecting the greater burden of caretaking and housework that single mothers face. Children over the age of two with a university-educated mother have a lower risk of stunting, possibly reflecting the role of formal education in facilitating the acquisition of knowledge—either directly or through expanded social networks—for more effective meal selection and feeding practices.

These analyses also suggest that nutrition drivers across sectors are complementary in their impact on child nutrition. In other words, children's nutrition stands to benefit more if public and private efforts work to create favorable environments for children across multiple domains, not just a single one. But as decision makers move toward defining how limited resources should be deployed to improve child nutrition, what initiatives should be prioritized?

Empirically, the results explored in this report suggest that the greatest reduction in stunting prevalence would occur if significant progress were made on two fronts: improving prenatal conditions and improving food security and diversity. Combined, suboptimal conditions in these two domains account for nearly 50 percent of the cases of stunting in children under the age of two years and 42 percent of the cases of stunting in children between the ages of two and five years. In the former case, greater focus is needed on efforts to support the nutrition and health of expecting mothers and adolescents to improve birth outcomes, including access to contraception to give women greater ability to exercise their fertility preferences. In the latter case, this means supporting efforts to ensure that children regularly consume a range of foods that deliver key micronutrients, including access to protein-dense perishable foods (such as meat or eggs) and the adoption of technologies that facilitate their consumption (such as refrigeration). Consumption of such foods is especially important when children reach the age of six months and their dietary intake needs to be supplemented significantly with energy and nutrients from solid or semisolid foods.

In areas where birth outcomes and food security are generally favorable (such as areas with a low prevalence of preterm or low birthweight newborns and diets that incorporate diverse food sources), stakeholders might examine ways to improve the safety and reliability of the drinking water supply and sanitation and wastewater systems. One aspect of the home care environment that is not associated with stunting according to this analysis—but nevertheless is important for the cognitive development of children—is stimulation through reading and play. Nationally, only 39 percent of children under the age of two both are read to and get play time with their caretaker, so more direct interventions to improve learning and schooling outcomes might include encouraging cognitive stimulation for children through outreach, education, and investment in early childhood development.

NOTES

The chapter is an abridged version of the analyses conducted as part of this study and also published in Capanzana, Demombynes, and Gubbins (2020).

1. The INTERGROWTH-21st project established the first international, multiethnic standard including well-dated pregnancies from eight geographically defined populations. This standard can be used to describe optimal and aspirational fetal growth around the world.

2. This indicator allows for delayed vaccination.
3. The studies used the following intervention groups: (1) water only: advocated the use of chlorine to treat water plus chlorine dispensers at communal points of access plus a 1-liter bottle of chlorine for use at home; (2) handwashing only: advocated handwashing with soap plus two permanent handwashing stations in the home; (3) sanitation only: advocated the use of latrines and safe disposal of child and animal feces into a latrine plus upgrade of the latrine facility (if necessary) plus sani scoop plus a child potty; (4) the water, sanitation, and hygiene interventions in combination; (5) nutrition counseling plus lipid supplementation; and (6) water, sanitation, and hygiene plus nutrition in combination.
4. Minimum dietary diversity is defined as the percentage of children 6–23 months of age who received foods from four or more food groups during the previous day. Seven food groups are considered: (1) grains, roots, and tubers; (2) legumes and nuts; (3) dairy products (milk, yogurt, and cheese); (4) flesh foods (meat, fish, poultry, and liver or organ meats); (5) eggs; (6) vitamin A–rich fruits and vegetables; and (7) other fruits and vegetables. A minimum acceptable diet is defined as children 6–23 months of age who receive a minimum acceptable diet (apart from breast milk). This indicator is composed of two fractions: (1) the proportion of breastfed children 6–12 months of age who had at least the minimum dietary diversity and the minimum meal frequency during the previous day and (2) the proportion of non-breastfed children 6–23 months of age who received at least two milk feedings and had at least the minimum dietary diversity not including milk feedings and minimum meal frequency during the previous day. This indicator has not improved since 2011 (when it was first measured).

   The share of children with a minimum acceptable diet was 12.1 percent in 2011, 6.4 percent in 2013, 18.6 percent in 2015, 13.4 percent in 2018, and 9.9 percent in 2019. The share of children with minimum dietary diversity was 21.6 percent in 2011, 15.5 percent in 2013, 29.2 percent in 2015, 23.0 percent in 2018, and 20.1 percent in 2019. Minimum meal frequency has been consistently high, so minimum dietary diversity is what is driving minimum adequate diet.
5. In contrast to the NDHS data, the NNS indicator of low birthweight prevalence uses the denominator of all living children (rather than all live births).
6. Among children under five, 30 percent are low birthweight, have a mother with low BMI, or have a mother with short stature. Children under five who are exposed to any one of these risk factors have 1.6 times the risk of stunting compared with children who are not exposed, controlling for age, sex, socioeconomic factors, and other determinants of postnatal stunting. Children with any two of these risk factors have 1.7 times the risk of stunting, and children with all three of these risk factors have 1.9 times the risk of stunting, controlling for other factors.
7. The contribution of a risk factor to a disease or a death is quantified using the population-attributable fraction, which is the proportional reduction in population disease or mortality that would occur if exposure to a risk factor were reduced to an alternative ideal exposure scenario (https://www.who.int/healthinfo/global_burden_disease/metrics_paf/en/).

REFERENCES

Black, Robert E., Cesar G. Victora, Susan P. Walker, Zulfiqar A. Bhutta, Parul Christian, Mercedes de Onis, Majid Ezzati, et al. 2013. "Maternal and Child Undernutrition and Overweight in Low-Income and Middle-Income Countries." *The Lancet* 382 (9890): 427–51.

Capanzana, Mario V., Gabriel Demombynes, and Paul Gubbins. 2020. "Why Are So Many Children Stunted in the Philippines?" Policy Research Working Paper 9294, World Bank Group, Washington, DC.

Chawanpaiboon, Saifon, Joshua P. Vogel, Anne-Beth Moller, Pisake Lumbiganon, Max Petzold, Daniel Hogan, Sihem Landoulsi, et al. 2019. "Global, Regional, and National Estimates of Levels of Preterm Birth in 2014: A Systematic Review and Modelling Analysis." *The Lancet Global Health* 7 (1): e37–e46. doi.org/10.1016/S2214-109X(18)30451-0.

Christian, Parul, Sun Eun Lee, Moira Donahue Angel, Linda S Adair, Shams E Arifeen, Per Ashorn, Fernando C Barros, et al. 2013. "Risk of Childhood Undernutrition Related to Small-for-Gestational-Age and Preterm Birth in Low- and Middle-Income Countries." *International Journal of Epidemiology* 42 (5): 1340–55. https://www.ncbi.nlm.nih.gov/pmc/articles/PMC3816349/.

Coates, Jennifer, Anne Swindale, and Paula Bilinsky. 2007. *Household Food Insecurity Access Scale (HFIAS) for Measurement of Food Access: Indicator Guide.* Version 3. Washington, DC: United States Agency for International Development and FANTA (Food and Nutrition Technical Assistance).

Denney, Liya, Imelda Angeles-Agdeppa, Mario V. Capanzana, Marvin B. Toledo, Juliana Donohue, and Alicia Carriquiry. 2018. "Nutrient Intakes and Food Sources of Filipino Infants, Toddlers, and Young Children Are Inadequate: Findings from the National Nutrition Survey 2013." *Nutrients* 10 (11): 1730. https://10.3390/nu10111730.

FNRI (Food and Nutrition Research Institute). 2011. *Seventh National Nutrition Survey.* Taguig City: Department of Science and Technology, FNRI.

FNRI (Food and Nutrition Research Institute). 2013. *Eighth National Nutrition Survey.* Taguig City: Department of Science and Technology, FNRI.

FNRI (Food and Nutrition Institute). 2015. *2015 Updating Survey Results.* Taguig City: Department of Science and Technology, FNRI.

Headey, Derek, Kalle Hirvonen, and John Hoddinott. 2018. "Animal Sourced Foods and Child Stunting." *American Journal of Agricultural Economics* 100 (5): 1302–19. https://doi.org/10.1093/ajae/aay053.

Iannotti, Lora, Chessa K. Lutter, Christine P. Stewart, Carlos Andres Gallegos Riofrío, Carla Malo, Gregory Reinhart, Ana Palacios, et al. 2017. "Eggs in Early Complementary Feeding and Child Growth: A Randomized Controlled Trial." *Pediatrics* 140 (1): e20163459.

Katz, Joanne, Anne C. C. Lee, Naoki Kozuki, Joy E. Lawn, Simon Cousens, Hannah Blencowe, Majid Ezzati, et al. 2013. "Mortality Risk in Preterm and Small-for-Gestational-Age Infants in Low-Income and Middle-Income Countries: A Pooled Country Analysis." *The Lancet* 382 (9890): 417–25.

Lee, Anne C. C., Joanne Katz, Hannah Blencowe, Simon Cousens, Naoko Kozuki, Joshua P. Vogel, Linda Adair, et al. 2013. "National and Regional Estimates of Term and Preterm Babies Born Small-for-Gestational-Age in 138 Low-Income and Middle-Income Countries in 2010." *The Lancet Global Health* 1 (1): e26–36. https://doi.org/10.1016/S2214-109X(13)70006-8.

Lee, Anne C. C., Naoko Kozuki, Simon Cousens, Gretchen A. Stevens, Hannah Blencowe, Mariangela F. Silveira, Ayesha Sania, et al. 2017. "Estimates of Burden and Consequences of Infants Born Small-for-Gestational-Age in Low and Middle Income Countries with INTERGROWTH-21st Standard: Analysis of CHERG Datasets." *BMJ* 358 (August 7): j3677.

Özaltin, Emre, Kenneth Hill, and S. V. Subramanian. 2010. "Association of Maternal Stature with Offspring Mortality, Underweight, and Stunting in Low- to Middle-Income Countries." *JAMA* 303 (15): 1507–16. doi:10.1001/jama.2010.450.

Prendergast, Andrew J., and Jean H. Humphrey. 2014. "The Stunting Syndrome in Developing Countries." *Paediatrics and International Child Health* 34 (4): 250–65.

PSA (Philippine Statistics Authority). 2017. *Philippines National Demographic and Health Survey 2017.* Quezon City: PSA; Rockville, MD: ICF.

Skoufias, Emmanuel, Katja Vinha, and Ryoko Sato. 2019. *All Hands on Deck: Reducing Stunting through Multisectoral Efforts in Sub-Saharan Africa.* Africa Development Forum. Washington, DC: World Bank and Agence Française de Développement. https://openknowledge.worldbank.org/handle/10986/32037.

Skoufias, Emmanuel, Katja Vinha, and Ryoko Sato. Forthcoming. "Reducing Stunting through Multisectoral Efforts in Sub-Saharan Africa." Forthcoming in *Journal of African Economies.*

UNICEF (United Nations Children's Fund). 1990. *Strategy for Improved Nutrition of Children and Women in Developing Countries.* UNICEF Policy Review. New York: UNICEF.

World Bank. 2018a. "Making Growth Work for the Poor: A Poverty Assessment for the Philippines." World Bank Group, Washington, DC. http://documents.worldbank.org/curated/en/273631527594735491/Making-growth-work-for-the-poor-a-poverty-assessment-for-the-Philippines.

World Bank. 2018b. "Operationalizing a Multi-Sectoral Approach for the Reduction of Stunting in Indonesia: An Application Using the 2007 and 2013 Riskesdas." World Bank, Washington, DC. http://documents.worldbank.org/curated/en/docsearch/report/114207.

5 Agriculture, Diets, and Nutrition

ABSTRACT Agriculture should have an essential role in any effort to improve the nutritional outcomes of Filipino mothers and children. Currently, poorer Filipinos eat a diet heavy in rice, with low levels of diversity and limited protein. They consume insufficiently nutritious diets due to a combination of low incomes, poor choices, and high prices of nutritious foods, such as vegetables and fruits, which typically cost more in the Philippines than in other countries in the region. Analyses of the links between household diets and nutritional outcome conducted as part of this study found that the consumption of fruits and protein-rich foods improves nutritional outcomes for children, adolescents, and adults. A higher share of protein-rich foods to total food consumption is correlated with a lower probability that a household has a stunted, wasted, or underweight child under five, a thin adolescent, or an adult with a low body mass index. Therefore, for the agriculture sector to contribute to improvements in nutritional outcomes will require not only promoting the diversification of agriculture at both the national and the household levels, but also addressing dietary preferences and economic access to nutritious foods.

IMPORTANCE OF AGRICULTURE IN NUTRITION

Agricultural development plays an important role in improving nutrition, not least because agricultural growth is generally pro-poor (World Bank 2008). Investments in agriculture help alleviate poverty, improve food security, and prevent undernutrition, especially since 75 percent of the world's poor live in rural areas and work in agriculture. A study by Headey (2001) using a global data set from 1960 onward concluded that (a) agricultural growth generally has had a large and significant effect on reducing stunting, whereas nonagricultural growth has had no significant effect on stunting (results did not hold for India); (b) agricultural growth has had a very strong effect on increasing the daily energy supply, especially at lower levels of initial daily energy supply;

(c) past agricultural growth has not had a robust effect on improved dietary diversity, accounting for less than the effect of nonagricultural growth; and (d) increased food production is an important link between agricultural growth and nutrition when overall food production is low. The final two conclusions are based mainly on past interventions, which explicitly sought to increase food production without improving dietary diversity, so their relative impact on the quantity, rather than the quality, of food is not surprising.

The link between agriculture and nutrition can, however, be tenuous: it all depends on whether the "right" kind of agricultural interventions are pursued or not. For example, agriculture's effect on poverty reduction may be limited in countries with extremely high inequality and a large class of landless or smallholder farmers. The effect may also be limited in countries where the agriculture sector is dominated by nonfood or cash crops (such as tobacco, coffee, or cotton). Furthermore, even in countries where the sector produces food crops, they may be heavily skewed toward basic cereals, which are relatively low in nutritional content and unlikely to improve dietary diversity. Finally, agriculture may even have unintended negative consequences, including negative effects on the nutrition of women and children or on the health of farmers due to the improper handling of agrochemicals, water contamination, or an enlarged habitat for infectious disease vectors.

A growing literature has emphasized the potential for interventions to increase and diversify food production at home, as these interventions allow households to gain control over food and nutrition security. Recent reviews of the literature by Dizon, Josephson, and Raju (2019) and Pandey, Dev, and Jayachandran (2016) show that interventions, such as home gardens, and production of fish, poultry, or livestock positively influence the pathways between agriculture and nutrition. In particular, increased consumption of home-produced food tends to increase dietary diversity and is associated with increased agricultural income. For all of the various interventions, the evidence suggests that having access to a type of food, be it vegetables or animal products, tends to increase its consumption (Bageant, Liu, and Diao 2016; Irfanullah et al. 2008; Jones et al. 2005; Murshed-E-Jahan and Pemsl 2011; Murty, Rao, and Bamji 2016; Nielsen, Roos, and Thilsted 2003), enabling families to sell their excess production (Murty, Rao, and Bamji 2016; Rahman and Sousa-Poza 2010; von Braun et al. 2005; Wilcox et al. 2014) and potentially improving their incomes (Rahman and Sousa-Poza 2010). These issues tend to be more complex than they might first appear (see the discussion of rice-producing net rice buyers). The question of whether production diversification leads to better welfare outcomes has been investigated elsewhere—for example, in Ethiopia, where crop diversification has been found to reduce poverty, and in Bangladesh, where crop diversification has led to improved diet diversity (Islam et al. 2018; Michler and Josephson 2017).

AGRICULTURE IN THE PHILIPPINES

In recent years in the Philippines, the share of agriculture in national gross domestic product (GDP) declined, while the share of services increased. Whereas in 1997 the agriculture sector accounted for approximately 20 percent of value added, in 2017 it accounted for only 10 percent (figure 5.1, panel a). The economy is now driven largely by the services sector, which currently contributes 70 percent of value added. The share of workers employed in agriculture has also declined, from about 40 percent of employment in 1997 to only about 25 percent in 2017 (figure 5.1, panel b).

FIGURE 5.1

Structural transformation of the Philippine economy, 1995–2017

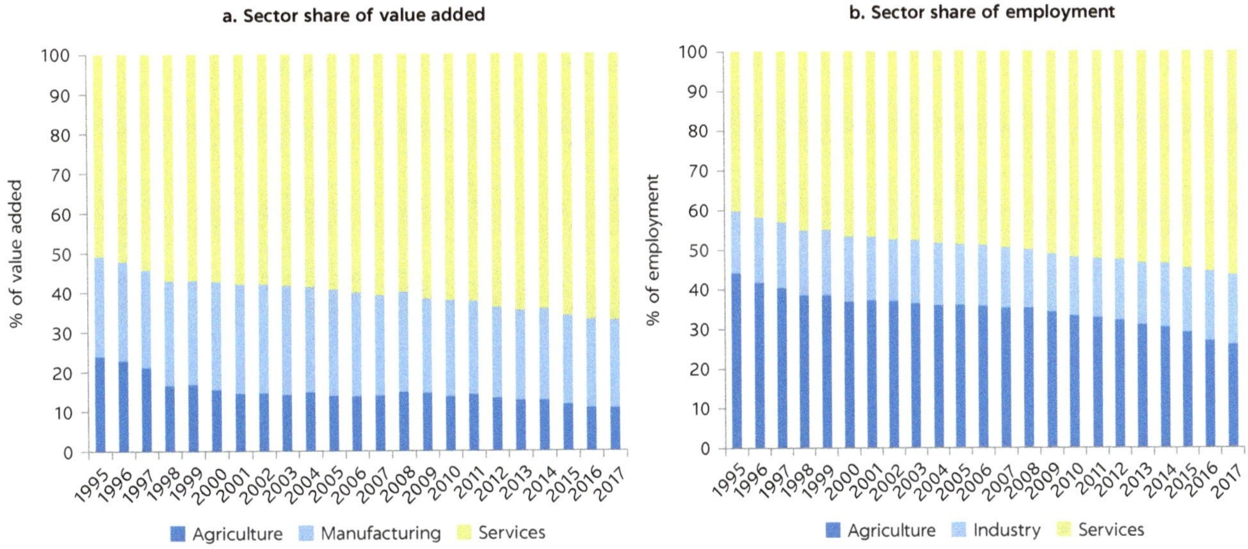

Source: World Bank 2018.

Nevertheless, a considerable share of households still rely on agriculture, primarily in the northeast and southwest areas of the country. According to the 2015 Family Income and Expenditure Survey (FIES), 17 percent of households rely on agriculture for their main source of income, defined as at least 50 percent of income sourced from agriculture (PSA 2015b). Some regions are more agriculture-oriented than others. In the Autonomous Region in Muslim Mindanao (ARMM), 63 percent of households rely on agriculture for their main source of income. This is the only region where a majority of households depend primarily on agriculture for income (map 5.1, panel a). The ARMM is followed by Cagayan Valley, where 41 percent of households rely on agriculture.

Rice farming still predominates among crop-producing households. According to the 2015 Labor Force Survey, 8 percent of households have at least one family member engaged in rice farming as their main occupation (or 4.3 percent if restricted to households whose main source of income is agriculture, based on the FIES) (PSA 2015c). In contrast, 5 percent have at least one member in fruit production, 4 percent in other cereal production, 2 percent in vegetable cultivation, 1 percent in roots and tubers, and another 1 percent in sugar. Rice-farming households are spread throughout the country, with the largest shares in Cordillera Administrative Region (CAR), Cagayan Valley, and Western Visayas, with 23 percent, 18 percent, and 16 percent of households, respectively, in rice farming (map 5.1, panel c).

Some rice-producing households buy more rice from markets than they produce: they are net rice buyers. Based on data from the 2015 FIES, 11 percent of households are rice-producing households (including those for whom rice production is not the main activity for any household member). Similarly, 8 percent of households are net rice sellers. Thus, 3 percent of households are both rice-producing households and net buyers of rice. The proportion of rice-producing net rice buyers can be high in some regions (map 5.1, panel d). In CAR, 32 percent of households produce rice, and about half of these households (16 percent) are also net rice buyers. In MIMAROPA, 24 percent produce rice, and 7 percent are also net rice buyers. And in Western Visayas, 20 percent of households are rice-producing, but 7 percent are both rice producers and net rice buyers.

MAP 5.1

Households engaged in agriculture, vegetable and fruit farming, and rice farming and net rice sellers in the Philippines, by region, 2015

a. Share of agricultural households

b. Share of households growing fruits and vegetables

c. Share of rice-farming households

d. Share of net rice sellers

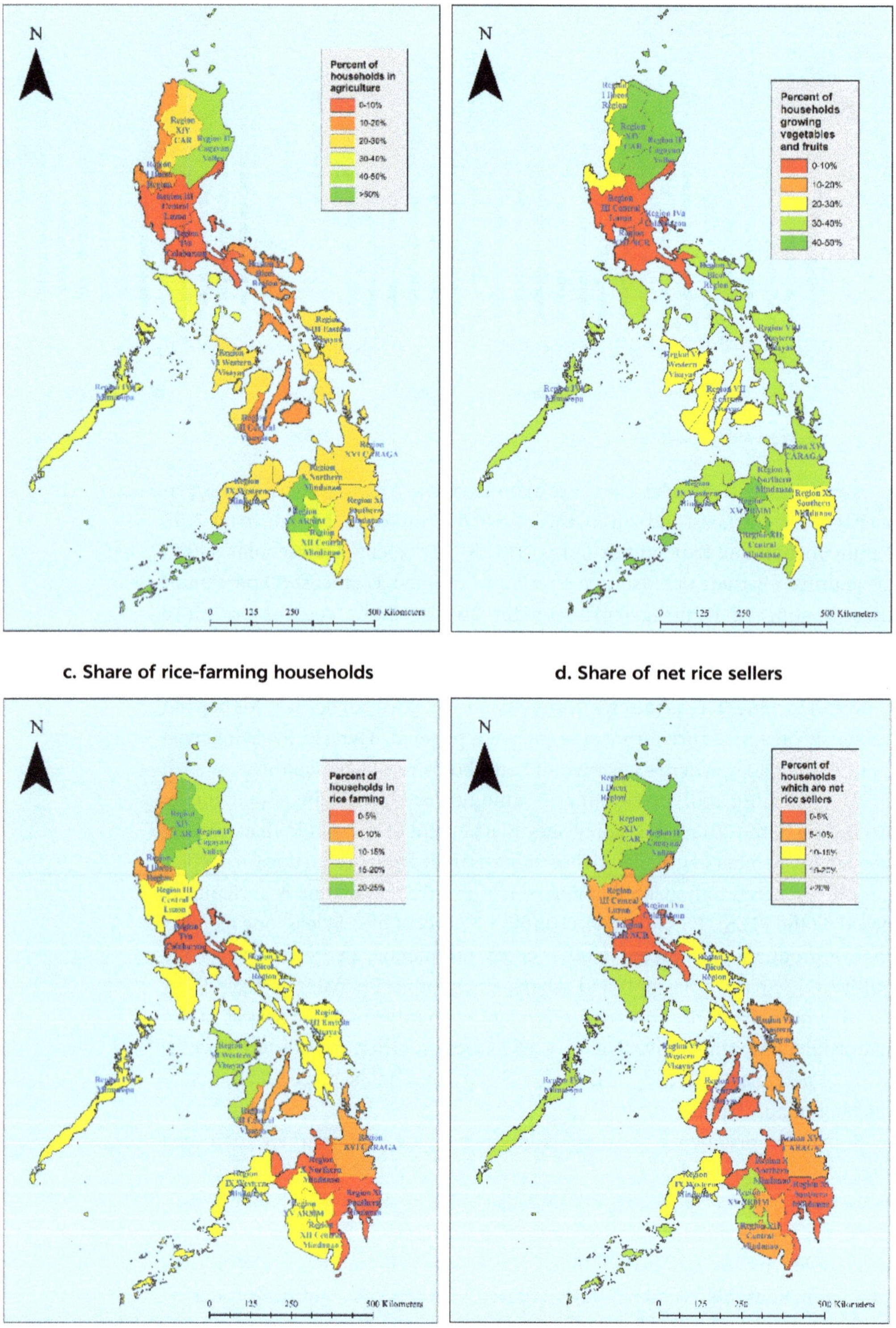

Sources: For panels a, b, and d, the 2015 Family Income and Expenditure Survey (PSA 2015b). For panel c, the 2015 Labor Force Survey (PSA 2015c).

Overall, rice remains at the forefront of significant government policy and spending decisions. Within the overall budget of the Department of Agriculture, a disproportionate share of support is still targeted to rice farmers. Under the Department of Agriculture's budget for fiscal year 2020, the rice program received 48 percent of the budget allocated for production support services; 53 percent of funds for extension support, education, and training services; 35 percent for agriculture equipment and facilities provision; 49 percent for research and development; and 88 percent for irrigation services. The vast majority of the budget of the National Irrigation Agency is devoted to single-crop rice production schemes. All of this support is for a crop that contributes only about 18 percent of the value of agricultural production. Meanwhile, the budget for some categories of expenditures on public goods that will be important to attain the policy goals of the Department of Agriculture's "New Thinking"[1]—such as research, market development (other than roads), and extension—are relatively low and declining.

Massive policy support notwithstanding, food expenditure on rice continues to be higher because consumer prices are higher than levels observed elsewhere in the region. The poor spend roughly 19 percent of their total food expenditure on rice. In July 2018, 1 kilogram of rice cost ₱43 in Philippine supermarkets. Consumers in Vietnam were paying the equivalent of ₱21. Rice prices have fallen substantially since passage and approval of the Rice Liberalization Act (Republic Act no. 11203), but farmgate prices have fallen farther than consumer prices. Overall, the high price of rice has crowded out more nutritious foods (figure 5.2), especially among the diets of poorer households. The factors contributing to the price of rice (and more nutritious foods) are multiple, although most stem directly from policies, including restrictions on food imports, restrictions on land use and land market development, restrictions on entry into the freight and logistics sector, concentration of irrigation development almost entirely on rice, and relative neglect of food crops other than rice and the public goods needed to develop those subsectors.

FIGURE 5.2

Food expenditures of the bottom income quintile in the Philippines, 2003, 2006, 2009, 2012, and 2015

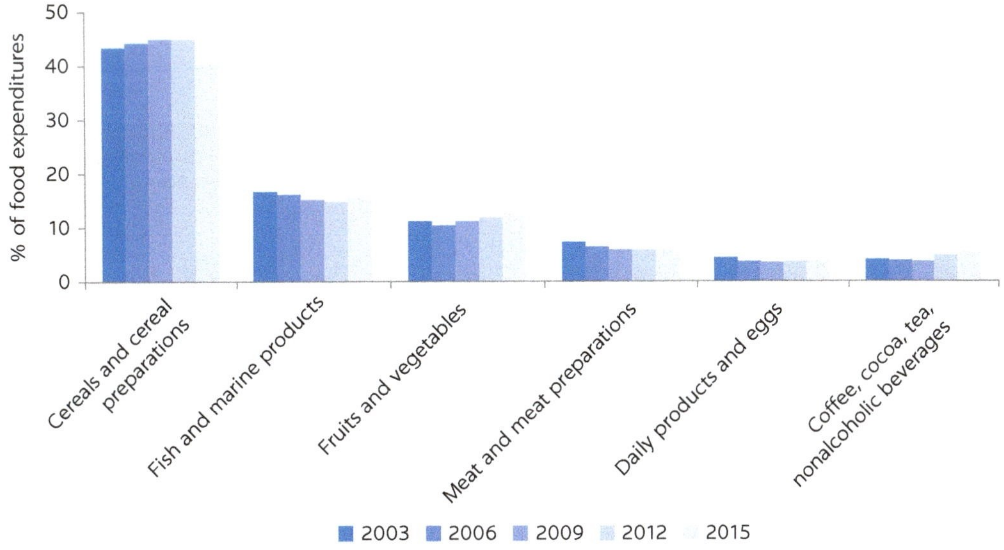

Source: The 2015 Family Income and Expenditure Survey (PSA 2015b).

Good nutrition is more expensive in urban than in rural areas. On average, urban consumers pay 10 percent more for a nutritionally adequate diet than their rural counterparts do. At the extreme, Metro Manila residents pay a 69 percent premium. Inadequate logistics partly explain the failure of horticulture value chains to expand, resulting in poor diets (World Bank 2020). In essence, government policies have protected farmers at the expense of consumers (or, more precisely, the 90 percent of Filipinos who are net buyers of rice). The protected value chain for rice has not become an efficient primary producer; in particular, milling and logistics remain inefficient. In sum, these policies have resulted in very high rice prices for consumers, crowding out more nutritious (more expensive) foods from the diet of a large segment of the population. Efforts to achieve self-sufficiency in staple food calories have not yielded nutritional security.

Fruits and vegetables are produced throughout the country. In CAR in the north and ARMM in the south, half of households produce some fruits and vegetables. Relatively fewer households produce fruits and vegetables in National Capital Region (NCR) or in regions closer to the capital, such as CALABARZON and Central Luzon.

Yet the agriculture sector comprises more than crops, its four subsectors being crop farming, livestock rearing, fishing, and forestry activities. Considering only households that derive most of their income from agriculture, 16 percent (of all households) do some crop farming, 10 percent rear some livestock, 6 percent do some fishing, and 16 percent do some forestry activities (figure 5.3, panel a). Households tend to engage simultaneously in a few of these subsectors. Among agricultural households, 53 percent engage in activities in three of the four subsectors, and 28 percent engage in activities in all four subsectors (figure 5.3, panel b).

Agricultural households are typically poorer than other households. In the Philippines, 41 percent of agricultural households are poor, compared with only 11 percent of nonagricultural households. The average per capita income for agricultural households is ₱31,962, which is less than half that of nonagricultural households, ₱75,172. Agricultural households are poorer regardless of the subsector in which they are engaged. For households in crop farming, livestock rearing, fishing, or forestry activities, the poverty rates are at or above 40 percent. Although the poverty rate is slightly lower for rice-farming households (33 percent) than for other agricultural households, it is still higher than for nonagricultural households.

FIGURE 5.3

Agriculture subsectors in the Philippines, 2015

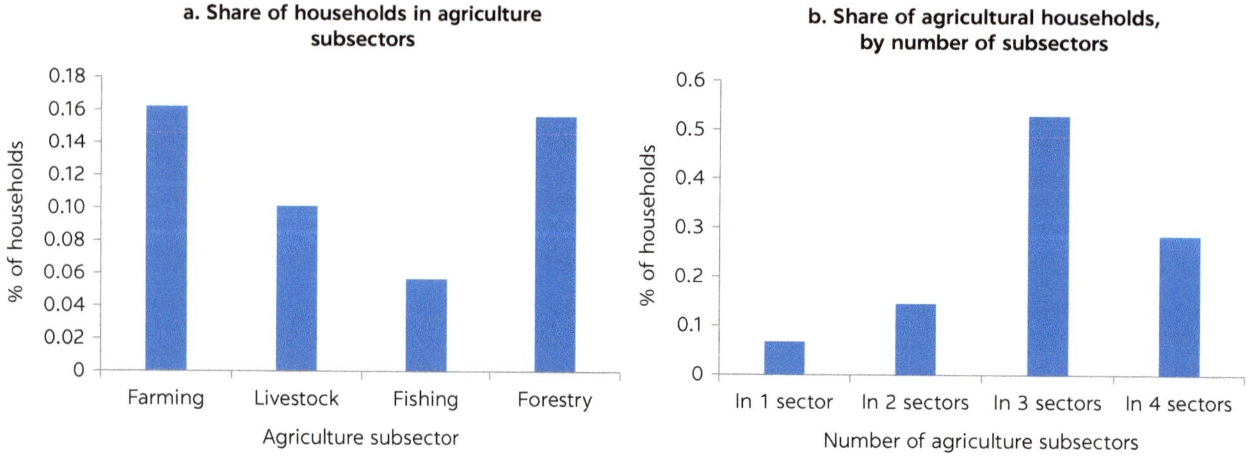

Source: The 2015 Family Income and Expenditure Survey (PSA 2015b).

DIVERSIFICATION OF AGRICULTURAL PRODUCTION AND MARKET ACCESS

An average agricultural household in the Philippines conducts roughly four agricultural activities, demonstrating some diversification of production. According to calculations using 2015 FIES data, among agricultural households (those whose main source of income is agriculture), the average household conducts 3.9 agricultural activities out of a total of 31 possible activities.[2] Bicol, CAR, and Western Mindanao have among the most diverse agricultural production, with agricultural households conducting, on average, 5.0 to 5.5 activities (map 5.2, panel a). In contrast, Central Luzon and NCR are home to the least diversified agricultural households (on average, conducting fewer than 1.5 activities).

Only 36 percent of barangays (districts or neighborhoods) have a marketplace where trading is conducted at least once a week, suggesting weak access to markets in many parts of the country. The Barangay Census conducted in 2015 asked whether a marketplace or building exists where trading activities are carried out at least once a week in the barangay (PSA 2015a). Of the 2,938 barangays, 36 percent have such a market. Apart from NCR, where many such marketplaces exist, barangays in the southern regions of the country are also more likely to have such markets: particularly ARMM, where 42 percent of barangays have such a marketplace, Northern Mindanao (43 percent), Central Mindanao (46 percent), Southern Mindanao (49 percent), and Western Mindanao (50 percent) (see map 5.2, panel b).

MAP 5.2

Production diversity and market access in the Philippines, by region

a. Agricultural production diversity | **b. Proportion of barangays with food markets in each region**

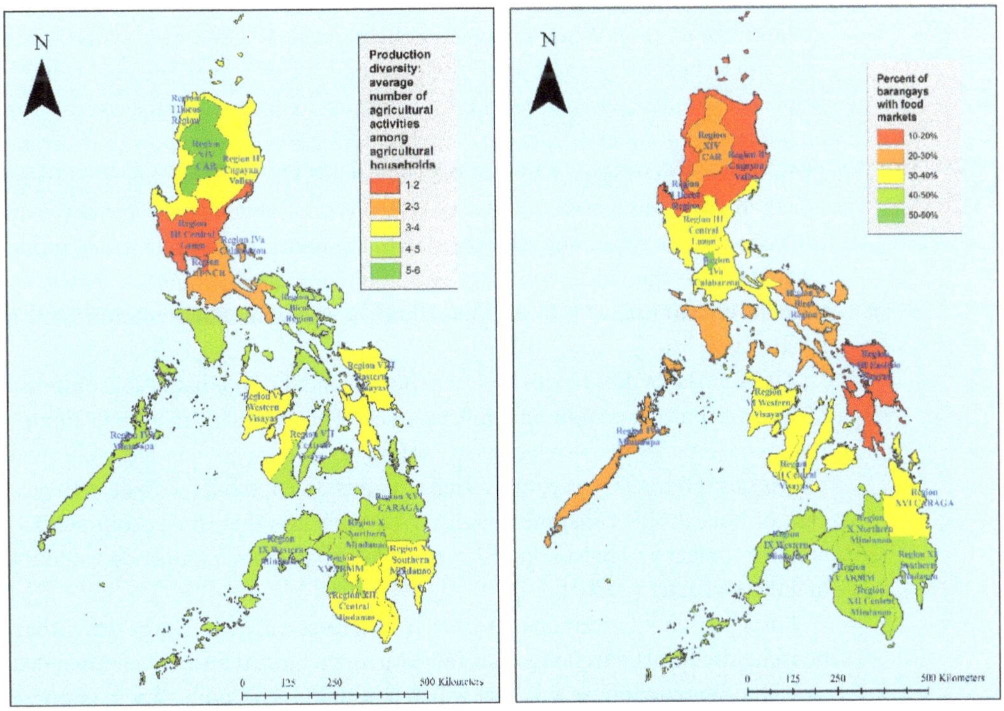

Sources: For panel a, the 2015 Family Income and Expenditure Survey (PSA 2015b). For panel b, the 2015 Census of Population—Barangay Schedule (PSA 2015a).

In contrast, the proportion of barangays with such a marketplace is lowest in the northern regions of the country, such as in Ilocos (10 percent), Cagayan Valley (15 percent), or Eastern Visayas (15 percent).

Agricultural households in regions with less access to markets tend to generate a more diverse range of products. NCR has low production diversity, but a very high proportion of barangays with market access. Southern Mindanao is similar to NCR: both have relatively low production diversity (3.37 activities), but relatively high access to markets (49 percent of barangays). In contrast, in some regions, production diversity might serve to compensate for the lack of access to markets. CAR has only 26 percent of barangays with a market but has the most diverse household production of all regions, with 5.5 activities, on average. Similarly, Bicol has only 24 percent of barangays with access to a market, but agricultural households in that region conduct 5.0 activities, on average.

DIETS OF FILIPINO HOUSEHOLDS

Enabling the consumption of diverse nutritious diets is one of the key pathways through which agriculture improves nutritional outcomes. Higher household diet diversity has been positively associated with better nutritional outcomes, particularly for stunted and underweight children. In the Philippines, according to the 2015 FIES, Filipinos consume 159 percent of the recommended amount of starchy staples (particularly rice) and only 22 percent of the recommended amount of vegetables, 10 percent for fruits, 12 percent for eggs, 79 percent for meat and pulses, 33 percent for milk and milk products, 29 percent for fats and oils, and 69 percent for sugar and sweets (figure 5.4).

Compared with the diet recommended in the country's food-based dietary guidelines, Filipinos are consuming 59 percent more starchy staples than the recommended amount and 78 percent fewer vegetables than the recommended amount (figure 5.4). When comparing the poorest 40 percent of households with the richest 40 percent, both the poor and the rich overconsume starchy staples and underconsume vegetables, fruits, and eggs to a similar extent. For example, the poorest 40 percent consume 88 percent less than the recommended amount of eggs, whereas the richest 40 percent consume 87 percent less than the recommended amount of eggs. With vegetables, the gap between the poor and the rich is slightly larger, with the poorest 40 percent consuming 82 percent less than the recommended amount of vegetables and the richest 40 percent consuming 74 percent less than the recommended amount: still a striking gap.

There are large differences between the rich and the poor in the consumption of meat and pulses and milk and milk products. The poorest 40 percent of households consume 48 percent less meat and pulses and 82 percent less milk (and milk products) than the recommended amounts. In contrast, the richest 40 percent of households consume roughly 7 percent less than the recommended amount of meat and pulses and 52 percent less than the recommended amount of milk (and dairy products).

Rural households overconsume starchy staples to a greater degree than urban households. Rural households consume 67 percent more than the recommended amount of starchy staples, whereas urban households consume 49 percent more than recommended. Urban households underconsume meat and pulses less than rural households. Urban households consume 10 percent less than the

FIGURE 5.4
Consumption of food groups in the Philippines, according to the country's food-based dietary guidelines

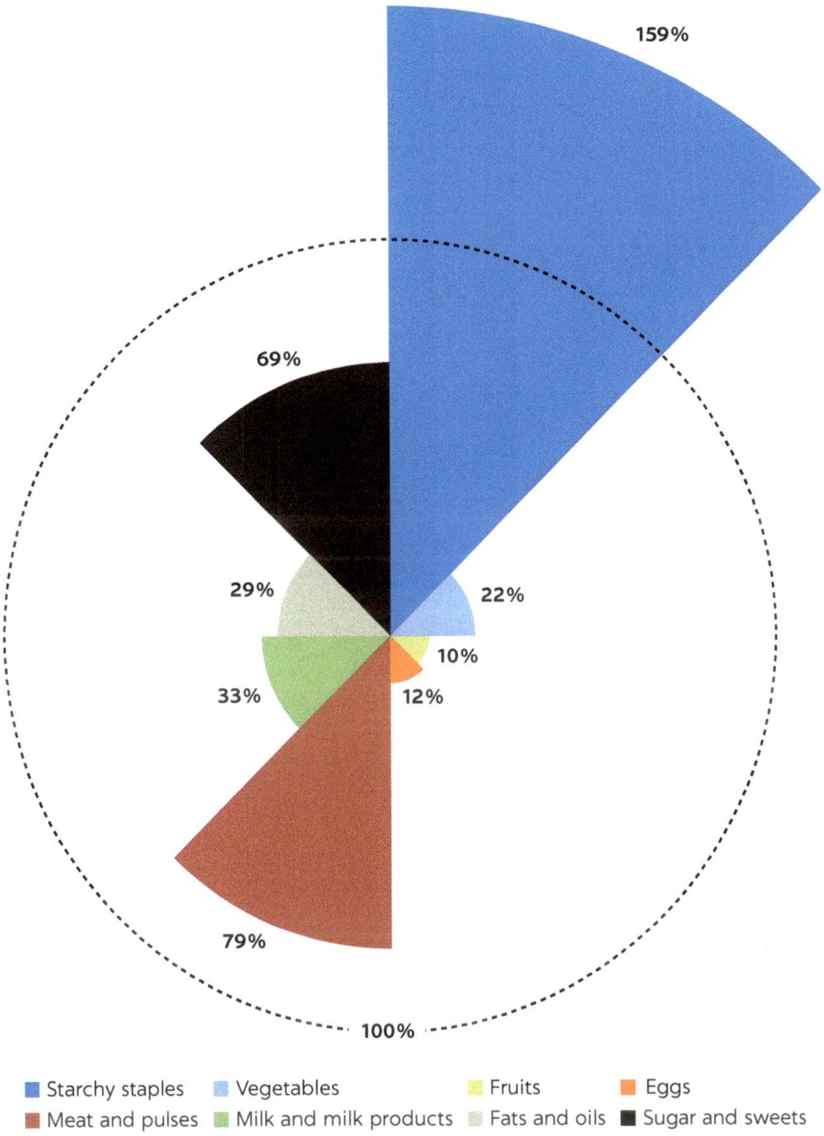

Source: The 2015 Family Income and Expenditure Survey (PSA 2015b).
Note: The Food and Nutrition Research Institute issues food-based dietary guidelines for the Philippines.

recommended amount of meat and pulses, while rural households consume 30 percent less than the recommended amount.

Based on analyses conducted as part of this study, market access is associated with comparatively higher consumption of protein and fruits, but to a lesser extent for agricultural households than for nonagricultural households. Having a regular marketplace for trading in the barangay, or nearby, improves protein and fruit consumption. However, this positive correlation is muted for households engaged in agriculture (table 5.1, columns 1 and 3). This finding suggests that enhancing access to markets improves dietary diversity, but that agricultural households are generally disconnected from markets (and have less cash for transactions), even when markets are nearby. Among protein foods, there are

TABLE 5.1 **Regressions: Production diversification, market access, and food consumption**

INDICATOR	SHARE OF GRAMS			
	PROTEIN (1)	VEGETABLES (2)	FRUITS (3)	HDDS (4)
In agriculture	−0.019***	−0.002**	−0.005***	−0.237***
	(0.001)	(0.001)	(0.001)	(0.060)
Income share in agriculture	0.009***	0.013***	−0.001	−0.562***
	(0.002)	(0.002)	(0.001)	(0.108)
Production diversification	−0.003***	−0.000	−0.000***	0.028***
	(0.000)	(0.000)	(0.000)	(0.008)
Market in barangay	0.010***	−0.002***	0.002***	0.189***
	(0.001)	(0.001)	(0.000)	(0.036)
In agri-X diversification	0.001***	−0.001***	0.001***	0.006
	(0.000)	(0.000)	(0.000)	(0.011)
In agri-X market	−0.003*	0.004***	−0.002***	−0.131*
	(0.001)	(0.001)	(0.001)	(0.070)
Income	0.002***	0.000***	0.001***	0.016***
	(0.000)	(0.000)	(0.000)	(0.003)
Total grams	−0.007***	−0.002***	−0.000	0.051**
	(0.001)	(0.000)	(0.000)	(0.022)
Constant	0.140***	0.079***	0.017***	9.157***
	(0.001)	(0.001)	(0.001)	(0.058)
Observations	41,104	41,104	41,104	32,590
R-squared	0.269	0.056	0.102	0.047
Mean of outcome	0.132	0.075	0.028	9.056

Sources: Calculations based on the 2015 National Nutrition Survey (FNRI 2015), 2015 Family Income and Expenditure Survey (PSA 2015b), the 2015 Labor Force Survey (PSA 2015c), and the 2015 Census of Population—Barangay Schedule (PSA 2015a).
Note: Dependent variables are the HDDS, and nutrition outcomes are defined as whether at least one person in the household experiences the specified undernutrition problem. *In agriculture* is defined as a household whose main income is derived from agriculture. *Production diversification* is the sum of agricultural activities. *Market in barangay* indicates whether a regular marketplace exists in the barangay or within 2 kilometers of the barangay. *Income* is per capita income in thousands of pesos. Region dummies are included as regressors. Robust standard errors are in parentheses.
HDDS = household dietary diversity score.
***$p<0.01$ **$p<0.05$ *$p<0.10$

interesting nuances. The positive effects of markets on meat consumption are largest for nonagricultural households, but the effects on fish consumption are largest for agricultural households. However, unlike market access, production diversification among agricultural households is not associated with substantial changes in the share of protein and fruit consumption.

Access to markets is also correlated with a more diverse diet, but again less so for agricultural households than for nonagricultural households. Unlike with the protein and fruit components of food consumption, production diversification is also positively related to diet diversity. However, the size of this correlation is small, especially relative to the size of the negative correlation between being in agriculture and the household dietary diversity score (HDDS) and the size of the positive correlation between having market access and the HDDS (table 5.1, column 4). However, the various correlations with diet diversity are much lower than the various correlations with share of protein food consumption and share of fruit consumption.

DIET OF HOUSEHOLDS ENGAGED IN AGRICULTURE

Analyses conducted for this study revealed that a household engaged in agriculture has a lower share of protein and fruit consumption and lower dietary diversity (HDDS).[3] But the magnitudes are small. Table 5.2 presents regression results that estimate the correlation between engaging in agriculture and the consumption share of protein-rich foods (meat, eggs, fish, and milk) (column 1), vegetables (column 6), and fruits (column 7). Households in agriculture consume a lower share of protein-rich foods and fruits than nonagricultural households, even after controlling for income, total grams of food consumption, and region dummies. The correlation between agriculture and share of consumption of nutritious foods is, however, not particularly large. The reduction in the share of protein in food, for example, is a 1.6 percentage point reduction, which is equivalent to a 12 percent reduction in its share (relative to the mean share of protein foods, 13 percent). The reduction in the share of fruits is a 0.3 percentage point reduction, which is equivalent to an 11 percent reduction (relative to the mean share of fruit consumption, 3 percent). The correlation between agriculture and HDDS is −0.29, which is equivalent to only a 3 percent reduction in the HDDS.

In addition, the share of household income from agriculture is correlated with the same food consumption variables. While 17 percent of households are defined as agricultural households (defined particularly as those who earn most of their income from agriculture), many more households (another 50 percent)

TABLE 5.2 Regressions: Agriculture and food consumption

INDICATOR	PROTEIN FOODS (1)	MEAT (2)	EGGS (3)	FISH (4)	MILK (5)	VEGETABLES (6)	FRUITS (7)	HDDS (8)
In agriculture	−0.016***	−0.011***	−0.001***	−0.002***	−0.002***	−0.002***	−0.003***	−0.292***
	(0.001)	(0.001)	(0.000)	(0.001)	(0.000)	(0.001)	(0.000)	(0.043)
Income share in agriculture	−0.016***	−0.018***	−0.004***	0.012***	−0.005***	0.010***	0.001	−0.359***
	(0.002)	(0.001)	(0.000)	(0.001)	(0.000)	(0.001)	(0.001)	(0.085)
Income (10 thousands)	0.002***	0.001***	0.000***	0.000***	0.001***	0.000***	0.001***	0.016***
	(0.000)	(0.000)	(0.000)	(0.000)	(0.000)	(0.000)	(0.000)	(0.003)
Total grams (thousands)	−0.007***	−0.002**	−0.001***	−0.004***	−0.000	−0.002***	−0.000	0.051**
	(0.001)	(0.001)	(0.000)	(0.000)	(0.000)	(0.000)	(0.000)	(0.022)
Constant	0.142***	0.067***	0.015***	0.051***	0.010***	0.079***	0.018***	9.240***
	(0.001)	(0.001)	(0.000)	(0.001)	(0.000)	(0.001)	(0.001)	(0.056)
Observations	41,539	41,539	41,539	41,539	41,539	41,539	41,539	32,853
R-squared	0.260	0.310	0.133	0.058	0.123	0.055	0.099	0.046
Mean of outcome	0.132	0.057	0.012	0.053	0.010	0.075	0.028	9.056

Sources: Calculations based on the 2015 Family Income and Expenditure Survey (PSA 2015b), the 2015 Labor Force Survey (PSA 2015c), 2015 National Nutrition Survey (FNRI 2015), and the 2015 Census of Population—Barangay Schedule (PSA 2015a).

Note: Dependent variables are total grams of consumption of a food group to total grams of adult male equivalent food consumption. *In agriculture* is defined as a household whose main income source is derived from agriculture. *Income* is per capita income in thousands of pesos. Region dummies are included as regressors. Robust standard errors are in parentheses. HDDS = household dietary diversity score.

***$p<0.01$ **$p<0.05$ *$p<0.10$

earn some, but not most, of their income from agriculture. Households with a higher share of income from agriculture also have a lower share of protein-rich food consumption, but a higher share of vegetable consumption, which is consistent with the aforementioned descriptive results. However, the negative correlation between the share of household income from agriculture and food consumption (or diet quality) is similarly small. For example, moving from no income derived from agriculture to all income derived from agriculture reduces the share of protein in food consumption by only 1.6 percentage points or 14 percent, and it reduces the HDDS by only 0.34 percentage point or 4 percent. The finding that agriculture is more strongly negatively correlated with share of protein or fruit consumption than with the HDDS demonstrates that the relationships are more about the intensive margin (eating more meat) than about the extensive margin (consuming a new food group).

COST OF A NUTRITIOUS DIET IN THE PHILIPPINES

To estimate the cost of a nutritious diet in the Philippines, the "cost of the recommended diet" (CoRD) methodology was applied using 2015 FIES data (annex 5A describes the methodology). The CoRD measures the minimum cost of using available foods to meet dietary recommendations, such as food-based dietary guidelines, commonly depicted as food pyramids. Such guidelines recommend a quantity to be consumed of each food group (within a culturally acceptable diet), both to meet nutritional needs and to prevent diet-related noncommunicable disease.

The CoRD approach shows that the minimum cost of the recommended diet substantially exceeds what households spend on food, on average (figure 5.5). In 2015 CoRD was ₱68 per adult per day. In contrast, households spent approximately ₱48 per adult per day on food. This crude comparison between CoRD and actual food spending suggests a gap of about 30 percent.

Breaking down spending by food group, the gap between actual and recommended food expenditure is primarily due to low spending on eggs, fruits, and vegetables. Figure 5.5 shows the cost and spending for each of the seven food groups. Households are spending, on average, much more on starchy staples and meat (in this context taken to include fish and nuts) than the minimum needed to meet the recommended dietary intake of those food groups. The overspending on meat (including fish and nuts) is probably because the items selected by the CoRD method are cheap, such as shellfish and peanuts. In contrast, households are spending, on average, less on all other food groups, namely, vegetables, fruits, eggs, milk (and milk products), and fats and oils.

The gap between CoRD and actual food spending varies across regions. The CoRD calculations for each region were compared with food expenses per adult male equivalent for that region to calculate the percentage difference between CoRD and actual food expenses. These gaps are presented in figure 5.6. In CAR, Caraga, Central Luzon, and MIMAROPA, the gap between CoRD and actual food expenses is 25 percent or less, whereas in Bicol, Cagayan Valley, and Ilocos, the gap is 35 percent or higher. In Cagayan Valley, the gap is 56 percent.

Insufficient consumption of nutritious food is the result of a combination of low income, poor food choices, and high price of nutritious foods. In this section, we consider why certain nutritious foods are relatively expensive in the Philippines. Headey and Alderman (2019) compare the price of nutritious and less nutritious foods across countries using food price data from the 2011 International Comparison Program (ICP) for 657 standardized food items across

FIGURE 5.5
CoRD and food expenses in the Philippines, by food group, 2015

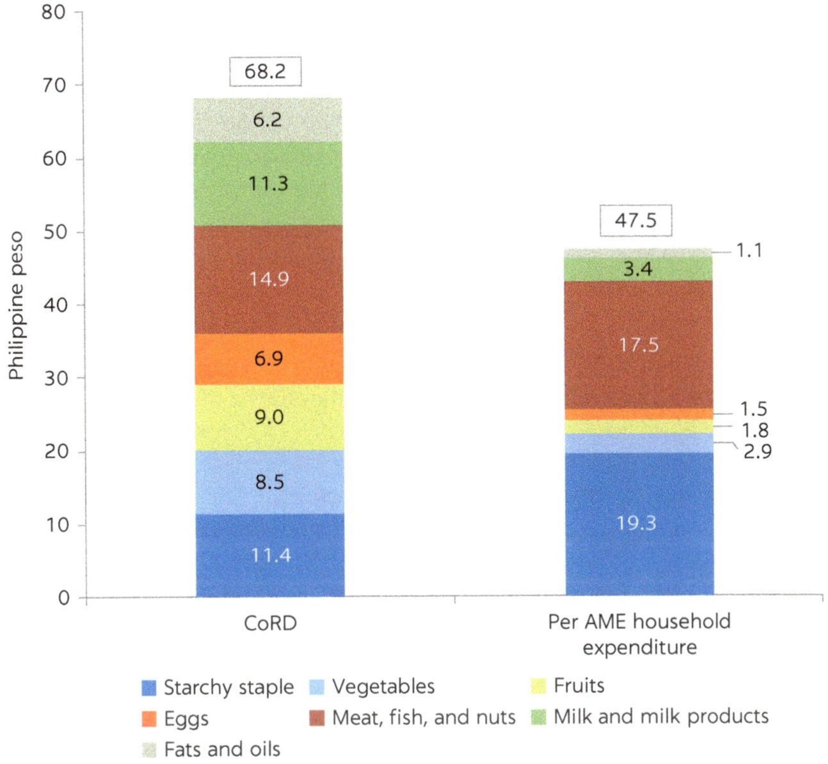

Source: The 2015 Family Income and Expenditure Survey (PSA 2015b).
Note: AME = adult male equivalent. CoRD = cost of the recommended diet.

FIGURE 5.6
Gap between CoRD and food spending in the Philippines, by region, 2015

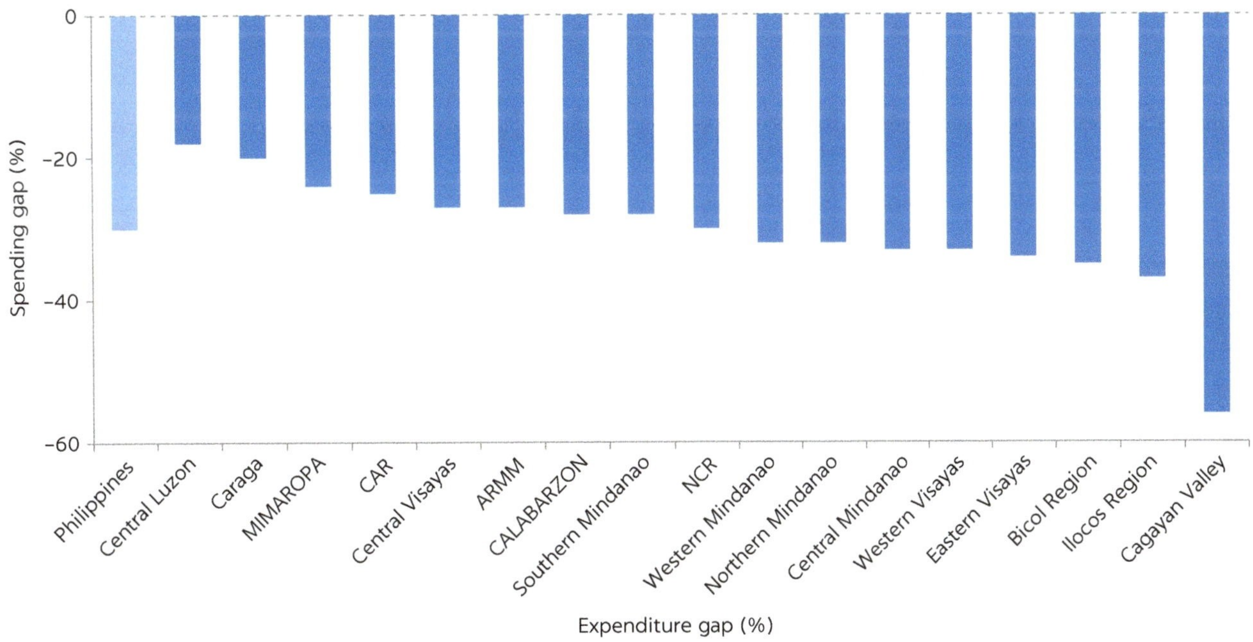

Source: The 2015 Family Income and Expenditure Survey (PSA 2015b).
Note: ARMM = Autonomous Region in Muslim Mindanao. CALABARZON = Cavite, Laguna, Batangas, Rizal, and Quezon. CAR = Cordillera Administrative Region. MIMAROPA = Occidental Mindoro, Oriental Mindoro, Marinduque, Romblon, and Palawan. NCR = National Capital Region.

176 countries (World Bank 2011). A key feature of the ICP data is the degree of standardization across food items. The ICP definitions for a food item include quantity, quality, weight, packaging, and processing, as well as other features of the product. This level of detail ensures that a given food item is comparable across countries, as is the price collected for that item. Food items are classified into 29 food groups and then aggregated into four broad food categories: starchy staples (which includes 9 of the 29 food groups), vegetable foods, animal-sourced foods, and a group of less nutritious foods that are high in sugar, salt, and fat. Drawing from these analyses, we calculate the price per calorie by food group for the Philippines and other countries (see annex 5B for a description of the methodology).

The prices of five out of seven vegetable food groups are higher in the Philippines than in low- and middle-income countries or Southeast Asia as a whole. Figure 5.7 presents the price per 1,000 kilocalories of vegetable foods in

FIGURE 5.7

Price per 1,000 kilocalories of vegetable and animal-sourced foods in select regions

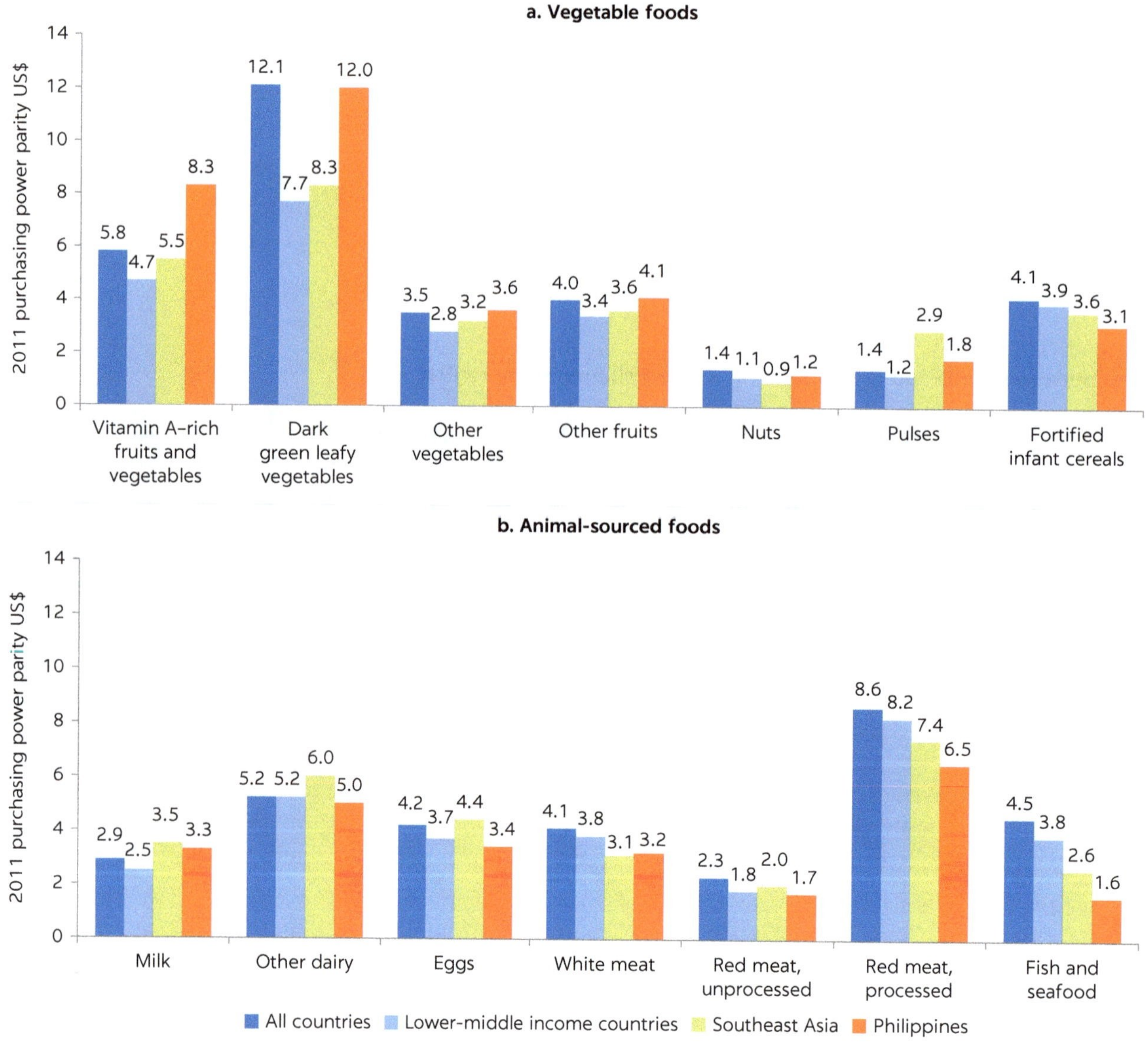

Source: Headey and Alderman 2019.

FIGURE 5.8

Price per 1,000 kilocalories of sugar-rich, salt-rich, and fat-rich foods

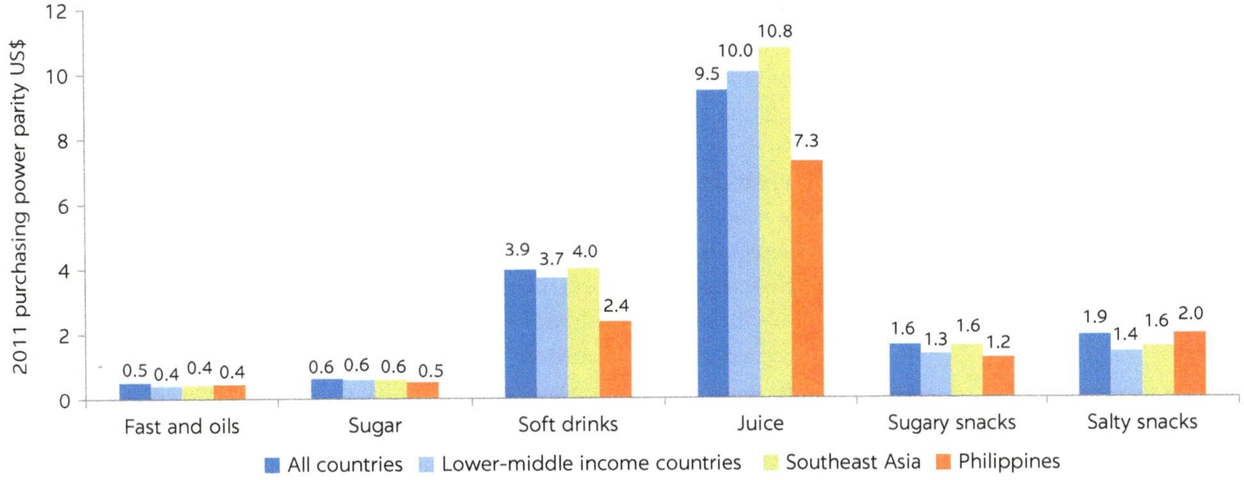

Source: Headey and Alderman 2019.

panel a and the price of animal-sourced foods in panel b, for all countries, lower-middle income countries, Southeast Asia, and the Philippines. In particular, the price per calorie for vitamin A–rich fruits and vegetables, dark green leafy vegetables, other vegetables, other fruits, and nuts is higher in the Philippines than in lower-middle income countries and Southeast Asia. The price per calorie for most vegetables and fruits in the Philippines more closely resembles the global average. The price per calorie of pulses and fortified infant cereals is, however, cheaper in the Philippines than in Southeast Asia.

The price per calorie of all animal-sourced food groups is lower in the Philippines than in lower-middle income countries. Compared with Southeast Asia, the price per calorie of all animal-sourced food groups is also lower in the Philippines, except for white meat, for which the price per calorie in the Philippines and Southeast Asia is similar.

COST OF LESS NUTRITIOUS DIETS

Figure 5.8 presents the price per calorie of six less nutritious foods that are high in sugar, salt, or fat. Fats and oils and sugar are relatively cheap sources of calories both globally and in the Philippines. These two food groups are an even cheaper source of calories than staples. For example, sugar in the Philippines costs US$0.51 per 1,000 kilocalories, whereas staples cost US$0.76. In addition, sugary drinks, such as soft drinks and juice, and sugary snacks are all cheaper in the Philippines than in all other countries (including in low- and middle-income countries or Southeast Asia). For example, in the Philippines, the price per 1,000 kilocalories is US$2.36 for soft drinks, US$7.27 for juice, and US$1.23 for sugary snacks. Meanwhile, in Southeast Asia, the price per 1,000 kilocalories is US$3.99 for soft drinks, US$10.76 for juice, and US$1.60 for sugary snacks. Even for low- and middle-income countries, the respective prices are US$3.70 (soft drinks), US$10.03 (juice), and US$1.34 (sugary snacks).

HOUSEHOLD AGRICULTURAL PRACTICES, DIETARY DIVERSITY, AND NUTRITIONAL OUTCOMES

Analyses were undertaken on a data set comprising the 2015 FIES, the 2015 Labor Force Survey, the 2015 National Nutrition Survey, and the 2015 Census of Population and Housing—Barangay Schedule. This analysis found that households engaged in agriculture have a higher probability of stunting, wasting, underweight (for children, low weight-for-age), or underweight (for adults, low body mass index, BMI) (table 5.3). An agricultural household experiences a 6.4 percentage point higher probability that a child in the household is stunted, equivalent to an 18 percent increase in probability (relative to the mean of households with stunted children, 36 percent). As noted, engagement in agriculture is correlated with comparatively lower consumption of protein-rich foods and fruits; hence, the inference that the negative correlation between engaging in agriculture and poor nutritional outcomes is at least partly due to poor food consumption by agricultural households. But poor food consumption in agricultural households is probably not the only pathway through which the negative correlation between engaging in agriculture and nutrition materializes.

Households that consume a more diverse diet have better nutrition outcomes, but the correlation is small (table 5.4). An increase in HDDS is positively correlated with child nutrition outcomes: stunting, wasting, and low weight-for-age for children or low BMI for adults. The impacts are, however, small in magnitude—for example, increasing HDDS by one more food group (of 12 possible groups) reduces the probability of stunting by 0.7 percentage points, equivalent to only a 2 percent reduction in the probability that a child from the household is stunted.

TABLE 5.3 **Regressions: Agriculture and nutrition outcomes**

	CHILDREN			ADOLESCENTS	ADULTS
INDICATOR	STUNTING (1)	WASTING (2)	UNDERWEIGHT (3)	THINNESS (4)	UNDERWEIGHT (5)
In agriculture	0.064***	0.027**	0.067***	0.005	0.022**
	(0.019)	(0.011)	(0.018)	(0.008)	(0.008)
Income share in agriculture	0.014	−0.027	−0.001	−0.009	0.043***
	(0.035)	(0.021)	(0.032)	(0.016)	(0.015)
Income	−0.016***	−0.004***	−0.014***	−0.006***	−0.006***
	(0.002)	(0.001)	(0.002)	(0.001)	(0.000)
Total grams	−0.059***	−0.013*	−0.037***	−0.021***	−0.016***
	(0.013)	(0.007)	(0.012)	(0.006)	(0.004)
Constant	0.406***	0.102***	0.281***	0.224***	0.272***
	(0.023)	(0.014)	(0.021)	(0.012)	(0.010)
Observations	8,193	8,193	8,193	22,206	32,830
R-squared	0.057	0.008	0.046	0.019	0.020
Mean of outcome	0.356	0.077	0.240	0.143	0.195

Sources: Calculations based on the 2015 National Nutrition Survey (FNRI 2015), 2015 Family Income and Expenditure Survey (PSA 2015b), the 2015 Labor Force Survey (PSA 2015c), and the 2015 Census of Population—Barangay Schedule (PSA 2015a).

Note: Dependent variables are nutrition outcomes, defined as whether at least one person in the household experiences the specified undernutrition problem. *In agriculture* is defined as a household whose main source of income is derived from agriculture, *Income* is per capita income in thousands of pesos. Region dummies are included as regressors. Robust standard errors are in parentheses.

***$p<0.01$ **$p<0.05$ *$p<0.10$.

TABLE 5.4 Regressions: Household dietary diversity score (HDDS) and nutrition outcomes

	CHILDREN			ADOLESCENTS	ADULTS
INDICATOR	STUNTING (1)	WASTING (2)	UNDERWEIGHT (3)	THINNESS (4)	UNDERWEIGHT (5)
HDDS	−0.007***	−0.003*	−0.006***	0.000	−0.003***
	(0.002)	(0.001)	(0.002)	(0.001)	(0.001)
Income	−0.017***	−0.004***	−0.015***	−0.006***	−0.006***
	(0.003)	(0.001)	(0.002)	(0.001)	(0.000)
Total grams	−0.058***	−0.013*	−0.036***	−0.021***	−0.015***
	(0.013)	(0.007)	(0.012)	(0.006)	(0.004)
Constant	0.488***	0.127***	0.348***	0.220***	0.311***
	(0.031)	(0.019)	(0.028)	(0.015)	(0.013)
Observations	8,194	8,194	8,194	22,206	32,830
R-squared	0.055	0.008	0.044	0.019	0.019
Mean of outcome	0.356	0.077	0.240	0.143	0.195

Sources: Calculations based on the 2015 National Nutrition Survey (FNRI 2015), 2015 Family Income and Expenditure Survey (PSA 2015b), the 2015 Labor Force Survey (PSA 2015c), and 2015 Census of Population—Barangay Schedule (PSA 2015a).
Note: Dependent variables are nutrition outcomes, defined as whether at least one person in the household experiences the specified undernutrition problem. Independent variables are the HDDS. Poor is defined as a household that falls below the poverty line. Region dummies are included as regressors. Robust standard errors are in parentheses.
***p<0.01 **p<0.05 *p<0.10.

A more detailed analysis of the link between household diets and nutritional outcome revealed that the consumption of protein-rich foods and fruits improves nutrition outcomes for children, adolescents, and adults. A higher share of protein-rich foods to total food consumption is correlated with a lower probability of having a stunted, wasted, or underweight child under five in the household; a lower probability of thinness among adolescents; and a lower probability of underweight in adults (table 5.5). The estimated correlations are quite large. For example, going from a 0 percent to a 25 percent share of protein in food consumption reduces the probability that a child in the household is stunted by 20 percentage points (a fourth of the estimate −0.79), which is equivalent to a 55 percent reduction in the probability of having a stunted child (relative to the mean of households with stunted children, which is 36 percent). Further analyses showed that the large correlation between protein-rich food and stunting is driven largely by meat and milk as opposed to fish and eggs.

Fruit consumption is also correlated with lower probabilities of poor nutrition outcomes, such as wasting, low child weight-for-age, thinness, or low adult BMI. As noted for protein foods, the magnitude of the correlations between fruit consumption and nutrition outcomes can be large. For example, going from a 0 percent to a 25 percent share of fruits in food consumption reduces the probability that a child in the household is wasted by 6 percentage points, which is equivalent to an 81 percent reduction in the probability (relative to the mean of households with wasted children, which is 7.7 percent).

In contrast, the share of vegetable consumption has no statistically significant correlation with child nutrition outcomes. Although a higher share of vegetable consumption is negatively correlated with adolescent thinness, it is positively correlated with low adult weight, suggesting that vegetable consumption might be crowding out the calories needed to meet the calorific needs of adults. Further analyses revealed that vegetables have a negligible correlation with child undernutrition outcomes, regardless of whether the vegetables are high in vitamin A or not.

TABLE 5.5 **Regressions: Food consumption and nutrition outcomes**

	CHILDREN			ADOLESCENTS	ADULTS
INDICATOR	STUNTING (1)	WASTING (2)	UNDERWEIGHT (3)	THINNESS (4)	UNDERWEIGHT (5)
Protein foods	−0.788*** (0.110)	−0.141** (0.060)	−0.535*** (0.098)	−0.223*** (0.048)	−0.298*** (0.043)
Vegetables	0.042 (0.157)	−0.028 (0.086)	−0.097 (0.138)	−0.204*** (0.074)	0.202*** (0.060)
Fruits	−0.316 (0.224)	−0.250** (0.118)	−0.470** (0.196)	−0.285** (0.120)	−0.427*** (0.080)
Income	−0.012*** (0.002)	−0.003*** (0.001)	−0.011*** (0.002)	−0.005*** (0.001)	−0.005*** (0.000)
Total grams	−0.072*** (0.013)	−0.016** (0.007)	−0.048*** (0.012)	−0.025*** (0.006)	−0.017*** (0.004)
Constant	0.526*** (0.028)	0.127*** (0.017)	0.378*** (0.025)	0.272*** (0.014)	0.312*** (0.012)
Observations	8,193	8,193	8,193	22,206	32,826
R-squared	0.062	0.009	0.048	0.021	0.022
Mean of outcome	0.356	0.077	0.240	0.143	0.195

Sources: Calculations based on the 2015 National Nutrition Survey (FNRI 2015), 2015 Family Income and Expenditure Survey (PSA 2015b), the 2015 Labor Force Survey (PSA 2015c), and the 2015 Census of Population—Barangay Schedule (PSA 2015a).
Note: Dependent variables are nutrition outcomes, defined as whether at least one person in the household experiences the specified undernutrition problem. Independent variables are the ratio of grams of consumption of a food group to total grams of adult male equivalent food consumption. Income is per capita income in thousands of pesos. Region dummies are included as regressors. Robust standard errors are in parentheses.
***$p<0.01$ **$p<0.05$ *$p<0.10$

Aflatoxin contamination is another possible mechanism in the relationship between agriculture and nutrition in the Philippines (box 5.1).

CONCLUSIONS AND RECOMMENDATIONS

Although the diversification of agriculture is a long-standing policy goal of the government of Philippines, traditional crops, such as rice, still dominate. Over the past two decades, the relative shares of noncrop agricultural production—livestock, poultry, and fisheries—have fallen, with fisheries showing the sharpest percentage drop (World Bank 2020). Therefore, it is not surprising that the average food intake is high in cereals and tubers and low in fruits and vegetables compared with Pinggang Pinoy, a food guide that uses a familiar food plate model to convey the right food group proportions on a per meal basis. This consumption pattern is consistent across socioeconomic strata. There is no doubt that social and cultural factors might play a role in this consumption pattern, but economic factors are key: it is expensive for Filipinos to diversify their diets and include more nutritious foods. While most, if not all, Filipino households can

BOX 5.1

Aflatoxin exposure and childhood stunting

Fungal infections of food with species of *Aspergillus* can lead to contamination with the mycotoxin aflatoxin, which causes stunted growth and delayed development in children and liver carcinoma and eventual death in adults; these species are highly toxic to animals as well. Aflatoxins are toxic secondary metabolites of *Aspergillus* molds that contaminate foods, such as maize, rice, and legumes. Aflatoxins are among the more serious chemical food contaminants (such as dioxin aflatoxin, cyanide present in cassava, and peanut allergens) contributing to the burden of disease (Moy and Miller 2016). They are associated with the most global disability-adjusted life years (n = 636,869). There is growing evidence of a relationship between aflatoxins and childhood stunting. Although only a small number of observational studies have been conducted, they have found a strong association between aflatoxin exposure and growth restriction (Leroy 2013).

Climatic conditions, high temperature, and high relative humidity in the Philippines favor growth of the *Aspergillus* fungi. Contamination in agricultural crops, food, and feed commodities is a serious problem in the country. Harvest of staple cereals normally coincides with the rainy season, resulting in high grain moisture, processing and storage problems, and potentially rapid formation and buildup of mycotoxins. Aflatoxins are frequently detected in Philippine products, such as rice, corn, copra (dried coconut), peanuts, and coffee beans, at levels above the country limit (Sales and Yoshizawa 2005). The literature on the Philippines focuses principally on aflatoxin contamination in food and feeds and the serious threat to human and animal health. By contrast, there has been little exploration of the impacts on growth retardation in children. Therefore, more research is needed to investigate the potential impact of aflatoxin in Filipino diets on children's nutritional outcomes. Meanwhile, aggressive monitoring of aflatoxin contamination is urgently needed, with more awareness campaigns and the provision and use at scale of aflatoxin testing kits in regional laboratories.

afford a diet that meets their energy needs (primarily due to their rice-heavy diet), more than one-third would not be able to afford a diet that meets their nutritional needs. Poverty is the key factor here.

Therefore, for the agriculture sector to contribute to improvements in the persistently high levels of malnutrition in the country, the following recommendations need to be considered.

Promote the diversification of production in the agriculture sector and expand the sector with a focus on value addition and specialization in key select regions

Owing to long-standing trade restrictions on rice imports, an inherent bias toward domestic rice production was maintained within a noncompetitive rice market. The recent groundbreaking reforms of rice trade policy pave the way for two eventualities: encouraging diversification of production to higher-value crops and lowering prices for consumers. These reforms would benefit consumers and rice farmers alike, many of whom are net rice buyers. In the context of these reforms, the government should continue to support farmers formerly engaged predominantly in rice farming to make a transition into higher-value food production (box 5.2). Trade reforms are expected to lower the price of rice and thereby remove a powerful constraint on the food budget of many consumers, enabling them to afford a more diverse basket of food. While the Philippine economy evolves away

BOX 5.2

Policy recommendation to support production diversification

Nutritional outcomes could be improved with the right policies in place. For too long, food security has been interpreted in the Philippines as being equivalent to rice self-sufficiency. To achieve that goal, administrations over the decades have been intervening heavily in the production and distribution of rice. In 1972 the National Food Authority was established as the lead government agency for regulating rice marketing, including licensing and quotas on international trade (on both the import and the export sides). Its original mandate included strong participation in rice marketing, involving the procurement of palay and the distribution of subsidized milled rice to consumers.

Rice policy has long been a contentious subject in the legislature. The reform momentum reached a turning point when the Rice Liberalization Act was passed by Congress in 2018 and signed into law in early 2019. The law abolished the quota system and opened up importation of rice to private traders, subject only to customs duties and sanitary and phytosanitary regulations. The law was an important first step to promote diversification. A second important step was to introduce the "New Thinking" for agriculture, a strategy based on pillars, such as modernization, industrialization, consolidation, and infrastructure development. However, public spending on agriculture is still focused on rice. A recent World Bank report, *Transforming Philippine Agriculture: During COVID-19 and Beyond* (World Bank 2020), suggests shifting away from a focus on specific crops and toward improving the overall resilience, inclusiveness, competitiveness, and sustainability of the sector. It also suggests shifting to a more demand-driven sector, with adjusted modalities of government support, stronger evidence-based decision making, and a greater focus on public goods. These reforms would lead to a more diversified sector with strong food value chains, affordable and nutritious food, and a vibrant rural economy.

from agricultural production, a few regions will continue to focus and maintain a comparative advantage in agricultural production. For these regions, the focus should be on enhancing specialization and value addition.

Promote access to markets for consumers and invest in infrastructure that lowers the cost of trade and transportation

This report shows that access to markets improves the consumption of more nutritious foods, such as protein-rich foods and fruits. Thus, although lowering the cost of nutritious foods might be impactful, a fundamental issue remains: the need to improve physical access to markets with diverse and nutritious foods. This need is particularly evident in the Philippines, a country where trade and transportation are challenging, given its geography of many islands.

Promote fortification as an entry point for improving nutrient intake in the short term

Only 2 percent of the national rice supply is fortified, despite strong legislation, dating back to 1952, that mandates fortification of rice with iron. Fortification is highly cost-effective and has been more successful at preventing micronutrient deficiencies in the general population (such as women of reproductive age) than other micronutrient interventions, such as voluntary supplementation or dietary diversification. However, the main difficulty in implementing this intervention in other countries has been resistance on the part of industry to mandatory fortification. Enforcement of fortification by governments can be perceived as being in conflict with the aim of fostering a positive environment for industry in the interests of economic development. Therefore, even though the government mandate for food fortification is a step in the right direction, it will be effective only if it is enforced and resources are made available to implement it. Mandatory fortification of salt, as implemented in other Southeast Asia countries, would serve as an important case study.

Promote a package of nutrition-specific and nutrition-sensitive interventions targeted to agricultural households

This chapter shows that agricultural households have poorer diets and poorer nutrition outcomes, even after controlling for income and total food consumption. Diversifying household production and improving access to markets are two possible areas of intervention for agricultural households. However, the analysis shows that diversifying agricultural production at the household level has a minimal relationship with increasing the diversity of household diets. Moreover, in areas lacking access to a market, agricultural households seem to have worse access than the average household in that area, suggesting that more has to be done to connect agricultural households to markets. Such efforts can take the form of investment in farm roads and connectivity. Diversifying agricultural production at the household level may help diversify diets, but as an isolated policy it should only be regarded as a strategy to help the most remote agricultural households, those for whom a transition out of extremely basic self-sufficiency is not feasible in the short run. Finally, although improved diets and enhanced incomes are vitally important, they can, in and of themselves, only address certain causal factors behind the poor nutritional outcomes of agricultural households. A more holistic package of nutrition-specific and nutrition-sensitive interventions targeted at agricultural households is urgently needed.

ANNEX 5A. METHODOLOGY FOR CALCULATING THE COST OF RECOMMENDED DIET

The CoRD is calculated as follows:

- Of the 212 food items surveyed in FIES 2015, 111 food items are excluded because they (a) do not belong to one of the seven food groups identified in the dietary guidelines (62 items), (b) are less nutritious, such as salted eggs and tocino (bacon) (13 items), or (c) are "other" items (36 items).
- Annual quantity purchased and total value spent on the remaining 101 food items are from the 2015 FIES data set. For each household in the data set, unit values for each food item are calculated by dividing the total value spent by the total quantity purchased.
- These unit values are converted into price per gram and then aggregated on the basis of various subnational areas, by taking the median price per gram for each food item across households nationally, for each region, for each province, or for each municipality. The 2015 FIES covers 17 regions, 85 provinces, and 1,145 municipalities.

TABLE 5A.1 **Price per gram of food group and selected items for national CoRD**

FOOD GROUP	TWO CHEAPEST ITEMS	PRICE PER EDIBLE GRAM (₱)
Rice, rice products, corn, root crops, bread, noodles	Bread (pandesal), rice (National Food Authority)	0.035
Vegetables	Camote tops (sweet potato), okra	0.028
Fruits	Papaya, coconut	0.060
Eggs	Fresh hen eggs	0.138
Fish, shellfish, meat and poultry, dried beans and nuts	Shellfish, peanuts	0.109
Milk and milk products (powder)	Powdered milk, evaporated milk	0.320
Fats and oils	Margarine, coconut oil	0.177

Source: Calculations based on the 2015 Family Income and Expenditure Survey (PSA 2015b).

- Food items in the survey are organized according to the seven food groups specified in the dietary guidelines (excluding water and beverages and sugar and sweets). The serving size for each type of food is determined by the serving portions of common foods, as stated in the guidelines.
- The median price per gram for each food item at different levels is converted to price per edible gram, which is calculated by multiplying the price per gram by the edible portion of that food. Information on edible portion is taken from the Philippine Food Composition Tables (FNRI 2021). The price per serving for each food item is then calculated by multiplying the price per edible gram by the corresponding serving size (table 5A.1).
- For each food group (except the egg group), the price per serving is the average of the two food items with the lowest price per serving within that food group. For the egg group, only the price of "eggs (fresh, chicken)" is considered. In addition, for the starchy staple group, "rice (National Food Authority)" is not selected alongside "rice (regular)" because they are essentially the same item except for the source. The table presents the price per (edible) gram nationally for each of the seven food groups and specifies which are the two cheapest items selected for each food group nationally.
- The average price per serving for each food group is multiplied by the recommended number of servings according to the dietary guidelines (which is the average of the lower- and upper-bound recommended servings). This calculation yields the minimum cost of the recommended consumption for each food group. Finally, these costs across the food groups are added up so as to yield CoRD (nationally and for each region, province, and municipality).

ANNEX 5B. DETAILED EXPLANATION OF THE CALCULATION OF PRICE PER CALORIE

Headey and Alderman (2019) calculate relative calorie prices (RCPs) defined as the price per calorie of a given food group relative to the price per calorie of a basket of staples. More specifically, for a given food group, an RCP is calculated as the ratio of the average of the three cheapest food items in that food group against the country-specific staple price index. The staple price index is the weighted average of the prices of food groups in the category of starchy staples, where the weights are equal to the calorie share of consumption of that food group in a given country. The RCP has several attractive features. First, conceptually, it captures the relative cost of diversifying out of cereals and into any specific nonstaple food group. Second, the measure is unit free and does not rely on or require adjustments for cost-of-living differences or generic inflation to make cross-country comparisons.

For the purposes of this report, however, the RCPs from Headey and Alderman (2019) are converted back into (non-cereal-relative) price per calorie by multiplying the RCPs for each food group with the staple price index, which is equal to the cost per 1,000 kilocalories of the basket of staples (in 2011 purchasing power parity US dollars). This conversion allows the price per calorie of a food group in the Philippines to be compared with the price per calorie of the same food group in other countries, without the differences being determined by differences in the price of staples across countries. This is particularly important because the price index for staples is higher in the Philippines than in comparable countries. For example, the cost per 1,000 kilocalories of staples in the Philippines is US$0.76, which is similar to the global average of US$0.75, but much higher than the average for lower-middle-income countries, which is US$0.55, or the average for Southeast Asia, which is US$0.53.

NOTES

1. The Department of Agriculture has articulated a conceptual framework to realize the "New Thinking" vision. The framework consists of eight paradigms: agricultural modernization, industrialization, export promotion, farm consolidation, infrastructure development, road map development, securing budget and investments, and legislative support.
2. For crops, the 12 possible activities are palay (paddy rice), corn, other cereal, fruits, vegetables, cassava, camote (sweet potato), coconut, other fruits and vegetables, tobacco, coffee, and other crops. For livestock, the 8 possible activities are pigs, cattle, chicken, carabao (water buffalo), other livestock and poultry, milk, eggs, and other products. For fish, the 6 possible activities are fish and other products, fry gathered, shells and other products gathered, fish harvested, oysters and mussels harvested, and other products harvested. For forest activities, the 5 possible activities are charcoal, firewood, logs, other forest products, and wild animals or birds.
3. The household-level analyses conducted for these data used a combination of four data sets. Data from the 2015 FIES and the Labor Force Survey were used to characterize household economic activities and household food consumption (PSA 2015b, 2015c), the 2015 National Nutrition Survey was used to describe diet quality and nutrition outcomes (FNRI 2015), and the 2015 Census of Population—Barangay Schedule was used to determine the presence of markets in a barangay (PSA 2015a).

REFERENCES

Bageant, Elizabeth, Yanyan Liu, and Xinshen Diao. 2016. "Agriculture-Nutrition Linkages and Child Health in the Presence of Conflict in Nepal." IFPRI Discussion Paper 1515, International Food Policy Research Institute, Washington, DC.

Dizon, Felipe, Anna Josephson, and Dhushyanth Raju. 2019. "The Nutrition Sensitivity of Food and Agriculture in South Asia." Policy Research Working Paper WPS 8766, World Bank Group, Washington, DC. http://documents.worldbank.org/curated/en/945551551887112580/The-Nutrition-Sensitivity-of-Food-and-Agriculture-in-South-Asia.

FNRI (Food and Nutrition Research Institute). 2015. *2015 Updating Survey Results.* Taguig City: Department of Science and Technology, FNRI.

FNRI (Food and Nutrition Research Institute). 2021. "Philippine Food Consumption Tables." FNRI, Department of Science and Technology, Manila. https://i.fnri.dost.gov.ph/fct/library.

Headey, Derek. 2001. "Turning Economic Growth into Nutrition-Sensitive Growth." IFPRI 2020 Conference Paper 6, International Food Policy Research Institute, Washington, DC. http://www.ifpri.org/sites/default/files/publications/2020anhconfpaper06.pdf.

Headey, Derek, and Harold Alderman. 2019. "The Relative Caloric Prices of Healthy and Unhealthy Foods Differ Systematically across Income Levels and Continents." *Journal of Nutrition* 149 (11): 2020–33.

Irfanullah, Haseeb, Ahana Adrika, Zakir Ahmed Khan, and Abdur Rashid. 2008. "Introduction of Floating Gardening in the North-Eastern Wetlands of Bangladesh for Nutritional Security and Sustainable Livelihoods." *Renewable Agriculture and Food Systems* 23 (2): 89–96.

Islam, Abu Hayat Md Saiful, Joachim von Braun, Andrew L. Thorne-Lyman, and Ahmed U. Akhter. 2018. "Farm Diversification and Food and Nutrition Security in Bangladesh: Empirical Evidence from Nationally Representative Household Panel Data." *Food Security* 10 (3): 701–20.

Jones, Katherine M., Shelia E. Specio, Parvati Shrestha, Kenneth H. Brown, and Lindsay H. Allen. 2005. "Nutrition Knowledge and Practices and Consumption of Vitamin A–Rich Plants by Rural Nepali Participants and Non-participants in Kitchen-Garden Program." *Food and Nutrition Bulletin* 26 (2): 198–208.

Leroy, J. L. 2013. "Child Stunting and Aflatoxins." In *Aflatoxins: Finding Solutions for Improved Food Safety,* edited by Laurian J. Unnevehr and Delia Grace. Washington, DC: International Food Policy Research Institute.

Michler, Jeffrey D., and Anna L. Josephson. 2017. "To Specialize or Diversify: Agricultural Diversity and Poverty Dynamics in Ethiopia." *World Development* 89 (January): 214–26.

Moy, G. G., and J. D. Miller. 2016. "Aflatoxin Update." IUFoST Scientific Information Bulletin, IUFoST (International Union of Food Science and Technology), Toronto. http://www.iufost.org/iufostftp/IUFoST %20SIB%20%20-%20Aflatoxin%20Update.April%202016.pdf.

Murshed-E-Jahan, Khondker, and Diemuth E. Pemsl. 2011. "The Impact of Integrated Aquaculture-Agriculture on Small-Scale Farm Sustainability and Farmers' Livelihoods: Experience from Bangladesh." *Agricultural Systems* 104 (5): 392–402.

Murty, P. V. V. S., M. Vishnuvardhan Rao, and Mahtab S. Bamji. 2016. "Impact of Enriching the Diet of Women and Children through Health and Nutrition Education, Introduction of Homestead Gardens and Backyard Poultry in Rural India." *Agricultural Research* 5 (2): 210–17.

Nielsen, Hanne, Nanna Roos, and Shakuntala H. Thilsted. 2003. "The Impact of Semi-Scavenging Poultry Production on the Consumption of Animal Source Foods by Women and Girls in Bangladesh." *Journal of Nutrition* 133 (11, Suppl. 2): 4027–30.

Pandey, Vijay L., S. Mahendra Dev, and Usha Jayachandran. 2016. "Impact of Agricultural Interventions on the Nutritional Status in South Asia: A Review." *Food Policy* 62 (July): 28–40.

PSA (Philippine Statistics Authority). 2015a. *2015 Census of Population—Barangay Schedule.* Quezon City: PSA.

PSA (Philippine Statistics Authority). 2015b. *Family Income and Expenditure Survey.* Quezon City: PSA.

PSA (Philippine Statistics Authority). 2015c. *Labor Force Survey.* Quezon City: PSA, July.

Rahman, K. M. M., and A. Sousa-Poza. 2010. "Food Consumption and Nutritional Status of Vulnerable People Rearing Livestock in Bangladesh." *Bangladesh Journal of Agricultural Economics* 33 (1-2): 41–56.

Sales, Anthony, and Takumi Yoshizawa. 2005. "Updated Profile of Aflatoxin and Aspergillus Section Flavi Contamination in Rice and Its By-products from the Philippines." *Food Additives and Contaminants* 22 (5): 429–36. doi:10.1080/02652030500058387.

von Braun, Joachim, Ashok Gulati, Peter Hazell, Mark W. Rosegrant, and Marie Ruel. 2005. "Indian Agriculture and Rural Development: Strategic Issues and Reform Options." IFPRI Issue Brief 35, International Food Policy Research Institute, Washington, DC.

Wilcox, Clair Sophia, Stephanie Grutzmacher, Rebecca Ramsing, Amanda Rockler, Christie Balch, Marghuba Safi, and James Hanson. 2014. "From the Field: Empowering Women to Improve Family Food Security in Afghanistan." *Renewable Agriculture and Food Systems* 30 (1): 15–21.

World Bank. 2008. *World Development Report 2008: Agriculture for Development.* Washington, DC: World Bank.

World Bank. 2011. International Comparison Program (ICP) 2011 DataBank database. World Bank, Washington, DC. https://databank.worldbank.org/source/international-comparison-program-(ICP)-2011.

World Bank. 2018. World Development Indicators database. Washington, DC: World Bank.

World Bank. 2020. *Transforming Philippine Agriculture: During COVID-19 and Beyond.* Washington, DC: World Bank.

6 Knowledge, Beliefs, and Practices of Health Workers and Caregivers on Child Stunting in the Philippines

ABSTRACT Declines in the rate of child stunting in the Philippines have decelerated, making it hard for the country to achieve its targets on nutritional outcomes. An aspect that has not yet been fully explored is the role of knowledge and beliefs about important markers of child undernutrition, such as stunting, that are held by caregivers, on the one hand, and health workers, on the other. While the knowledge and beliefs of most Filipino health workers are consistent with accepted practices, important deviations from consensus views exist, and these deviations are correlated with worse self-reported service delivery outcomes at local health centers. Therefore, any endeavor to improve service delivery in the Philippines must consider the beliefs of frontline workers.

THE IMPORTANCE OF KNOWLEDGE, BELIEFS, AND PRACTICES ON CHILD NUTRITION

An aspect of the nutrition challenge that has not yet been fully explored is the role of knowledge and beliefs about important markers of child undernutrition, such as stunting, on the part of caregivers, on the one hand, and policy makers and frontline policy implementers, on the other.

Globally, the importance of the beliefs and behaviors of caregivers toward child nutrition is better understood, especially in the realm of feeding practices—for example, some countries have strong notions of "good" versus "bad" foods for pregnant women and young children as well as if and how much to feed children during bouts of illness (Raman et al. 2016). However, less is known about how the knowledge and beliefs of caregivers regarding the markers of undernutrition, such as stunting, may influence feeding and other caregiving and health-monitoring practices.

Similarly, the knowledge, beliefs, and practices of health workers are important because they may have considerable influence over how caregivers and their families perceive and experience health and nutritional care and consequently whether and how they seek and access care. For instance, care that is not framed or explained in a way that leads to acceptance by caregivers and families may lead to dissatisfaction with the health system. In addition, beliefs of health workers can directly influence the quality of care and the effectiveness of efforts to promote maternal and child health and nutrition (Mannava et al. 2015). The strength of a health worker's beliefs will affect whether or not growth is monitored consistently; counseling is offered on optimal feeding and caring practices for infants and young children; or essential micronutrients, such as iron and folic acid, vitamins, and zinc, are provided.

From an international perspective, the quality of health workers' knowledge about nutrition—and, by extension, their counseling skills—has been a concern (Sunguya et al. 2013). Historically, medical training has not included adequate, updated nutrition training; as a result, health workers trained at most medical training institutions have lacked adequate knowledge of nutrition. These health workers may also lack the competence and skills to provide advice about basic nutrition. Evidence is available on how in-service nutrition training has a positive impact on health workers' knowledge of nutrition, nutrition counseling skills, and management of child undernutrition. However, little evidence exists on whether the beliefs of health workers affect their delivery of nutrition services and, if so, how.

This chapter discusses the knowledge, beliefs, and practices of health workers and caregivers with respect to stunting among children in the Philippines—in particular, their beliefs about the root causes of stunting—using primary data collected through qualitative interviews. A method used by cognitive anthropologists, called cultural consensus modeling or CCM (Romney, Weller, and Batchelder 1986), is adjusted and then used to measure mental models related to stunting. CCM is a mixed-method technique for estimating the "culturally correct" answers to a series of questions about belief; it is used to test whether there is a dominant group belief as well as to calculate each respondent's degree of sharing and agreement with the group (Weller 2007). A key feature of CCM is its emic approach, meaning the adoption of the respondent's perspective, using his or her own words to understand culture and construe meaning.[1] The CCM method involves several steps. The first is a free (random) listing of key terms by respondents (such as all possible causes of stunting). The second requires respondents to sort these terms into broader categories. Subsequently, respondents rate these categories on several dimensions, such as importance, controllability, and changeability, in quantitative surveys. The pattern of responses to the series of questions reveals whether the group harbors a singular belief system or a mental model.

The results of a large-scale quantitative survey implemented among health and nutrition workers are then used to delve deeper into the worldviews held by frontline workers and how these beliefs relate to service provision in local health centers in the Philippines.

KNOWLEDGE, BELIEFS, AND PRACTICES OF CAREGIVERS AND HEALTH WORKERS

The results of the qualitative interviews show that both caregivers and health workers believe that genetics or hereditary factors are an important cause of stunting, along with undernutrition. However, in an initial written exercise ("list as many factors, things, events, and relationships that you can think of that you think affect a person's height"), the majority of caregivers and health workers listed undernutrition as an important cause of stunting. Undernutrition is aggregated for terms reflecting both the *quality* and *quantity* of food (for example, mentions of lack of food, nutrients, vitamins, and vegetables). The second most commonly listed cause was *heredity* (such as terms reflecting genes, heredity, and race), followed by lack of sleep and then low income or poverty.

However, the responses are inconsistent, as shown by a large number of caregivers who initially attributed stunting to undernutrition (in the written exercise), but during subsequent discussion concluded that genetics is a more powerful factor. One interpretation of this discrepancy is that it is a form of "blame avoidance" in which caregivers in a group avoid saying that having a malnourished child is a consequence (as they actually suspect) of inadequate parenting. An alternative explanation is that they hesitate to voice their true internalized beliefs about the genetic cause of stunting until somebody else in the group has mentioned it first (and thereby has socially sanctioned it).

> For me, I got my height from my mother—she's kind of short; my dad is tall. That is how I thought that maybe it is hereditary. There are also those who say, even among grandmothers and aunts, that it can be passed down. It's possible that it's not only from the parents. Even from other relatives, it can be passed down.
>
> — Caregiver of child younger than two years old, Digos City, Davao

> Judging by my children, it really is genes. My 15-year-old is taller than my husband. He is really tall; even my 13-year-old is just as tall as I am. But my 10-year-old ... it's not that he's just short, it's just that ... well, actually he is really short and fat. I said, "Where did he get that from?" Then my husband said, "You're still asking that? He got that from your siblings." It's because my siblings and my mom are not that tall. If the child is already beyond a certain age, then the child will not grow taller; that is because of his or her race.
>
> — Caregiver of child younger than two years old, Cotabato City, Maguindao

After genetics and nutrition, caregivers mentioned illness as a factor that directly inhibits child growth. Respondents claimed that this may affect nutrition indirectly since children who are sickly often have a poor appetite and therefore a limited intake of nutrients. For caregivers, certain factors may increase a child's susceptibility to disease, such as an unclean environment and poor diet and eating habits.

> Of course, if the environment is dirty, then clearly the child will contract many diseases. That will have a larger effect on the child's growth.
>
> — Caregiver of child younger than two years old, Borongan, Eastern Samar

Among the indirect causes of shortness in height, poverty is the most salient concern for caregivers since it has a huge impact on their ability to provide ample nutritious food.

> Sometimes, [we get up] at 12 noon, so in the late morning I'll just have coffee and bread. But sometimes in the afternoon, I'll cook porridge because I have nothing to buy viands with. Sometimes I do what I can to make enough for all of us.
>
> — Caregiver of child younger than two years old, Ilagan, Isabela

Although knowledge was not spontaneously mentioned, caregivers did consider it a potential factor that may hamper a child's growth, particularly when caregivers have inadequate knowledge of proper child nutrition.

> Sometimes the person taking care of the child lacks knowledge, like how it is with the first child, when the parent is still not used to it. For first timers, they do not know what to feed their child. They do not know what should be given to their child, what are the right things the child should be getting.
>
> — Caregiver of child younger than two years old, Borongan, Eastern Samar

The findings from discussions with Barangay (district or neighborhood) Health Workers (BHWs) are similar. Health workers identified genetics and nutrition as the two most important factors, but gave them "equal" importance in determining a child's height. This attitude reflects a tension between what is formally taught and local beliefs.

> For me, the number one factor that really affects height is the genes of the child. If we look at those who we say are poor, we soon see that there are tall people among them. So it really seems to be genes that affect the height of a child.
>
> — Barangay Health Worker, Borongan, Eastern Samar

> Yes, we accept [that we are short]. Particularly the Itas. Maybe the few who are not Itas will be tall. But if they are Itas, that is the race, that is their body build, so we're in the same boat as indigenous people.
>
> — Midwife, Sagada, Mt. Province

Other possible factors also came up during the discussion, but were given varying degrees of importance, as shown by the word cloud in figure 6.1. Health workers (but not caregivers) gave lack of adequate nutrition during pregnancy as well as the consequences of teenage pregnancy in general as reasons for stunting. Based on these and other factors identified during the focus group discussions with health workers, a conceptual framework was drawn indicating the relationship between the different reasons mentioned (figure 6.2).

FIGURE 6.1

Word cloud of causes perceived by Barangay Health Workers in the Philippines, based on intensity of their responses

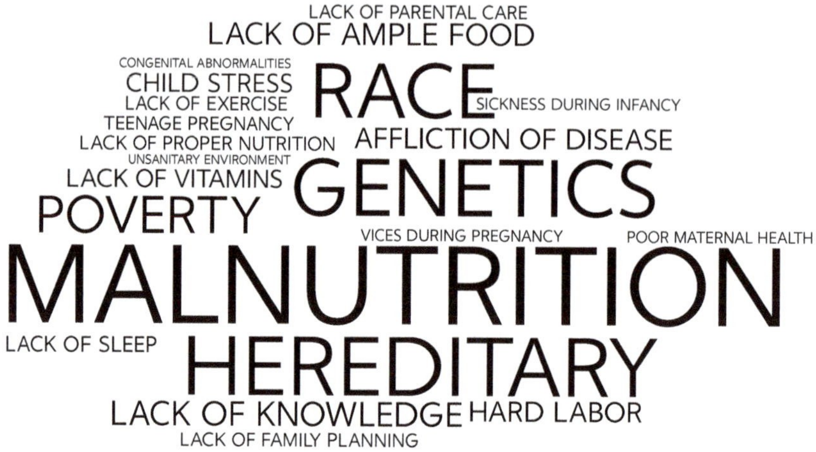

Source: Focus group discussions with Barangay Health Workers conducted as part of this study.

FIGURE 6.2

Relationships between causes of stunting, as perceived by Barangay Health Workers

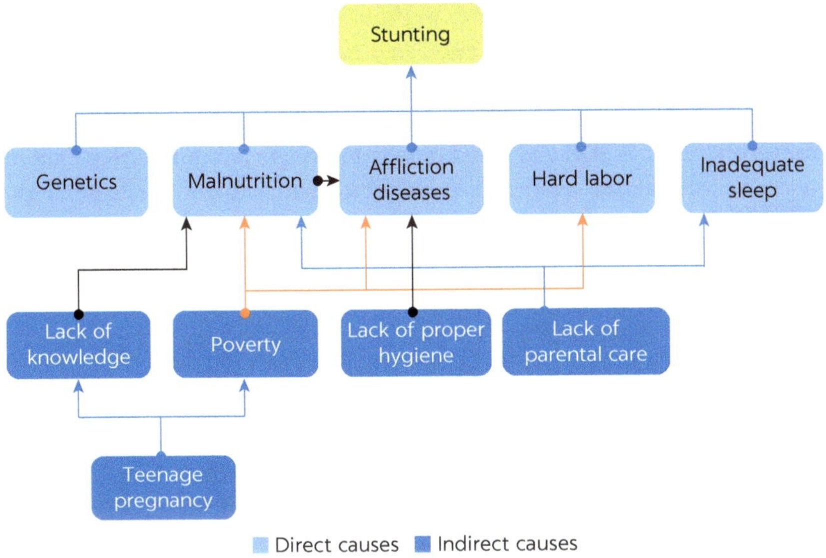

Source: Based on a survey of Barangay Nutrition Scholars and Barangay Health Workers conducted for this book.

OTHER BELIEFS: CONSEQUENCES OF STUNTING AND MONITORING GROWTH

The beliefs of caregivers and health workers about the consequences of stunting included longer-term impacts, such as low self-esteem and exclusion from employment opportunities involving height requirements. Caregivers mentioned worse prospects for marriage, while health workers mentioned lower cognitive abilities and issues during pregnancy for women. However, neither group regarded these consequences as being of great concern. Respondents highlighted counterexamples of individuals who were short but had achieved great success in life.[2]

When evaluating the growth of the child, greater importance is attached to monitoring the weight of the child than the height. Weight is accorded more importance because the effects of wasting are perceived to be more serious than the consequences of stunting (which is accurate in the sense that wasting, not stunting, is associated with increased risk of mortality). In their assessment of a child's development and well-being, both caregivers and health workers said that they monitor other indicators, including immunity from sickness, physical activity, and cognitive functions. However, some caregivers claimed that health workers only monitor a child's weight and rarely monitor the child's height, therefore strengthening these beliefs.

BELIEFS ABOUT WEIGHT GAIN DURING PREGNANCY

The qualitative interviews also uncovered the advice that health workers give to expecting mothers on the subject of weight gain during pregnancy, showing the importance of monitoring weight during pregnancy—as maternal weight gain serves as an indicator of the health of the unborn child. Although mothers are unsure of the exact weight that they are expected to gain each month, they do expect to be admonished by health workers if the weight gain appears to be excessive. Some respondents described an increase of about 5 to 15 kilograms as normal and an increase of more than 20 kilograms as excessive. Most health workers in the different survey areas agreed that a weight gain of up to 1 kilogram every month is ideal and that they monitor weight monthly during routine checkups. However, the mothers reported that health workers would often ask them to go on a diet if they had gained roughly 3 kilograms in a month, claiming that putting on too much weight may lead to complications during birth.

FINDINGS FROM A QUANTITATIVE SURVEY WITH HEALTH WORKERS

To test quantitatively which factors or set of factors may be most important in affecting child stunting, a large-scale survey was implemented with more than 5,000 health workers, including Barangay Nutrition Scholars (BNSs) and BHWs. Respondents rated the level of importance of each factor that may affect child height on a Likert scale, including all factors that were mentioned in the qualitative discussions. They also answered additional knowledge questions and reported the extent to which their local barangay health centers provide different services.

All respondents were asked a series of eight questions to determine their level of knowledge about infant-feeding practices and nutrition (table 6.1). The questions tested basic information with which all health workers were supposed to be reasonably familiar. Nutrition scholars typically provided more accurate responses than health workers, answering one additional question correctly on average (4.6 compared with 3.7). Nearly two-thirds of BNSs answered five or more questions correctly (out of eight), and the same percentage of BHWs answered at least half the questions correctly (four out of eight). More than half of all workers answered each question accurately, with one striking exception: a majority of both BNSs and BHWs thought that breast milk alone is sufficient for children ages 6–9 months. This is a crucial stage in the transition to complementary feeding. Workers were asked the rate of under-five stunting in the Philippines, which is 33 percent. The responses of BNSs were closer to the actual rate than the responses of BHWs. The BNSs, on average, believed the rate to be 36.6 percent, while BHWs, on average, believed it to be higher, at 43.7 percent.

However, when asked about weight gain during pregnancy, the results were more mixed.[3] Compared with nutrition scholars, health workers more often recommended that pregnant women "eat less food than normal." When asked about the "recommended" weight gain for women during pregnancy, nearly 47 percent of respondents either said that they did not know or did not respond to the question. Another 13 percent mentioned that there is no recommended weight gain for women during pregnancy. Compared with BNSs, more BHWs did not respond to the question or mentioned that there is no recommended weight gain. However, for the 40 percent of workers who responded, BNSs, on average, recommended a weight gain of 9.0 kilograms, while BHWs recommended 12.3 kilograms, on average.

Respondents were asked to rate 17 factors that may affect a child's height, and the ranked results are shown in table 6.2. The five most important factors that

TABLE 6.1 **Knowledge questions asked to Barangay Nutrition Scholars and Barangay Health Workers in the Philippines**

QUESTION OR STATEMENT	ANSWER	BARANGAY NUTRITION SCHOLARS	BARANGAY HEATH WORKERS
What are the causes of anemia among children? (multiple choice)	Lack of rice (% yes)	11.8	16.2
	Worm infestation (% yes)	20.1	18.7
	Lack of iron-rich food (% yes)	75.6	63.2
	Lack of fat (% yes)	6.4	4.9
	Lack of iodine (% yes)	21.4	16.5
	Unsure (% yes)	0.9	1.0
	Only selected "lack of iron-rich food" (%)	46.5	40.1
What causes night blindness in children? (multiple choice)	Lack of calcium (% yes)	5.5	11.1
	Lack of rice (% yes)	2.5	4.33
	Lack of vitamin A (% yes)	84.0	70.7
	Lack of vitamin C (% yes)	7.3	11.9
	Unsure (% yes)	1.0	1.4
	Only selected "lack of vitamin A" (%)	77.3	59.5
When should a mother initiate breastfeeding of her newborn child? (only one option selected)	Within one hour of giving birth (% yes)	71.1	62.1
	Between two and three hours of giving birth (% yes)	12.0	10.9
	After five hours of giving birth (% yes)	1.8	1.8
	On the second day of giving birth (% yes)	0.2	0.6
A child should be fed extra food when he or she has a cold, fever, or diarrhea.	True (% correct)	71.8	65.5
It is recommended that a mother breastfeed her child for at least two years.	True (% correct)	79.6	67.7
Breast milk alone is an adequate source of nutrition for a child older than six months and younger than nine months.	False (% correct)	40.1	21.1
Milk formula or canned milk is good for infants who are less than six months old.	False (% correct)	80.1	65.7
A child who is short for her age in the first two years can catch up in height with appropriate nutrition during adolescence.	True (% correct)	72.7	68.1

Source: Calculations based on a survey of Barangay Nutrition Scholars and Barangay Health Workers conducted for this book.
Note: Shaded cells show the percentage of accurate responses.

affect stunting, according to aggregated responses, indicate that the beliefs of respondents align with globally accepted views about the immediate causes (food consumed, disease environments), underlying causes (prenatal care, parental care and attention), and basic causes (poverty) of child height. Ethnicity and height of mother or father are not rated consistently as important factors.

However, the rankings of the factors change when respondents are asked to choose the three most important factors, and this difference is driven by the

TABLE 6.2 **Responses of Barangay Nutrition Scholars and Barangay Health Workers to the question, "To what extent does each of the following factors affect a child's height?"**

	OVERALL			BARANGAY NUTRITION SCHOLARS			BARANGAY HEALTH WORKERS		
FACTOR	OBS.	MEAN	RANK	OBS.	MEAN	RANK	OBS.	MEAN	RANK
Disease	4,584	0.683	1	2,386	0.700	1	2,198	0.664	1
Poverty	4,568	0.642	2	2,380	0.655	2	2,188	0.628	2
Food consumed	4,641	0.544	3	2,389	0.571	4	2,252	0.516	3
Prenatal care	4,539	0.527	4	2,363	0.572	3	2,176	0.478	4
Parental care and attention	4,550	0.511	5	2,368	0.553	5	2,182	0.465	5
Access to toilets and clean water	4,544	0.489	6	2,359	0.531	6	2,185	0.444	7
Exclusive breastfeeding	4,591	0.436	7	2,374	0.476	7	2,217	0.393	10
Sufficient sleep	4,544	0.429	8	2,370	0.444	8	2,174	0.412	9
Carry heavy loads	4,559	0.424	9	2,375	0.404	10	2,184	0.445	6
Help family livelihood	4,543	0.414	10	2,360	0.413	9	2,183	0.415	8
Destiny	4,499	0.291	11	2,334	0.258	11	2,165	0.326	11
Height of mother	4,604	0.283	12	2,390	0.258	11	2,214	0.310	12
Height of father	4,589	0.282	13	2,391	0.258	11	2,198	0.309	13
Faith	4,497	0.252	14	2,324	0.232	14	2,173	0.273	14
God	4,481	0.214	15	2,308	0.195	15	2,173	0.235	16
Ethnicity	4,646	0.207	16	2,408	0.180	16	2,238	0.236	15
Luck	4,491	0.182	17	2,332	0.156	17	2,159	0.210	17

Source: Calculations based on a survey of Barangay Nutrition Scholars and Barangay Health Workers conducted for this book.
Note: Means of normalized scores are computed as follows: does not affect = 0.0; slightly affects = 0.33; affects = 0.67; greatly affects = 1.0. OBS. = number of observations/respondents.

choices of BHWs. For the subsample of BNSs alone, however, although disease and poverty are still the two most important factors, prenatal care is the third most important factor.

One way of measuring such underlying constructs is through factor analysis. In factor analysis, it is assumed that such latent constructs cannot be measured directly but can be evaluated indirectly through the relationships observed in response patterns across a set of variables. Factor analysis of the responses to the set of belief questions on the causes of stunting uncovers the key underlying constructs (factors). These factors are, in effect, worldviews or mental models held by BNSs and BHWs, and they explain the patterns observed.

INTERPRETING MENTAL MODELS OF HEALTH WORKERS THROUGH RESPONSE PATTERNS

This analysis confirms the existence of a dominant worldview among health workers in the Philippines. Based on the factor loadings, four factors (mental models) emerge based on the items that load onto these factors:

- *Prescribed practices,* including responses such as "quality and quantity of food," "parental care and attention," "prenatal care," "breastfeeding," "access to toilet and water," and "sufficient sleep."

- *Genetics,* including responses such as "ethnicity of parents," "height of mother," and "height of father."
- *Poverty,* including responses such as "poverty," "helping with family livelihoods," "carrying heavy loads," and "affliction of disease."
- *Faith and fate,* including responses such as "destiny," "God's will," "faith and prayer on the part of parents," and "luck."

Indexes created from these groups of beliefs tell two very different stories for nutrition scholars and health workers in different regions of the Philippines.[4] Figure 6.3 shows the standardized means of these four belief indexes. For BNSs in most regions (except for SOCCSKSARGEN), the prescribed practices and poverty indexes are positive, indicating greater agreement with the items in these indexes. The faith and fate index is usually negative, indicating the least agreement with these factors. Agreement with genetics-related causes is also low and similar to the faith and fate index, with exceptions in CALABARZON and Davao, where it is higher.

The figure for BHWs is starkly different; across all regions, agreement with the faith and fate index and the genetic index is always higher than agreement with the prescribed practices and poverty indexes.

Interpreting response patterns through factor analysis revealed four underlying constructs, which are interpreted as mental models or worldviews. The first and most consequential factor includes prescribed practices typically recommended for better child health, which can be interpreted as the main worldview for health workers. However, several additional views emerged, including views that health workers hold with respect to genetics, poverty, and faith or fate.

FIGURE 6.3

Means of standardized belief indexes for Barangay Nutrition Scholars and Barangay Health Workers, by region

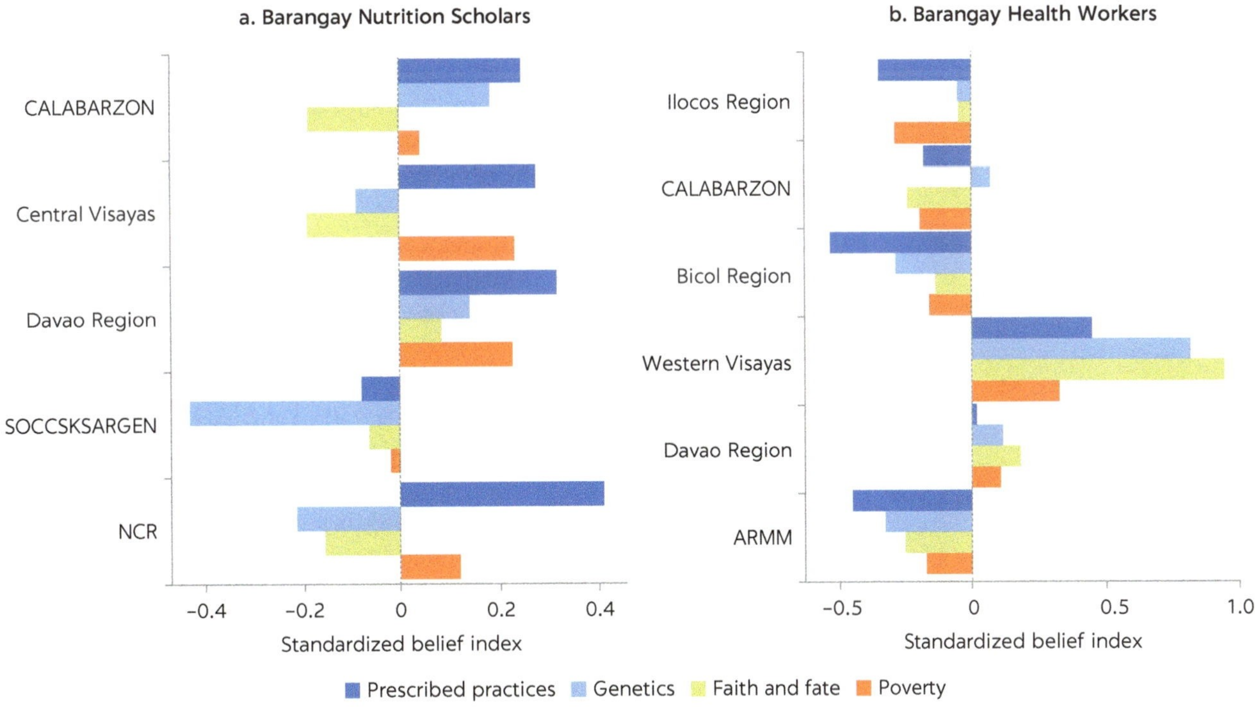

Source: Survey of Barangay Nutrition Scholars and Barangay Health Workers conducted for this book.
Note: ARMM = Autonomous Region in Muslim Mindanao. CALABARZON = Cavite, Laguna, Batangas, Rizal, and Quezon. NCR = National Capital Region. SOCCSKSARGEN = South Cotabato, Cotabato, Sultan Kudarat, Sarangani, and General Santos.

BHWs are more likely to hold these additional views than BNSs. In summary, while most health workers reported the accepted determinants of child health, some reported beliefs that deviate from conventional views. These deviations deserve further investigation.

HOW KNOWLEDGE AND BELIEFS RELATE TO SERVICE DELIVERY AT LOCAL HEALTH CENTERS

While uncovering deviations from the expected worldview is important in and of itself, can these worldviews also influence health worker behavior, such as the services offered at local (barangay) health centers?[5]

Eight questions were asked about the advice given to pregnant women and mothers of young children on breastfeeding and complementary feeding; provision of iron and folic acid and vitamin A supplements; and monitoring and measurement of height, weight, and growth. According to the responses, the two least-reported services carried out at local health centers were the measurement of height for children under two years old and the provision of vitamin A supplements for children under five. However, there was high agreement on measurement of the weight of children and women as well as the distribution of other supplements, such as iron and folic acid tablets. As an indicator of health and well-being, more frequent weight measurement (rather than height measurement) is consistent with findings from the qualitative data. There is also a high level of agreement with the assertion that advice is given about exclusive breastfeeding and complementary feeding.

To explore the variation in self-reported service delivery, a standardized index was created for all eight services reported by health workers. A regression analysis of standardized belief and knowledge indexes on a standardized index of all of the service questions was then conducted to explore the relationship across these variables. Figure 6.4 shows the individual coefficients on the relationship between each service delivery question and each belief and knowledge grouping for BNSs.[6] The figure shows that stronger adherence to belief in "prescribed practices" and greater health worker knowledge are associated with greater self-reported service delivery at local health centers, across all questions about service delivery. A stronger belief in poverty-related causes of stunting shows a positive association with greater service delivery, although this relationship is weaker. Conversely, a stronger belief in poverty- and genetics-related causes of stunting is negatively associated with self-reported service delivery.

THE IMPLICATIONS OF DIFFERENT BELIEFS AND LEVELS OF KNOWLEDGE ON CHILD STUNTING

Stunting rates have not declined significantly in recent years in the Philippines. Methods were drawn from cognitive anthropology to measure and interpret the deep-seated beliefs of different stakeholders. Initial qualitative discussions with caregivers, health workers, and policy makers showed that, while factors related to a lack of nutrition and appropriate maternal and child care were often cited as important reasons for child malnutrition, genetic and racial reasons were foremost for several stakeholders—and the discussions revealed strong tensions between the two, especially for health workers.

FIGURE 6.4

Relationship between knowledge, beliefs, and service delivery among Barangay Nutrition Scholars

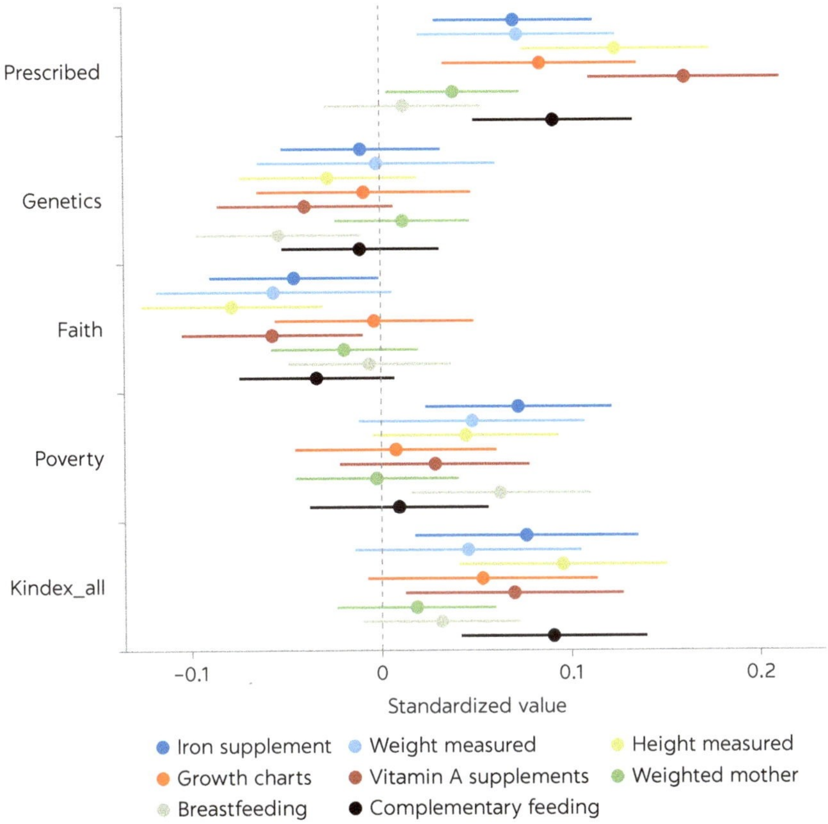

Source: Calculations based on a survey of Barangay Nutrition Scholars and Barangay Health Workers conducted for this book.
Note: Kindex_all = the standardized index of all the knowledge questions that were asked.

To understand the importance ascribed to the beliefs uncovered in these discussions, self-administered surveys were conducted with more than 5,000 frontline health workers (BNSs and BHWs). Analysis of the response patterns suggests that four underlying worldviews (or mental models) are at play. The predominant worldview adheres to conventional prescribed practices in improving child health outcomes and includes nutrition alongside prenatal care and parental attention to infants. However, respondents held additional views, including genetic and racial factors, faith- and fate-based factors, and factors related to poverty and the disease environment. These views, along with knowledge of health workers, are strongly correlated with self-reported service provision at the local barangay health centers—views predicated on prescribed practices and poverty are positively correlated with service provision, while views predicated on genetics and faith are negatively correlated.

These findings demonstrate the societal implications of the levels of knowledge and the different worldviews held by health workers. While most health workers command sufficient knowledge and subscribe to views that are consistent with conventional practices in improving child health, a minority of workers also agree with views on child stunting, including genetic and racial factors alongside faith- and fate-based factors. BHWs and BNSs who have more robust, evidence-based knowledge and beliefs are more likely to work in facilities that provide better (self-reported) maternal and child nutrition services. Conversely, BHWs and BNSs who also see child height as a question of genetics, faith, or fate are less likely to work in facilities that provide better maternal and child nutrition services. Comparisons between these beliefs and actual stunting rates from the 2018 Expanded National Nutrition Survey suggest that the mental models, knowledge, and services are better in provinces with lower-than-average stunting rates and worse in provinces with higher stunting rates (FNRI 2018). Profiling of health workers based on the different worldviews suggests that views on genetics and faith or fate can coexist with conventional wisdom on child health. The relative intensity of these beliefs, rather than the presence or absence of a set of beliefs, can influence service delivery at local health centers.

The analysis also highlighted differences between the worldviews of health workers and nutrition scholars. BHWs were much more likely to agree with views ascribing child height to factors predicated on genetics and faith or fate than were BNSs. These findings are not unexpected. Nutrition scholars receive more focused training on nutrition than health workers, and this training is reflected in their belief models and knowledge responses, which tend to be better aligned with health practices. Lacking this technical input, health workers more often reflect the belief systems of their own communities. These results may have implications, given the roles that BHWs and BNSs play in local health systems in the Philippines. While nutrition scholars carry out more focused work based on their training and perform tasks related to nutrition services, health workers are often asked to work on a much broader range of health services. Because there are more BHWs than BNSs, in practice, both groups of community health workers participate in each other's programs, depending on the need for manpower. Hence, health workers assist in providing vitamin A supplements, while nutrition scholars help out during immunization days. It is not inconceivable for BHWs to be asked to take on nutrition-related assignments, even with minimal or no training on the task and with supervision most likely from the midwife or even the nutrition scholar.

If the beliefs and mental models of health workers (as well as caregivers and policy makers) are to be changed, innovative training exercises constitute a useful direction for future research and will have to be tested carefully. Recent literature from the behavioral sciences offers some guidance; however, such interventions will still need to be customized and adapted to the local context and topic. It is possible to change mental models through critical reflection, discussion, and exposure to alternative worldviews. For example, sessions could be held in which participants are able to discuss in an open environment, express their beliefs and actions, and observe the beliefs and actions taken by others. These sessions can be made more engaging if participants can role-play reactions to different scenarios or view entertaining audiovisual materials with compelling narratives. It is important for such sessions to be highly participative as well as to show that other persons are also being exposed to this new set of ideas.

THE WAY FORWARD

More innovative and competency-based training of Barangay Health Workers and Nutrition Scholars is urgently needed in the Philippines. These health workers have to be able to command adequate knowledge of nutrition, shift beliefs toward acceptable practices, and communicate their knowledge effectively so as to bring about sound behavioral change. Education and communication on nutrition must be investigated and improved at the level of the training curriculum as well as that of in-service education, such that any beliefs that deviate from conventional practices regarding child nutrition can be addressed.

How might these results be of use to the Department of Health (DOH), which is ultimately responsible for the country's health outcomes and on whose shoulders rests the burden of reducing childhood stunting? Several possible actions, particularly in the crisis situation brought about by the COVID-19 pandemic, could be pursued. As the world learns to live with the virus that causes COVID-19, nutrition could be positioned as a way of strengthening the immune system so that people can be better protected and respond more appropriately to treatments, including the anticipated COVID-19 vaccines. It is crucial for frontline health workers, such as BNSs and BHWs, to be equipped with updated nutrition knowledge and skills to respond to these emerging health and nutrition needs.

The training and supervisory support provided to nutrition scholars is far more systematic than the support provided to health workers. The DOH might consider providing nutrition training to BHWs through the National Nutrition Council. Such training would ensure consistency in the content and methods of training and might be more efficient than providing a separate training process for BHWs. The DOH could support cross-training to enable BHWs to attend BNS training or support regional-level training to be delivered by academic institutions. The National Nutrition Council has used the latter approach for its training of nutrition scholars. After receiving training, health workers could be supervised by the nutrition action officer for nutrition-related activities and performance.

While training will be necessary, it may not be sufficient to ensure that these health workers have the capacity to implement stunting reduction programs. In this regard, the DOH could consider reviewing the roles and expectations of community health workers. They play vital roles in the health system but are not given the recognition and benefits they deserve, which explains the low motivation that was apparent in poor-nutrition regions. Issues that need to be addressed could include ensuring their security of tenure as well as formulating and enforcing standards for their qualifications, recruitment, training, performance, compensation, and retention. The Department of Interior and Local Government has initiated efforts to promote and encourage local government units and local chief executives to consider the service retention of BNSs.

This chapter has focused on the beliefs, knowledge, and practices of BNSs and BHWs regarding the nutrition-specific actions they undertake. BNSs, as part of their community functions, are also expected to participate in nutrition-sensitive programs, and they need to be supported in this role. The DOH, together with other government agencies, can provide incentives for the attainment of nutrition-related milestones, particularly those related to the Sustainable Development Goals, such as reductions in stunting and wasting. The incentives can be cross-cutting—for example, to support the achievement of better diet diversity through an agricultural crop diversification program. The Department of Agriculture crop diversification program has been enhanced in response to the effects of COVID-19 on the food supply chain. The DOH could complement this initiative by including an incentive to link this program to a complementary feeding program that BNSs and

BHWs could both implement and use to monitor nutritional outcomes of the program's beneficiaries.

The power of beliefs and knowledge to influence action can be harnessed by taking a broader approach involving both national and local governments. The scope of actions on nutrition and support for them extend beyond the DOH. Enhanced training of BNSs and BHWs will mark a key first of many responses to the National Nutrition Council's call for an "all of government, all of society" approach to achieving better nutrition.

NOTES

This chapter is an abridged version of the research conducted for this book and also published as an HNP Discussion Paper (Mbuya et al. 2020).

1. The quotes in this chapter were translated from the original language.
2. This is an accurate counterpoint to a usually simplified (and false) notion that being short is a negative outcome or occurrence that will damage an individual's life course. The sole negative physical outcome for short height (causally related) is an increased risk for cephalopelvic disproportion among women. It is critical for all programming and training on child stunting to focus on providing an accurate understanding of stunting in the first two years of life as a proxy for underlying negative conditions in the child's environment that are associated with stunting (for example, delayed cognitive development). Linear growth retardation and stunting are associated with—but, based on available evidence, do not cause—delayed child development, reduced earnings at adulthood, and chronic diseases.
3. According to the Clinical Practice Guidelines on Maternal Nutrition and Supplementation issued by the Philippine Obstetrical and Gynecological Society (POGS 2013), weight gain for Filipino pregnant women should be as follows (based on weight before pregnancy): if of normal weight, 25–35 pounds; if underweight, 28–40 pounds; if overweight, 15–25 pounds; if obese, 11–20 pounds. Therefore, weight gain of 9.0 kilograms (19.8 pounds) for a woman of normal weight would not meet these guidelines, but a weight gain of 12.3 kilograms would (27.0 pounds).
4. Indexes are created by aggregating the items that load onto each of the four factors and standardizing them.
5. Workers were asked if the services are delivered in the health centers where they work, in order to avoid asking directly whether they have performed these services themselves. This approach was taken to minimize social desirability bias in self-reported service delivery behavior. However, reported service delivery is still interpreted as being influenced by whether individual health workers deliver the services themselves and as indicative of the behavior of individual health workers.
6. Indexes were created based on the main response patterns identified and discussed earlier—that is, standardized indexes were created for each of the following groupings: prescribed practices, genetics, faith, and poverty. Results shown are coefficients from ordinary least squares regressions controlling for several health worker characteristics and the poverty rate as well as responses from the same barangay and region.

REFERENCES

FNRI (Food and Nutrition Research Institute). 2018. *2018 Expanded National Nutrition Survey.* Taguig City: Department of Science and Technology, FNRI.

Mannava, Priya, Kelly Durrant, Jane Fisher, M. Chersich, and S. Luchters. 2015. "Attitudes and Behaviors of Maternal Health Care Providers in Interactions with Clients: A Systematic Review." *Global Health* 11 (August 15): 36. doi:10.1186/s12992-015-0117-9.

Mbuya, Nkosinathi, Iman Sen, Gabriel Demombynes, and Varun Gauri. 2020. *Mind over Matter in the Philippines: A Study of Key Stakeholders' Perceptions of Childhood Stunting.* Health Nutrition, and Population (HNP) Discussion Paper. Washington, DC: World Bank.

POGS (Philippine Obstetrical and Gynecological Society). 2013. "Clinical Practice Guidelines on Maternal Nutrition and Supplementation." POGS, Quezon City.

Raman, Shanti, Rachel Nicholls, Jan Ritchie, Husna Razee, and Samaneh Shafiee. 2016. "Eating Soup with Nails of Pig: Thematic Synthesis of the Qualitative Literature on Cultural Practices and Beliefs Influencing Perinatal Nutrition in Low and Middle Income Countries." *BMC Pregnancy and Childbirth* 16: Art. PMC4964025. doi:10.1186/s12884-016-0991-z.

Romney, A. Kimball, Susan C. Weller, and William H. Batchelder. 1986. "Culture and Consensus: A Theory of Culture and Informant Accuracy." *American Anthropologist* 88 (2): 313–38.

Sunguya, Bruno F., Krishna C. Poudel, Linda B. Mlunde, David P. Urassa, Junko Yasuoka, and Masamine Jimba. 2013. "Nutrition Training Improves Health Workers' Nutrition Knowledge and Competence to Manage Child Undernutrition: A Systematic Review." *Frontiers in Public Health* 1 (September 24): 37. doi: 10.3389/fpubh.2013.00037.

Weller, Susan C. 2007. "Cultural Consensus Theory: Applications and Frequently Asked Questions." *Field Methods* 19 (4): 339–68.

7 Synergies and Opportunities for Nutrition in the Health Sector

ABSTRACT In addition to its overall responsibility for overseeing most of the nutrition-specific interventions, the health sector is also involved in activities to tackle the causes of undernutrition that relate to communicable and noncommunicable diseases. This chapter reviews the role of the health sector in delivering nutrition-specific interventions, the role of programs targeted at reducing communicable and noncommunicable disease, and the services that could contribute to the country's fight against undernutrition.

NUTRITION GOVERNANCE

The National Nutrition Council (NNC) was created in 1974 as the highest policy-making and coordinating body on nutrition, with a mandate to formulate an integrated national program on nutrition through the enactment of policies and programs. It is composed of a Governing Board and a Secretariat.[1] The Philippines was one of the first countries to set up a governance structure for nutrition separate from health or any of the other government bureaucracies at that time. At the outset, the NNC was directly under the Office of the President, a testament to the high profile accorded to nutrition during the Marcos administration. Since the start, NNC has had a strong community focus for its policies and interventions and a fairly substantial budget.

The Local Government Code, enacted in 1991, decentralized the delivery of health services to local government units (LGUs). The expressed objective was to make government more responsive to the people's needs, but an underlying sentiment was to strengthen local governments sufficiently in order to prevent a single strongman from establishing another dictatorship.

For the NNC, this meant that the functions and multisectoral composition of the NNC had to be replicated at subnational levels. Regional, provincial, city, municipal, and barangay (district or neighborhood) nutrition committees are organized to manage and coordinate the planning, implementation, monitoring, and evaluation of local nutrition action plans, which, in parallel to national processes, are a component of the local development plan. Local chief executives serve as chairpersons of their respective nutrition committees. Nutrition action officers are designated or appointed to conduct the day-to-day operations of the local nutrition program.

From a highly centralized service delivery arm, the NNC had to shift to an advocacy mode to motivate LGUs to develop local nutrition plans and implement local nutrition programs. With devolution, the accountability for nutrition outcomes shifted to the LGUs. However, their capacity to deliver nutrition services varies enormously. NNC efforts to provide structure and guidance through policies, advocacy, and incentives are constrained by limitations on the frontline resources for which LGUs are responsible. Motivated by its inclusion in the Scaling Up Nutrition Network, the NNC has renewed its focus on preventing stunting through stronger engagements with the LGUs (SUN Movement 2015).

SYNERGIES BETWEEN HEALTH AND NUTRITION

The potential synergies between health and nutrition, recognized instinctively at the individual level, begin to have a real impact when recognized explicitly and built into programs. The major goals and achievements of the health sector are curative, preventive, and promotive. They encompass development policies for better service quality, capacity building of staff at all levels, and enhancement of essential health and nutrition services. The Department of Health (DOH) and the NNC, in cooperation with other government agencies, has developed an extensive list of initiatives to address the nutritional needs of the Filipino population across different age groups (figure 7.1).

Nutrition and nutrition-related programs are guided by the Philippine Plan of Action for Nutrition (PPAN), a strategy for LGU implementation of nutrition programs for the period 2017–22 (NNC 2013). Specific programs target the nutritionally vulnerable, such as children below the age of five years, pregnant and lactating mothers, as well as individuals age 60 and above. Initiatives, such as

FIGURE 7.1

Illustration of interrelationships among agencies cooperating for nutrition programs in the Philippines

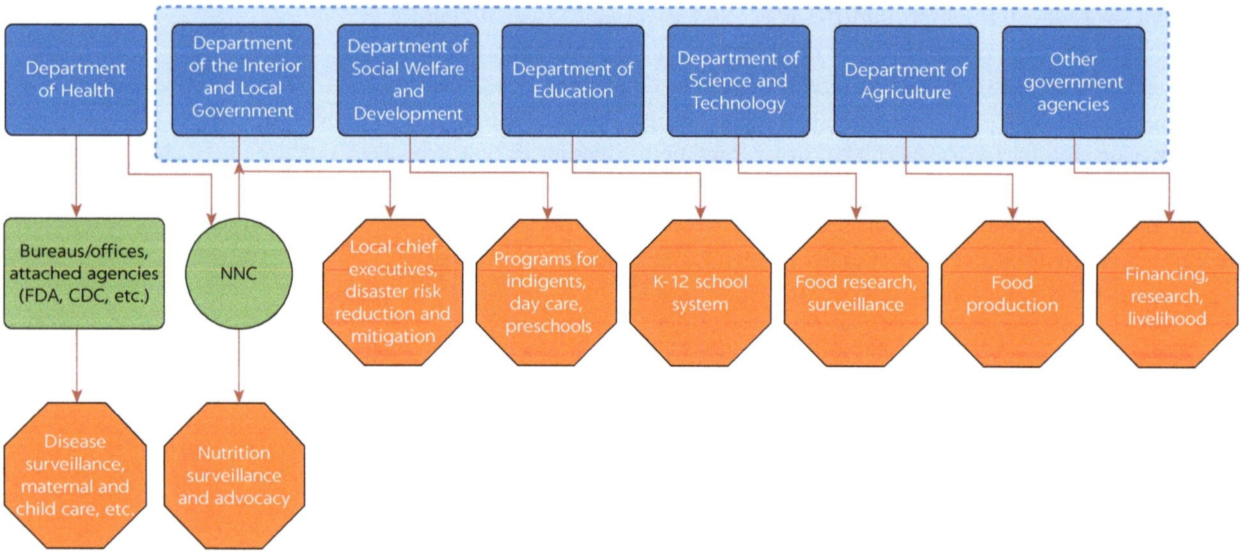

Source: World Bank.
Note: CDC = Centers for Disease Control and Prevention. FDA = Food and Drug Administration. NNC = National Nutrition Council.

food fortification and nutrition in emergencies, cater to the needs of the general population, while other programs are intended to support nutrition surveillance and health promotion. These programs are planned and their outcomes are assessed at the national level, but their implementation depends on the priorities and capacities of the local governments ultimately responsible for service delivery. This fragmented form of governance has an impact on the consistency and efficiency of the programs and therefore on nutritional outcomes.

Multisectoral coordination is needed to enable the delivery of nutrition outcomes, which means that interagency coordination is required at different levels of governance from the national ministerial level, at the top, down to the barangay, on the frontlines. Problematic interagency coordination and implementation can lead to confusion about health-seeking behavior, while introducing a new intervention or modifying an existing one can lead to fatigue on the part of local government implementers. Redundancy of effort arises when agencies try to generate new programs or initiatives rather than revive or reinforce existing initiatives or piggyback on programs already mandated by existing legislation.

The ongoing COVID-19 pandemic aggravates this sociocultural context by limiting mobility and reducing income, with a negative effect on food security and access to health and nutrition services. Measures taken to contain and mitigate the COVID-19 pandemic are having profound effects on children's health and nutrition. While much of the focus has been on testing, tracing, and treating individuals likely to have the disease, it is equally urgent to meet children's needs now, because their growth and development cannot be postponed. As part of an integrated mid- to long-term response to the pandemic, giving priority to nutrition through the first 1,000 days and identifying multisectoral opportunities for child nutrition would be both strategic and pragmatic. This chapter identifies the opportunities for child nutrition in health programs.

NUTRITION-SPECIFIC INTERVENTIONS AND APPROACHES

Global evidence suggests that effective delivery of a set of 10 high-impact nutrition interventions, focused on the first 1,000 days of life, can significantly reduce childhood undernutrition (and stunting in particular). In 2013, on the basis of this evidence, *The Lancet* published its Series on Maternal and Child Nutrition, recommending 10 nutrition-specific interventions to be implemented at scale in countries with high rates of undernutrition (Bhutta et al. 2013) (box 7.1). (Nutrition-specific interventions are defined as those that improve the quality of maternal and child diets and reduce infections by addressing immediate and some underlying causes of undernutrition.) If these interventions were scaled up to 90 percent coverage, they could reduce stunting by an estimated 20 percent. However, a key challenge for many countries, including the Philippines, is to build sufficient implementation capacity to scale up the recommended interventions, taking into consideration local and sectoral challenges while maintaining high-quality services. These interventions need to be accessible precisely where they are needed. Therefore, they need to be delivered through well-coordinated community-based primary care services as part of a well-designed maternal and child health and nutrition program.

The Philippines has been implementing all of these interventions (except for maternal multiple micronutrient supplementation) as discrete programs, with implementation conducted at varying levels and intensities. The lack of a clearly defined minimum comprehensive package of evidence-based interventions has

BOX 7.1

Evidence-based nutrition-specific interventions

Preconception

- Preconception folic acid supplementation or fortification

Pregnancy

- Maternal multiple micronutrient supplementation
- Maternal balanced energy and protein supplementation
- Maternal calcium supplementation

Early infancy and young childhood

- Promotion of breastfeeding
- Appropriate complementary feeding
- Vitamin A supplementation
- Preventative zinc supplementation
- Management of severe acute malnutrition
- Management of moderate acute malnutrition

contributed to the fragmentation of their implementation at the local level. For maternal and child health, the DOH has sought to put together comprehensive packages based on stages of the life cycle (DOH 2011b). Despite this effort, the components have been implemented and tracked individually. Table 7.1 summarizes the status of these nutrition-specific interventions with regard to some governance indicators.

NUTRITION-SPECIFIC INTERVENTIONS AND APPROACHES IN THE PHILIPPINES

Barangay Nutrition Scholar Program and Operation *Timbang* Plus

The Barangay Nutrition Scholar (BNS) Program is a human resource development endeavor aligned with the PPAN (NNC 2020a). The BNS Program seeks to recruit and train community volunteers to act as Barangay Nutrition Scholars throughout the country. Each barangay is required to have one BNS whose primary responsibilities include monitoring the nutritional status of children under the age of five and coordinating nutrition activities throughout the community.

Barangay Nutrition Scholars identify malnourished children in the community through the growth-monitoring program known as Operation *Timbang* Plus (OPT Plus). Annual anthropometric measurement and weighing of children, especially those of preschool age, are vital for identifying and classifying children with malnutrition. While conducting OPT Plus, BNSs also interview parents and caregivers about their feeding and child care practices and determine what resources are available to the family and community for helping improve a child's health and nutritional status. They also refer parents and caregivers for counseling, if a quarterly reweighing indicates that a child's growth is faltering or other adverse nutritional outcomes are detected. In addition to conducting OPT Plus, they may organize mothers' classes, provide nutrition counseling on exclusive breastfeeding and complementary feeding, spearhead community

TABLE 7.1 **Nutrition-specific interventions with corresponding policies, implementation coverage, monitoring system, and oversight persons or agencies**

INTERVENTION	POLICY	SCOPE OF IMPLEMENTATION	METHOD FOR TRACKING OUTCOMES	OVERSIGHT AGENCY
Prenatal iron plus folic supplementation	Republic Act no. 11148 (2018)	National: pregnant mothers	FHSIS	DOH, local health officer
Maternal energy plus protein supplementation	Republic Act no. 11148 (2018)	Select LGUs: pregnant mothers	LGU records	LGU, local nutrition action officer
Maternal calcium supplementation	Republic Act no. 11148 (2018)	National: pregnant mothers	LGU records	Local health officer
Micronutrient powder	DOH Department Memorandum no. 2011-0303 (2011)	National: children 6–12 months	FHSIS	DOH, local nutrition action officer
Breastfeeding promotion	Republic Act no. 10028 (2010); Republic Act no. 11148 (2018)	National: children 0–24 months	FHSIS, ENNS	DOH, local nutrition action officer, health officer
Appropriate complementary feeding	Republic Act no. 11148 (2018)	National: children 6–24 months	FHSIS, ENNS	DOH, local nutrition action officer
Vitamin A supplementation (*Garantisadong Pambata* and maternal supplementation)	Administrative Order no. 36 s.2010 (2010); Republic Act no. 11148 (2018)	National: children 6–59 months	FHSIS	DOH, local nutrition action officer
Zinc supplementation	Administrative Order no. 2007-0045 (2007)	National: children 6–59 months	FHSIS (in the context of the provision of oral rehydration solution)	DOH, local health officer
Management of moderate acute malnutrition	PIMAM protocol (2011); Republic Act no. 11148 (2018)	Select LGUs: all children assessed with moderate acute malnutrition	LGU records	DOH, local nutrition action officer
Management of severe acute malnutrition	PIMAM protocol (2011); Republic Act no. 11148 (2018)	Select LGUs: all children assessed with severe acute malnutrition	LGU records	DOH, local nutrition action officer
Barangay Nutrition Scholar Program	Presidential Decree no. 1569 (1978)	National: all deployed Barangay Nutrition Scholars	NNC	NNC, local health officer, local nutrition action officer, district or city nutrition program coordinator
Nutrition in emergencies	NNC Governing Board Resolution (2009)	Select affected LGUs	LGU records	NNC, Department of Social Welfare and Development, health offices
Food fortification	Republic Act no. 8976 (2000)	National: general population	ENNS (iodine only)	DOH, FDA, DTI

Sources: Congress of the Philippines 2000, 2010, 2018; DOH 2007, 2010, 2011a, 2011c; FNRI 2019; Government of the Philippines 1978; NNC 2009.
Note: DOH = Department of Health. DTI = Department of Trade and Industry. ENNS = Expanded National Nutrition Survey. FDA = Food and Drug Administration. FHSIS = Field Health Services Information System. LGU = local government unit. NNC = National Nutrition Council. PIMAM = Philippine Integrated Management of Acute Malnutrition.

feeding and community gardening programs, and work with health care providers to facilitate the provision of deworming, immunization, and other health services for the target age group.

As of 2020, 49,779 BNSs are deployed in 39,942 barangays nationwide. They are supervised by 400 district or city nutrition program coordinators working with local health departments.

Food Fortification Program

The Food Fortification Program of the DOH seeks to address nutrient deficiencies, specifically deficiencies in iodine, vitamin A, and iron, through the production and promotion of fortified foods and staples, such as salt, flour, sugar, cooking oil, and rice (DOH 2020e). The first legislative initiative in this field was Republic Act no. 8172: An Act Promoting Salt Iodization Nationwide and for Other Purposes (also known as the ASIN Law, *asin* being the local term for salt), which was signed into law on July 24, 1995 (Congress of the Philippines 1995). Under this law, all involved in the salt industry, including producers, distributors, and retailers, are required to make iodized salt available to the general population. Food establishments, such as restaurants and food manufacturers, are required to use iodized salt exclusively in cooking and processing. Guidelines on the use of iodine in salt support the regulatory actions of the National Salt Iodization Program. Iodine deficiency has since declined substantially (FNRI 2008, 2013).

A landmark policy for the Food Fortification Program was Republic Act no. 8976: An Act Establishing the Philippine Food Fortification Program and for Other Purposes, which mandated the fortification of sugar and cooking oil with vitamin A and the fortification of rice with iron (Congress of the Philippines 2000). This program calls for wheat flour to be fortified with both vitamin A and iron. By 2009, up to 50 percent of rice tested by the Food and Drug Administration was fortified with iron, 91 percent of cooking oil was fortified with vitamin A, and 99 percent of wheat flour was fortified with these two nutrients. Although further investigation is needed, food fortification is deemed to have contributed to declines in vitamin A deficiency and anemia in the general population.

An additional component of the act was creation of the *Sangkap Pinoy* Seal Program, an initiative to promote voluntary fortification of processed foods (literal translation: Filipino or indigenous ingredients). Manufacturers complying with food fortification requirements are entitled to place a special seal on their product packaging to encourage consumers to purchase and consume these fortified foods. As of 2008, only 11.6 percent of households were aware of the *Sangkap Pinoy* Seal Program, even though up to 99.2 percent of households surveyed were consumers of foods given this seal.

The program needs improvement. The fortification of rice with iron has faced several hurdles, including initially poor acceptance of the iron powder–coated rice grains, which became discolored when oxidized and had a suspicious odor and metallic flavor that did not appeal to consumers. Subsequent development using extrusion technology reduced these sensory problems, but consumer acceptance has been low and slow. Program monitoring is mandated by law to be undertaken by the Food and Drug Administration, but updates of coverage have not been made available regularly. The *Sangkap Pinoy* Seal has reportedly been co-opted by food manufacturers, which apply the seal to advertise claims that salty and sugary snacks are fortified, giving a nutritional halo to otherwise unhealthy foods. These claims have not been investigated thoroughly or monitored regularly.

Garantisadong Pambata

Garantisadong Pambata is a biannual week-long delivery of a package of health services to children from birth to 59 months of age. The Expanded *Garantisadong*

Pambata Program is guided by the principles of universal health care and seeks to provide a comprehensive, integrated package of health and nutrition services to children in different settings, such as the home, school, and health facilities (DOH 2020f). Nutrition-related services include vitamin supplementation, promotion of the use of iodized salt in home cooking, and reinforcement of sound feeding practices for infants and young children.

A key component of the Expanded *Garantisadong Pambata* Program is vitamin A supplementation, which is conducted biannually. Routine supplementation as well as therapeutic supplementation to prevent xeropthalmia and combat illnesses, such as pneumonia, are also given. Vitamin A supplementation is conducted routinely in community facilities, such as the local health center, or through routine home visits by volunteers and health workers. In the past, prior to routine supplementation through this program, massive one-time supplementation events were held to increase coverage.

On average, 76 percent of children 6–59 months old were given vitamin A supplements during the six months preceding the survey, but coverage varies widely among regions—from 45 percent in the Autonomous Region in Muslim Mindanao (ARMM) to 90 percent in Eastern Visayas (PSA 2017).

Nutrition in emergencies

The Philippines is an archipelago that is vulnerable to natural calamities, such as typhoons, earthquakes, and volcanic eruptions. Calamities worthy of note include Typhoon Haiyan (locally known as Yolanda) in 2013 and eruptions of Mayon Volcano in 2018 and Taal Volcano in 2020. In recent years, the country has also experienced human-induced disasters, such as armed conflict in Marawi in 2017. In light of these disasters, the National Nutrition Council has developed guidelines on nutrition in emergencies. The first iteration of these guidelines was approved in December 2009; an update was being drafted in 2019.

The current guidelines focus on planning and logistical support prior to emergencies, nutritional surveillance, as well as service delivery to the following priority groups: pregnant and lactating mothers, children below the age of five, children assessed to have low mid-upper-arm circumference or low weight-for-height, older persons, sick and injured persons, as well as persons living with human immunodeficiency virus (HIV)/acquired immunodeficiency syndrome (AIDS). Services to be delivered as part of nutrition in emergencies include feeding services for infants and young children, mass feeding in accordance with the most updated Sphere guidelines for humanitarian aid (Sphere 2018), micronutrient supplementation, and psychosocial care. The planned update, guided by policies such as Republic Act no. 10028 and Republic Act no. 11148, expands on service delivery to include adolescents, especially girls 11–19 years of age, as well as indigenous persons (Congress of the Philippines 2010, 2018). Emphasis is also accorded to the management of severe and moderate acute malnutrition as well as to continued surveillance. The planned policy delineates the role of local governments in providing nutrition services in emergencies, in line with the current disaster risk reduction and management framework implemented both nationally and locally. A recent update to the policy includes a section on service delivery in the Bangsamoro Autonomous Region in Muslim Mindanao (BARMM) to account for its unique government structure.

Philippine Integrated Management of Acute Malnutrition

In response to the need to establish a program for the community-based management of acute malnutrition, national guidelines were drawn up in 2011 (DOH 2011c). These guidelines, known as the Philippine Integrated Management of Acute Malnutrition (PIMAM), were not readily adopted for routine use locally due to logistical concerns, including the procurement and availability of commodities, such as ready-to-use therapeutic food. However, the PIMAM guidelines were useful in providing urgent nutritional interventions for children affected by disasters, such as the Bohol Earthquake and Typhoon Haiyan in 2013, as well as armed conflicts in Mindanao. These guidelines were also integrated into the urban planning of Davao in 2014.

Under the PIMAM guidelines, specific roles are delegated to the local government, under the direction of local nutrition action officers, to facilitate the provision of timely nutritional assistance to children assessed as having either severe or moderate acute malnutrition. Important activities, especially at the barangay level, include active and passive case finding, referral of cases with severe acute malnutrition to the nearest outpatient treatment facility, case registration, treatment, follow-up, and promotion of healthy nutrition practices. Specific criteria, including measurement of mid-upper-arm circumference, weight-for-height, and presence or absence of bipedal edema, are used to detect the presence of severe or moderate acute malnutrition. Treatment in the community or outpatient setting includes the provision of ready-to-use therapeutic food, routine antibiotics, deworming, vitamin A supplementation, and vaccination against measles. The PIMAM guidelines also cover the inpatient management of individuals with severe acute malnutrition or with complications, beginning from assessment and referral all the way to treatment and discharge. Special provision is made for malnourished infants under six months of age, to promote a return to exclusive breastfeeding.

Program reports indicate the following, but data on the geographic location of cases were not provided:

- A total of 2,285 cases of severe acute malnutrition were treated under the PIMAM guidelines in 2018; 1,295 of these were treated as outpatients, while 990 were treated as inpatients. Of the outpatient cases, 792 were cured, 7 died, 279 stopped treatment, and 185 were not cured. Among inpatients, 428 were cured, 62 died, 128 stopped treatment, and 197 were not cured.
- For 2019, a partial total of 2,951 cases of severe acute malnutrition were admitted to outpatient and inpatient programs. Of these, 1,845 were cured, 53 died, 455 stopped treatment, and 462 were not cured.

Infant and Young Child Feeding Program

The Infant and Young Child Feeding (IYCF) Program is crucial for ensuring good nutritional status for children under the age of five as well as for reducing mortality and morbidity in this age group (DOH 2020g). The first National IYCF Plan, formulated by the DOH in 2005, is patterned after the global strategy created by the World Health Organization (WHO) in 2003 (WHO 2003). The strategy was codified in Administrative Order no. 2005-0014: National Policies on IYCF, signed on May 23, 2005 (DOH 2005). Key points of the IYCF strategy include encouraging exclusive breastfeeding for children up to six months of age and appropriate complementary feeding practices, with continued breastfeeding for children 6–24 months of age.

Several important national policies support current IYCF efforts. One of these is Executive Order no. 51: National Code of Marketing of Breastmilk Substitutes, Breastmilk Supplements, and Other Related Products, more popularly known as the Milk Code of 1986 (Congress of the Philippines 1986). This executive order prohibits health facilities from promoting the use of infant formula with the intent of encouraging breastfeeding. This policy also regulates the marketing of infant formula and breast milk substitutes, particularly product labeling. Another key policy was the Republic Act no. 10028, known as the Expanded Breastfeeding Promotion Act of 2009 (Congress of the Philippines 2010). This law promotes rooming-in as a policy for mothers and babies delivering in health facilities. It urges health and nonhealth facilities to establish lactation stations with access to a clean lavatory and to provide seating and breast pumps. In addition, it entitles employees to lactation breaks in addition to the mandated lunch or break time to provide ample opportunities for breastfeeding or expressing milk.

Building on this legislation is Republic Act no. 11148 of 2018, also known as the Kalusugan at Nutrisyon ng Mag-Nanay Act (Congress of the Philippines 2018). The following groups fall under the purview of this policy: nutritionally at-risk individuals, especially pregnant and lactating women, teenage mothers, women of reproductive age, adolescent girls, and all Filipino children from birth to 24 months. With regard to IYCF, this law reinforces the role of lactation support as part of health and nutrition services at the community level and promotes the counseling and teaching of caregivers of children 6–24 months of age with regard to timely and appropriate introduction of complementary feeding while continuing breastfeeding. Other key services related to IYCF include the identification and management of moderate to severe acute malnutrition in children under two years of age, dietary supplementation, as well as growth and development monitoring.

The 2019 Expanded National Nutrition Survey (ENNS) found the following with regard to breastfeeding (FNRI 2019):

- 74 percent of infants experienced early initiation of breastfeeding.
- 58 percent were exclusively breastfed by six months of age, but only 35 percent were able to do so continuously from birth.
- The mean duration of exclusive breastfeeding was 4.4 months, and breastfeeding in total (exclusive plus continued after introduction of solid food) was 8.3 months.
- 54 percent of infants were still breastfeeding by 12 months, falling to 34 percent by 24 months.
- Only 10 percent of children ages 6–23 months were receiving the minimum acceptable diet, largely because of low diet diversity, particularly in the younger age groups.

Micronutrient Program

The Micronutrient Program of the Department of Health seeks to address specific micronutrient deficiencies, such as vitamin A, iodine, and iron (DOH 2020j). This program works hand in hand with other initiatives, such as the Expanded *Garantisadong Pambata* Program and the Food Fortification Program.

Independent of those programs, the Micronutrient Program provides therapeutic iron supplementation to anemic children ages 6–59 months as well as to pregnant and lactating mothers attending regular checkups at local health facilities. The program manual recommends the provision of iodine supplements for pregnant and postpartum women, vitamin A supplementation for postpartum patients, and iron supplementation for women of reproductive age (10–49 years) to prevent the onset of iron deficiency anemia (DOH 2011b).

Another important initiative of this program is the provision of micronutrient powder to be mixed into the food of children 6–23 months of age. This powder contains vitamins A, D, E, B1, B2, B6, B12, and C, niacin, folate, iron, zinc, copper, selenium, and iodine, designed for consumption once a day (DOH 2020d).

According to the Field Health Services Information System (FHSIS) 2018 data (DOH 2018), coverage of this program was as follows:

- 22 percent of children ages 6–11 months were given routine iron supplementation.
- 4 percent of children ages 12–59 months were given routine iron supplementation.
- 85 percent of anemic children ages 6–11 months were given therapeutic iron supplementation.
- 86 percent of anemic children ages 12–59 months were given therapeutic iron supplementation.
- 23 percent of children ages 6–11 months were given micronutrient powder.
- 39 percent of children ages 12–23 months were given micronutrient powder.
- 54 percent of pregnant mothers were given iron with folic acid supplementation.
- 53 percent of postpartum mothers were given iron with folic acid supplementation.
- 53 percent of postpartum mothers were given vitamin A supplementation.
- 13 percent of women ages 10–49 were given iron supplementation.

Calcium supplementation will be included in future monitoring under the FHSIS. The current target population for this intervention is 30 percent of pregnant women, prioritizing those with high-risk conditions, such as a history of hypertension or preeclampsia. As of 2019, 17.25 percent of pregnant women were given calcium supplementation (DOH 2019).

Operation *Timbang* Plus (growth monitoring program)

OPT Plus is a growth-monitoring program of the National Nutrition Council, which is conducted annually for children under the age of five (NNC 2020c) (*timbang* is the Tagalog word for "weight" or "weigh"). Data on height and weight are collected and collated, primarily to identify children in the community who are malnourished and thus eligible for supplementary feeding, food aid, and other interventions. Data from OPT Plus are also used to assess the community's overall nutrition status and the general impact of nutritional programs.

The 2019 OPT Plus covered every region of the Philippines except for the BARMM. Data on height and weight were used to assess the overall prevalence of stunting, wasting, and low weight-for-age in children in the target age group.

Some of the findings of the 2019 OPT Plus are as follows:

- Stunting prevalence was highest in the province of Samar, with 29 percent of children under the age of five found to have low height-for-age.

- Wasting was highest in the province of Palawan, with 7 percent of children under the age of five found to have low weight-for-height or weight-for-length.
- Underweight prevalence was highest in the province of Catanduanes, with 13 percent of children under the age of five found to have low weight-for-age.

Mother-Baby-Friendly Hospitals

The Mother-Baby-Friendly Hospitals accreditation is in line with Republic Act no. 10028: Expanded Breastfeeding Promotion Act of 2009 as well as Republic Act no. 7600: Rooming-In and Breast-feeding Act of 1992 (Congress of the Philippines 1992, 2010). Both of these policies seek to promote breastfeeding while a mother and her newborn baby stay in a health facility by enforcing rooming-in and early initiation of breastfeeding. Mothers who have undergone a caesarian section or delivered outside the health facility but were subsequently admitted must practice exclusive breastfeeding. Health care workers and other employees of the facility are also required to promote breastfeeding and enforce Executive Order no. 51, the Milk Code (Congress of the Philippines 1986). The use of breast milk substitutes and infant formulas is prohibited in health facilities, such as hospitals, lying-in clinics, and even health centers. Health care providers directly engaged in providing health and nutrition services to pregnant and postpartum mothers are required to discourage their use, unless medically indicated. This accreditation is also aligned with the PPAN, especially with regard to its goals for antenatal and postpartum nutrition as well as IYCF.

To attain the Mother-Baby-Friendly Hospital accreditation, a facility must adhere to the standards of the "Ten Steps to Successful Breastfeeding" that are part of the WHO Baby-Friendly Hospital Initiative, as revised in 2018 (WHO 2002, 2018b). The 10 steps include having a clearly posted and communicated breastfeeding policy on the premises, encouraging rooming-in and skin-to-skin contact between mother and baby, and coordinating discharge instructions so that the mother and child may have access to ongoing support and care in the community. Prior to accreditation, a facility must have a certificate of commitment that signifies a two-year window for the facility to implement the 10 steps and fulfill antenatal and postpartum care requirements. Following this two-year period, a facility can apply for a certificate of accreditation and undergo evaluation. A certificate of accreditation is valid for three years.

At present, 653 out of a targeted 1,180 facilities in the Philippines have been assessed. Of these, 488 have active certificates of commitment, while 165 have active certificates of accreditation. The reassessment of facilities has been postponed until 2021 due to the COVID-19 pandemic.

Gaps and opportunities in nutrition-specific programs

The Philippines has struggled to implement this growing number of programs given the discontinuous nature of governance—at national and subnational levels (at least two regions are considered autonomous: Cordillera Administrative Region and BARMM), with further subdivisions within local governments (cities and municipalities are separate from provinces). Through the enactment of national policies and guidelines, the presence of designated manpower at local levels, extensive advocacy, and infusion of resources (through commodities, training, and other forms of support), the national government has managed to impose some degree of structure on the execution of priority programs. Nevertheless, there is considerable variation in how LGUs operate nutrition programs, which can be exacerbated by changes in administration with every national and local election and, recently, by the COVID-19 pandemic.

Facilitative supervision is a major cross-cutting gap across all programs. Although the NNC has regional coordinators and nutrition action officers at the provincial and city or municipal levels, almost all (with the exception of regional coordinators) wear multiple hats (in addition to their nutritional role). The nutrition action officers are constrained to find sufficient time and focus (*tutok* in the local language) to provide the needed supervision. At the barangay level, all health and nutrition programs converge on the midwife, who usually has only minimal training on nutrition. The ratio of supervisors to BNSs, about 8 per 1,000, is clearly inadequate. Externally funded nutrition project staff are thus a welcome supplement to the workforce and often provide the much-needed focus and attention. However, they leave when the project ends, and the sense of focus tends to evaporate.

Truncation and fragmentation at higher levels of governance make it even more crucial for frontline nutrition workers—the BNSs—to be well trained, suitably equipped, and regularly updated. Since the BNS Program is a human resources development initiative, the biggest opportunity presents itself in the form of reinforcing and expanding the knowledge and skill sets of the BNSs. Nutrition scholars could be trained (1) to use alternative assessment measures, such as mid-upper-arm circumference, for rapid assessment of nutritional status; (2) to interpret, not just measure, weight gain in pregnancy; and (3) to assess families' food security status and resources for providing adequate nutrition for children under five. Given the limited number of BNSs in each local government unit, BHWs could be trained to deliver community-based nutrition programs, which would support the needs of frontline nutrition workers.

Surveillance is a need, not always met, that cuts across almost all of these programs. Opportunities to improve surveillance include providing feedback, expanding coverage, and improving the quality of data gathered. Reporting systems need to be aligned to allow for ready relay and use of the data, especially by the community health workers themselves, to enable a quick response. Socioeconomic and even behavioral factors contribute to difficulties with surveillance, especially in communities where services are provided mostly within health facilities. These factors include losses to follow-up, particularly when a child has completed the basic course of vaccinations. Immediate feedback would be particularly helpful in the areas of household food security, consumer behavior and beliefs regarding the feeding of infants and young children, and even media promotion of food supplements and breast milk supplements. The most recent OPT Plus missed the entire BARMM region, which has some of the highest rates of child malnutrition in the country.

Logistics and supply chain management problems are also evident, especially for LGUs with limited resources and in more remote or geographically isolated and disadvantaged areas. Improved logistics are particularly important for the Micronutrient Supplementation Program, where timely availability of supplements is crucial to meeting beneficiaries' needs. Another program requiring improved logistics is the Food Fortification Program. The challenge here is to improve the availability of fortified foods, especially in geographically isolated and disadvantaged areas.

Opportunities exist for many of these programs. The Food Fortification Program provides an opportunity to take advantage of newer food technologies that may make it possible to fortify other foods. The program could capitalize on the interest of the Department of Science and Technology in broadening its portfolio of fortified products and build capacity for food fortification at regional and provincial levels to make such products more accessible and harness local produce.

The Expanded *Garantisadong Pambata* Program provides opportunities not just for vitamin A supplementation, but also for the integration of nutrition programs intended to reach the same target beneficiaries. These opportunities include improving coverage for iron supplementation and micronutrient powder, follow-up and counseling of caregivers regarding IYCF practices, and growth monitoring. This integrated approach would facilitate client-based care and enable families to be more proactive when they need and seek care.

A good opportunity for client-based care may be possible through programs intended for women and girls. Iron and folic acid supplementation should be extended to all women ages 10–49 years, not only to ill or symptomatic patients seeking a consultation. This expansion is particularly crucial for folic acid, which is vitally needed when a woman may not yet be aware that she is pregnant. Pregnant women should be encouraged to seek prenatal care earlier and more often so that appropriate care and needed supplements can be provided in a timely manner. Apart from updating the status of accredited Mother-Baby-Friendly Hospitals, an opportunity exists to improve adherence to the tenth step, which is coordinating discharge of the mother and newborn to ensure follow-up in the community. In this regard, linking this hospital initiative with the community-based IYCF Program and the maternal care programs makes sense for improving continuity of care and efficiency in service delivery.

The establishment of the BARMM region in Mindanao, which is among the most vulnerable to child malnutrition, also presents opportunities for promoting good nutrition. Culturally sensitive interventions, such as the provision of halal food, are necessary in this region. This type of consideration represents a significant opportunity for coordinating with local civil and religious authorities to promote the acceptability and coverage of IYCF and management of moderate and severe acute malnutrition. The changing structure of BARMM governance is also an opportunity to integrate context-specific nutrition surveillance, such as the OPT Plus, as the health system in this area continues to evolve.

The COVID-19 pandemic

The COVID-19 pandemic and the resulting nationwide quarantine has restricted the mobility of health care workers as well as patients. Fear of contracting COVID-19 limits patients' opportunities and willingness to seek a consultation, especially for well-baby or routine services. Efforts to deliver nutrition in emergencies are hampered by the need for social distancing (how could or should anthropometric assessments be conducted safely?) and by difficulties in the distribution of commodities, compounded by the rechanneling of resources for the pandemic.

As successive waves of higher case numbers ripple throughout the archipelago, health care providers are still enjoined to provide the full complement of services as far as the quarantine permits. On May 11, 2020, the Department of Health issued a memorandum covering interim guidelines for delivering nutrition services during a pandemic, stipulating which services would be suspended or limited based on the level of community transmission (NNC 2020b). With the gradual lifting of the quarantine, opportunities have arisen to resume postponed routine nutrition interventions, such as surveillance. The NNC has provided guidance on the use of mid-upper-arm circumference for rapid assessment and is coordinating with national agencies and local governments to identify nutritionally at-risk persons and provide support for intervention. The government's push for universal internet connectivity to allow online classes creates opportunities for nutrition training and counseling, including the use of remote classrooms or other digital technology.

NUTRITION-SENSITIVE PROGRAMS

Although the outcomes of the following programs are not nutrition-specific, their services affect nutrition outcomes. These nutrition-sensitive initiatives may also serve as platforms for delivering nutrition-related activities as well as nutrition surveillance, especially those that operate in conjunction with other nutrition initiatives or target the same intended beneficiaries. An example of this tandem approach would be the *Unang Yakap* (meaning "the first embrace") or Essential Newborn Care Program, which is practiced in Mother-Baby Friendly Hospitals (WHO 2017).

Adolescent Health and Development Program

The Adolescent Health and Development Program was first instituted in April 2000 through Administrative Order no. 34-A s. 2000, which created the Adolescent Youth Health subprogram (DOH 2020a). The program created adolescent-friendly health facilities. These safe spaces serve as physical locations for counseling on health, nutrition, use of tobacco and alcohol, prevention of teenage pregnancy, HIV, sexually transmitted infections, and mental health. The prevention of teenage pregnancy is of particular importance, as mothers in their teens are more nutritionally at-risk than mothers in their 20s and are less likely to provide optimum feeding and support for their infants (FNRI 2015). With 47 births annually per 1,000 women ages 15–19, the Philippines has a higher teenage pregnancy rate than both the world as a whole (44) and the Association of Southeast Asian Nations region (33.5) (World Bank Group 2019).

Taking an integrated, client-based approach, adolescent-friendly health facilities could also serve as a staging point for the regular provision of iron and folic acid supplementation for young women. Teen-oriented nutrition and healthy diet sessions are part of the program, intended to address the increasing overweight and obesity rates in this age group. However, there have been few reports of program progress, and it is not known whether these nutrition opportunities are currently taking place.

Integrated Management of Childhood Illness Program

The Integrated Management of Childhood Illness (IMCI) Program is designed to cure and prevent disease in children under the age of five who are seen in the community or outpatient setting (DOH 2020h). The IMCI approach focuses on five conditions: pneumonia, diarrhea, malaria, measles, and malnutrition (WHO 2018a). Children with malnutrition frequently suffer from one or more of the other conditions and must be managed in the outpatient or home setting or be referred urgently to a tertiary facility. The IMCI is one of the first programs to integrate previously vertical programs with the intent of optimizing training opportunities for staff and providing more holistic care.

Some IMCI protocols fall under the purview of ongoing health programs of the DOH and NNC. The IMCI Program provides vitamin A supplementation to children with measles or persistent diarrhea and iron to sick children recuperating at home. The outcomes are also being monitored in the Micronutrient Supplementation Program and the Expanded *Garantisadong Pambata* Program. Counseling for mothers and caregivers on feeding practices falls under the current IYCF Program. Provision of ready-to-use therapeutic food for managing malnutrition is also emphasized not only in the IMCI but also in the IYCF, OPT Plus, and other programs assessing and treating moderate and severe acute malnutrition. Reports on the status and coverage of the IMCI in the Adolescent Health and Development Program are limited. The coverage of individual components of nutrition, such as vitamin A supplementation, IYCF, and zinc provision in diarrhea case management, are reported, but coverage of the program is not (table 7.2). Although staff have been trained nationwide, it is not known whether they are still implementing the program.

National Safe Motherhood Program

The National Safe Motherhood Program seeks to strengthen the provision of high-quality maternal and newborn services, with the aim of reducing maternal mortality and morbidity as well as poor perinatal and neonatal outcomes (DOH 2020k). Under this program, health facilities are trained in basic emergency obstetrics and newborn care practices, with more complicated or high-risk cases referred to centers that have comprehensive emergency obstetrics and newborn care services. Another key part of this program is ensuring that all pregnant mothers receive at least four antenatal visits. These visits are opportunities to provide nutrition services, such as iron and folic acid supplementation, as well as to assess mothers' nutritional status. Coverage of iron supplements has been

TABLE 7.2 **Key indicators of the Integrated Management of Childhood Illness Program in the Philippines, 2018**

INDICATOR	% OF CHILDREN
Share of children ages 0–59 months with diarrhea who were given oral rehydration solution	67.42
Share of children ages 0–59 months with diarrhea who were given oral rehydration solution or treatment with zinc	47.28
Distribution of low birthweight infants ages 2–5 months who were given a full dose of iron	68.14
Distribution of children ages 0–59 months with pneumonia who were given a complete treatment	96.31
Sick infants ages 6–11 months who were given vitamin A	51.55
Sick children ages 12–59 months who were given vitamin A	44.78
Anemic infants ages 6–11 months who were given iron	85.31
Anemic children ages 12-59 months who were given iron	86.27

Source: Field Health Service Information System 2018 data (DOH 2018).

quite good (92 percent), but information on the number of doses taken and whether folic acid was also received was not provided (PSA 2017). Postpartum visits, of which at least two are mandatory for each patient, provide an opportunity to encourage exclusive breastfeeding and address any nutritional concerns. As of 2017, the wide coverage of these measures—87 percent for antenatal visits and 86 percent for postpartum visits—suggests a large window of opportunity for implementing and strengthening nutrition services. Unfortunately, reports on maternal nutritional status are not routinely provided.

Unang Yakap (Essential Newborn Care) Program

The *Unang Yakap* (Essential Newborn Care) Program was made mandatory for hospitals and lying-in clinics in 2009. Four essential steps are followed in this protocol: immediate and thorough drying of the newborn, early skin-to-skin contact, properly timed cord clamping, and nonseparation of newborn from mother (to start early breastfeeding). Properly timed cord clamping is recommended to prevent iron deficiency anemia until the age of six months (WHO 2019). Early initiation of breastfeeding is also key in establishing exclusive breastfeeding as well as promoting bonding between mother and child. To achieve recommended nutrition in this age group, it would be useful to improve surveillance of these practices and monitor their impact on newborn health for up to six months.

Expanded Program on Immunization

The Expanded Program on Immunization (EPI) seeks to provide essential vaccines to Filipino children before they complete their first year of life (DOH 2020b). The following vaccines are administered under this program: BCG (Bacillus Calmette–Guérin) and hepatitis B after birth; two doses of the pentavalent vaccine for diphtheria, tetanus, pertussis (DTP), hepatitis B, and Hib (*Haemophilus influenzae* type B); three doses of the oral polio vaccine; and two doses of the vaccine for measles, mumps, and rubella. Pneumococcal and rotavirus vaccines also may be administered within the first year of life.

By 2018, up to 66 percent of Filipino children were considered fully immunized, having received the full EPI regimen before 12 months of age. More than 7 percent of children were also considered to be completely immunized, having fulfilled the EPI requirements, but having done so outside of the prescribed schedule. Vaccine coverage has been declining over the years, due to lack of follow-up as well as reduced focus by local governments on this program. EPI vaccines are given in conjunction with well-baby checkups or as part of house-to-house visits in mass vaccination campaigns. The EPI also provides an opportunity to conduct nutrition surveillance, assess the target population, and counsel caregivers. Visits for booster shots are opportunities for health care and nutrition providers to follow up with families regarding IYCF, especially exclusive breastfeeding for infants 0–6 months of age as well as complementary feeding for children 6–11 months of age.

Malaria Control Program

The Malaria Control Program has enabled 42 out of 81 provinces to be declared free of malaria. The program is presently focused on seven provinces still suffering from local transmission, with the aim of eliminating malaria in the country

TABLE 7.3 **Number of malaria cases and deaths in the Philippines, 2003–18**

YEAR	NUMBER OF CASES	NUMBER OF DEATHS
2003	48,400	162
2004	50,800	167
2005	46,300	150
2006	35,400	122
2007	36,200	73
2008	23,600	56
2009	19,900	24
2010	19,220	33
2011	9,610	12
2012	8,150	16
2013	7,720	11
2014	4,930	6
2015	8,100	20
2016	6,550	7
2017	3,990	4
2018	2,980	1

Source: DOH 2020i.
Note: Number of cases is rounded for each year.

by 2030. A sharp general downward trend in mortality and morbidity due to malaria has been observed, from 19,217 cases with 33 deaths recorded in 2010 to 2,976 cases with 1 fatality in 2018 (DOH 2020i, table 7.3).

At present, the Malaria Control Program emphasizes controlling vectors, increasing diagnostic capacity via microscopy, surveillance, and case finding, as well as making therapeutics, such as primaquine and artesunate, more readily available. This program offers an opportunity to monitor patients for anemia, especially secondary to *P. falciparum* infection. Although the matter still requires detailed evaluation, the success achieved in malaria control is credited with having contributed to the decline of anemia in the general population (figure 7.2).

Philippine National Family Planning Program

Population and family planning services can help limit population growth by reducing early pregnancies and lowering fertility rates (DOH 2020c). Birth spacing can reduce the incidence of maternal depletion syndrome, which can lead to low birthweight, anemia, and prematurity. The Philippine National Family Planning Program aims to ensure that families have access to medically safe, effective, and culturally acceptable modern methods of family planning. An important policy bolstering this program is Republic Act no. 10354: Responsible Parenthood and Reproductive Health Act of 2012 (Congress of the Philippines 2012). Reproductive health and family planning are also integrated into other services, such as the minimum initial service package in emergencies and disasters.

By 2018, the use of modern contraceptives throughout the country stood at almost 57 percent, indicating that more men and women are regularly using modern contraceptives. Client interactions for family planning present an

FIGURE 7.2

Prevalence of anemia in the Philippines, 1993–2013

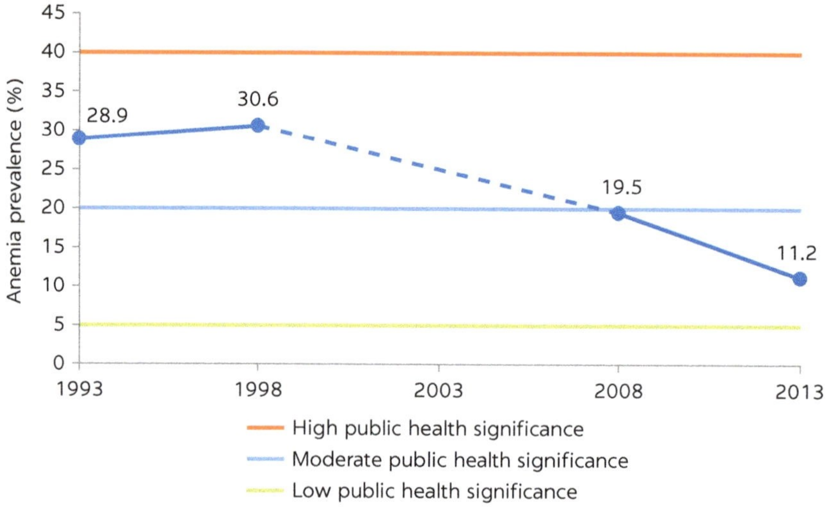

Source: The Eighth National Nutrition Survey: Biochemical (FNRI 2013).
Note: The dashed line indicates that for 10 years there were no data collected.

opportunity to deliver nutrition services, such as assessment of nutritional status, iron supplementation to women of reproductive age, and counseling on lifestyle changes and dietary modifications to prevent or reduce the risk of noncommunicable diseases.

DISCUSSION AND CONCLUSIONS

Health and nutrition programs and services operate in the Philippines within a devolved system that relies on interagency coordination with the National Nutrition Council and its local counterparts. Many nutrition interventions are targeted at children under five as well as pregnant and lactating mothers. These interventions include regular anthropometric assessment, vitamin and micronutrient supplementation, IYCF, and early initiation of breastfeeding in tertiary hospitals, lying-in clinics, and facilities offering care to pregnant mothers. Other programs are designed to meet specific needs among the general population, such as the Food Fortification Program as well as nutrition in emergencies and disasters.

However, these programs often lack sufficiently trained, adequately equipped, and updated staff to deliver nutrition services at the community level and have limited facilitative supervision. Updated surveillance of the status and coverage of programs is needed, not just for assessing impact at the national level, but also for guiding operations at the local level. Logistical constraints, such as poor supply chain practices, also hamper the timely delivery of products and services, such as vitamin supplementation and food fortification. Other gaps to consider include follow-up care, especially after the first year of life, as well as prevailing attitudes regarding the feeding of infants and young children, food supplementation, and micronutrient supplementation. The COVID-19 pandemic has exacerbated these gaps in surveillance and service delivery, as a consequence of quarantine restrictions.

Many opportunities for nutrition are centered around integrating nutrition services either by program or by intended beneficiaries through a client-based approach to care. Updating surveillance as well as improving the coverage and quantity of data gathered should elicit responsive guidance and support. A particular area of interest is the BARMM, because its political evolution and newly established health systems provide an opportunity to improve conditions where malnutrition is particularly severe.

Integrated, client-based care would maximize every opportunity to address nutrition with clients—whether it be at a health facility, in the community, or at home. Prenatal checkups, coordinated discharge from delivery facilities, and immunization visits are all facility-based opportunities to provide micronutrient supplementation, counseling, and support on IYCF and other nutrition interventions as well as to assess nutritional status. Outside of facility visits, follow-up may also entail activities within the community, such as house-to-house visits or mass promotion events and campaigns. These nutrition opportunities are enabled by the presence of legislation mandating and promoting IYCF practices, food fortification, and other nutrition programs. The ongoing COVID-19 pandemic may push providers to consider remote work and digital technology to facilitate training and, in due course, other nutrition interventions.

Nutrition-sensitive programs centered on specific population groups are key areas for surveillance as well as delivery of nutrition services. Target populations for these programs are broader than the basic categories of children under five and pregnant and lactating mothers. These programs extend the reach and potential benefits of nutrition interventions, particularly for adolescents, persons living in malaria-infested areas, and all adults of reproductive age irrespective of gender.

The recently enacted Universal Health Care Law (Republic Act no. 11223, s. 2019) provides several opportunities to promote nutrition (Congress of the Philippines 2019): (1) the integration of local health systems at the provincial level is intended to reduce the variance in LGU capacities to deliver nutrition services and allow provinces to provide oversight over municipality-level nutrition actions; (2) the proposed interoperable information system is intended to make it easier to track performance as well as to identify and troubleshoot problems early; and (3) the financing of primary care services, including nutrition, is delineated more clearly as being the responsibility of the DOH and the LGU, and health and nutrition programs are expected to be funded more sustainably and systematically under the law.

Health programs provide the best opportunities for both nutrition-specific and nutrition-sensitive components. Key requirements are to have explicit and measurable nutrition outcomes and to coordinate manpower and logistical support to take advantage of synergies and potential for integration.

NOTE

1. The members of the Governing Board are the secretary of health (chairperson), secretary of agriculture (vice chair), secretary of the interior and local government (vice chair), secretary of budget and management, secretary of education, secretary of labor and employment, secretary of science and technology, secretary of social welfare and development, secretary of trade and industry, and director general of the National Economic and Development Authority. In addition, the president appoints three nongovernmental organizations for two-year terms.

REFERENCES

Bhutta, Zulfiqar, Jai Das, Arjumand Rizvi, Michelle Gaffey, Neff Walker, Susan Horton, Patrick Webb, Robert Black, Lancet Nutrition Interventions Review Group, and Maternal and Child Nutrition Study Group. 2013. "Evidence-Based Interventions for Improvement of Maternal and Child Nutrition: What Can Be Done and at What Cost?" *The Lancet* 382 (9890): 452–77.

Congress of the Philippines. 1986. "Executive Order no. 51: National Code of Marketing of Breastmilk Substitutes, Breastmilk Supplements, and Other Related Products." *Official Gazette,* October 20, 1986. https://www.officialgazette.gov.ph/1986/10/20/executive-order-no-51-s-1986-2/#:~:text=%E2%80%93%20The%20aim%20of%20the%20Code,adequate%20information%20and%20through%20appropriate.

Congress of the Philippines. 1992. "The Republic Act no. 7600: The Rooming-in and Breastfeeding Act of 1992." Philippine Commission on Women, Manila. https://pcw.gov.ph/republic-act-7600-the-rooming-in-and-breast-feeding-act-of-1992/.

Congress of the Philippines. 1995. "Republic Act no. 8172: An Act Promoting Salt Iodization Nationwide and for Related Purposes." *Official Gazette,* December 20, 1995. https://www.officialgazette.gov.ph/1995/12/20/republic-act-no-8172/.

Congress of the Philippines. 2000. "Republic Act no. 8976: An Act Establishing the Philippine Food Fortification Program and for Other Purposes." Congress of the Philippines, Manila.

Congress of the Philippines. 2010. "Republic Act no. 10028: An Act Expanding the Promotion of Breastfeeding." *Official Gazette,* March 16, 2010. https://www.officialgazette.gov.ph/2010/03/16/republic-act-no-10028/.

Congress of the Philippines. 2012. "Republic Act no. 10354: An Act Providing for a National Policy on Responsible Parenthood and Reproduction Health." *Official Gazette,* July 23, 2012.

Congress of the Philippines. 2018. "Republic Act no. 11148: An Act Scaling up the National and Local Health and Nutrition Programs." *Official Gazette,* November 11, 2018. https://www.officialgazette.gov.ph/downloads/2018/11nov/20181129-RA-11148-RRD.pdf.

Congress of the Philippines. 2019. "Republic Act no. 11223, s. 2019: An Act Instituting Universal Health Care for All Filipinos, Prescribing Reforms in the Health Care System, and Appropriating Funds Therefor." *Official Gazette,* February 21, 2019.

DOH (Department of Health). 2005. "Administrative Order 2005-0014: National Policies on IYCF." DOH, Manila, May 23, 2005.

DOH (Department of Health). 2007. "Administrative Order no. 2007-0045: Zinc Supplementation and Reformulated Oral Rehydration Salt in the Management of Diarrhea." DOH, Manila.

DOH (Department of Health). 2010. "Administrative Order 36 s2010: Aquino Health Agenda (AHA): Achieving Universal Health Care for All Filipinos Goal." DOH, Manila.

DOH (Department of Health). 2011a. "Department Memorandum no. 2011-0303: Revised Policy on Micronutrient Supplementation to Support Achievement of 2015 MDG Targets to Reduce under Five and Maternal Mortality Deaths and to Address Micronutrient Deficiencies of the Population Groups." DOH, Manila.

DOH (Department of Health). 2011b. *The Maternal, Newborn, Child Health, and Nutrition Strategy: Manual of Operations."* Manila: DOH.

DOH (Department of Health). 2011c. "Protocol on the Philippine Integrated Management of Acute Severe Malnutrition (PIMAM)." Ver. 1 (draft for consideration), DOH, Manila.

DOH (Department of Health). 2018. "FHSIS Annual 2018." DOH, Manila. https://www.doh.gov.ph/sites/default/files/publications/FHSIS_Annual_2018_Final.pdf.

DOH (Department of Health). 2019. "FHSIS Report CY 2019." DOH, Manila. https://www.doh.gov.ph/index.php/health-statistics/field-health-service-information-system/fhsis-reports-cy-2019.

DOH (Department of Health). 2020a. "Administrative Order no. 34-A s 2000: Adolescent Health and Development Program." *Official Gazette,* December 28, 2020. https://www.doh.gov.ph/Adolescent-Health-and-Development-Program.

DOH (Department of Health). 2020b. "Expanded Program on Immunization." DOH, Manila. https://www.doh.gov.ph/expanded-program-on-immunization.

DOH (Department of Health). 2020c. "Family Planning Program." DOH, Manila. https://www.doh.gov.ph/family-planning.

DOH (Department of Health). 2020d. "FAQS: What Are the Substances in the Micronutrient Powder MNP Sachet?" DOH, Manila. https://www.doh.gov.ph/faqs/What-are-the-substances-in-the-Micronutrient-Powder-MNP-sachet.

DOH (Department of Health). 2020e. "Food Fortification Program." DOH, Manila. https://www.doh.gov.ph/food-fortification-program.

DOH (Department of Health). 2020f. "Garantisadong Pambata." DOH, Manila. https://www.doh.gov.ph/garantisadong-pambata.

DOH (Department of Health). 2020g. "Infant and Young Child Feeding." DOH, Manila. https://www.doh.gov.ph/infant-and-young-child-feeding.

DOH (Department of Health). 2020h. "Integrated Management of Childhood Illness." DOH, Manila. https://www.doh.gov.ph/integrated-management-of-childhood-illness.

DOH (Department of Health). 2020i. "Malaria Control Program." DOH, Manila. https://www.doh.gov.ph/malaria-control-program.

DOH (Department of Health). 2020j. "Micronutrient Program." DOH, Manila. https://www.doh.gov.ph/micronutrient-program.

DOH (Department of Health). 2020k. "National Safe Motherhood Program." DOH, Manila. https://www.doh.gov.ph/national-safe-motherhood-program.

FNRI (Food and Nutrition Research Institute). 2008. *National Nutrition Survey: Biochemical Component*. Taguig City: Department of Science and Technology, FNRI.

FNRI (Food and Nutrition Research Institute). 2013. *National Nutrition Survey: Biochemical Component*. Taguig City: Department of Science and Technology, FNRI.

FNRI (Food and Nutrition Research Institute). 2015. *2015 Updating Survey Results*. FNRI, Department of Science and Technology, Taguig City.

FNRI (Food and Nutrition Research Institute). 2019. *2019 Expanded National Nutrition Survey*. Taguig City: Department of Science and Technology, FNRI.

Government of the Philippines. 1978. "Presidential Decree no. 1569, s 1978: Strengthening the Barangay Nutrition Program by Providing for a Barangay Nutrition Scholar in Every Barangay, Providing Funds Therefor, and for Other Purposes." *Official Gazette*, June 11, 1978.

NNC (National Nutrition Council). 2009. "NNC Governing Board Resolution no. 1 Series of 2009: Adopting the National Policy on Nutrition Management in Emergencies and Disasters." NNC, Taguig City. https://www.nnc.gov.ph/phocadownloadpap/userupload/elavapie/NNC%20GB%20Reso%20no.%201%20s2009_NIEm.pdf.

NNC (National Nutrition Council). 2013. "Philippine Plan of Action for Nutrition (PPAN)." NNC, Taguig City, December 3, 2013. https://www.nnc.gov.ph/plans-and-programs/philippine-plan-of-action-for-nutrition-ppan.

NNC (National Nutrition Council). 2020a. "Barangay Nutrition Scholar (BNS) Program." NNC, Taguig City. https://www.nnc.gov.ph/plans-and-programs/barangay-nutrition-scholar-bns-program.

NNC (National Nutrition Council). 2020b. "Department Memorandum 2020-0237: Interim Guidelines for the Delivery of Nutrition Services in the Context of COVID-19 Pandemic." NNC, Taguig City. May 11, 2020.

NCC (National Nutrition Council). 2020c. "Operation *Timbang* Plus." NNC, Taguig City. https://www.nnc.gov.ph/plans-and-programs/philippine-food-and-nutrition-surveillance-system/operation-timbang-plus.

PSA (Philippine Statistics Agency). 2017. *National Demographic and Health Survey 2017*. Quezon City: PSA; Rockville, MD: ICF.

Sphere. 2018. *Sphere Handbook 2018*. Geneva: Sphere.

SUN Movement. 2015. "The History of the SUN Movement." Scaling Up Nutrition. https://scalingupnutrition.org/about-sun/the-history-of-the-sun-movement/.

WHO (World Health Organization). 2002. "The Mother and Child Health and Education Trust: Ten Steps to Successful Breastfeeding." WHO, Geneva. http://www.tensteps.org/.

WHO (World Health Organization). 2003. *Global Strategy for Infant and Young Child Feeding.* Geneva: WHO; New York: UNICEF.

WHO (World Health Organization). 2017. "*Unang Yakap*: Encouraging Breastfeeding from the Start." WHO, Geneva, August 4, 2017. https://www.who.int/philippines/news/feature-stories/detail/unang-yakap-encouraging-breastfeeding-from-the-start.

WHO (World Health Organization). 2018a. "Integrated Management of Childhood Illness Chart Booklet." WHO, Geneva. https://apps.who.int/iris/bitstream/handle/10665/104772/9789241506823_Chartbook_eng.pdf;jsessionid=2459A3817545C91FA28F945D7221CCB7?sequence=16.

WHO (World Health Organization). 2018b. "Ten Steps to Successful Breastfeeding (Revised 2018)." WHO, Geneva. http://apps.who.int/nutrition/bfhi/ten-steps.

WHO (World Health Organization). 2019. "Optimal Timing of Cord Clamping for the Prevention of Iron Deficiency Anaemia in Infants." WHO, Geneva, September 18, 2019. https://www.who.int/elena/titles/cord_clamping/en/.

World Bank Group. 2019. "Adolescent Fertility Rate (Births per 1,000 Women Ages 15–19)." World Bank Group, Washington, DC.

8 Optimizing *Pantawid* for Nutrition

ABSTRACT The *Pantawid Pamilyang Pilipino* Program, the Philippines' flagship safety net program, has shown great potential to improve nutrition outcomes for children living in poverty by providing cash assistance to households conditional on their adherence to health checkups and growth monitoring and by offering family development sessions that raise caregivers' knowledge and awareness of nutrition. During the early stages of program implementation, there was strong evidence that the program had a positive effect on nutrition outcomes. Over time, however, its impact on nutrition has faded for several reasons. This chapter proposes five key areas in which *Pantawid* can be strengthened to improve nutrition outcomes among children in poor and vulnerable households.

CAN *PANTAWID* IMPROVE NUTRITION?

The *Pantawid Pamilyang Pilipino* Program (translation: Bridging Program for the Filipino Family) aims to build the human capital of children living in poverty. The program provides conditional cash transfers (CCTs) to poor households to improve their health, nutrition, and education.[1] By investing in children's human capital, the program seeks to break the intergenerational cycle of poverty. Eligible households identified by *Listahanan*—the National Household Targeting System (or social registry)—commit to comply with education and health conditions. Since its introduction in 2007, the program has grown and is currently implemented in 145 cities and 1,483 municipalities, according to records of the Department of Social Welfare and Development (DSWD). As part of the national poverty reduction strategy, *Pantawid* has benefited more than 4 million households (close to 20 percent of the country's population), including 8.7 million children. It is estimated that the program was responsible for a quarter of the total poverty reduction in the country between 2006 and 2015 (Qian et al. 2018).

Beneficiary households receive cash benefits every two months upon verification of their compliance with conditions (figure 8.1 presents monthly program benefits and conditions as of January 2020). Health grants are provided

FIGURE 8.1

Summary of the *Pantawid* program rules

Source: Based on the *Pantawid Pamilyang Pilipino* Program Act (Republic Act no. 11310) in 2019 and its implementation rules and regulations.
Note: 4Ps = *Pantawid Pamilyang Pilipino* Program. DSWD = Department of Social Welfare and Development. GAA = General Appropriations Act. Php = Philippine pesos. SONA = State of the Nation Address. TRAIN law = Tax Reform for Acceleration and Inclusion law, officially cited as Republic Act No. 10963, the initial package of the Comprehensive Tax Reform Program. UCT = unconditional cash transfer.

for households where monitored family members (such as pregnant women and children ages 0–14 years) comply with health conditions. Education grants are given to households where school-age children (ages 3–18) comply with education conditions. *Pantawid* beneficiaries also receive benefits from other programs, including health coverage from the National Health Insurance

Program, a rice subsidy[2] for food security, and temporary assistance from the unconditional cash transfer program.[3]

The cash benefits—alongside the conditions stipulated under the program—help beneficiary families manage consumption flows and invest in their children's human capital. In 2017 the average beneficiary household received a six-month grant of ₱5,458 (US$107), which corresponds to about 6.6 percent of its pretransfer income in 2017 (10.2 percent for households in the bottom quintile). Following adoption of the *Pantawid* Act in 2019 and its implementation rules and regulations, the total amount of benefits increased in 2020. As an example, a household in receipt of a health grant with a child in junior high school used to receive ₱2,000 per payment (₱500 health grants and ₱500 for education grants per month, disbursed every two months); the same household is now entitled to receive ₱2,500 per payment (the health grant per household having increased from ₱500 to ₱750) upon compliance with all conditions.

Pantawid shows considerable potential to improve nutrition outcomes. Nutrition outcomes are determined by the quantity and quality of food consumption, access to health services and sanitation, and nutritional knowledge and practices. Although *Pantawid* does not directly address nutrition,[4] its conditional cash grants and support services can help reduce malnutrition (as illustrated in figure 8.2). In particular, the family development sessions (FDSs) are a major channel for disseminating information on good parenting and hygiene practices conducive to improved child health and nutrition.[5] The cash grants are provided mostly to women (about 86 percent). As women are usually the main caretakers of children, this grant constitutes an important channel through which *Pantawid* can affect nutrition outcomes.

By covering pregnant women and young children, the program targets the critical window of nutritional opportunity offered by the first 1,000 days of life. A large body of literature emphasizes the substantial costs of inaction during the early

FIGURE 8.2

Theory of change: *Pantawid's* pathways to potential nutrition-related impacts

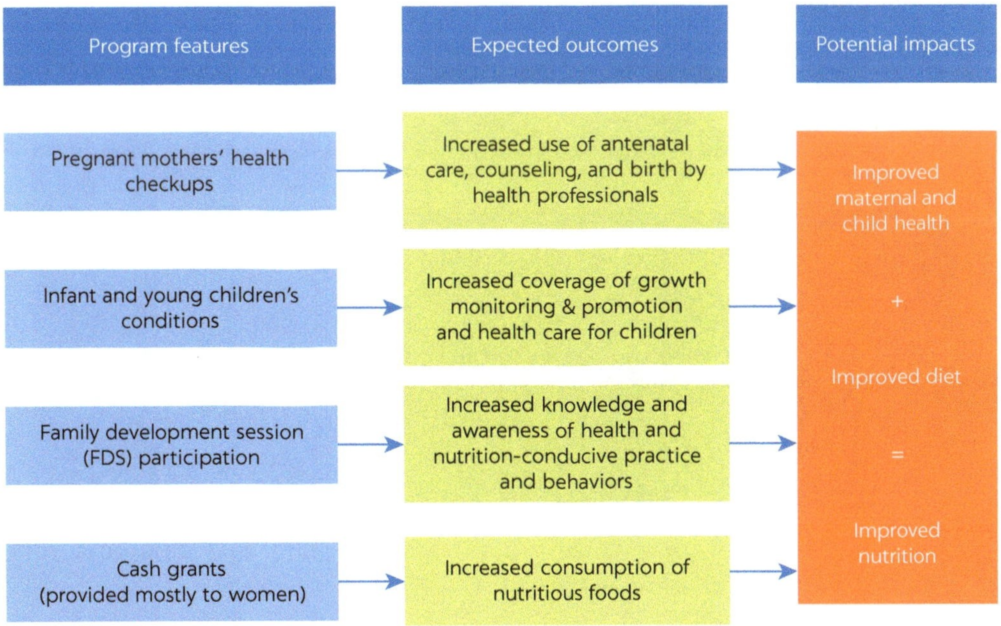

Source: Cho, Avalos, Kawasoe, and Rodriguez 2020.

years of child development, especially the first 1,000 days. Almost 70 percent of stunting occurs during the first 1,000 days of a child's life, with substantial long-term consequences for future educational and economic outcomes (Leroy et al. 2014). In the Philippines, stunting is associated principally with suboptimal prenatal conditions and inadequate food security and diversity (Capanzana, Demombynes, and Gubbins 2020). Undernutrition and disease in early childhood can also lead to impaired cognitive and brain development, weaker socioemotional skills, lower educational outcomes, and ultimately lower incomes (Galasso and Wagstaff 2018). Early childhood malnutrition thus leads to lost earnings for individuals and economywide consequences for countries—studies estimate productivity losses as high as 11 percent of gross domestic product (GDP) every year in Africa, Asia, and Latin America (Martínez and Fernández 2008).

As the country's flagship safety net program covering almost one-quarter of the population, *Pantawid* can have a large-scale impact. In 2007 *Pantawid* was piloted with 6,000 households. Since its formal launch in 2008, it has expanded to more than 4 million households, peaking at more than 4.4 million in 2014 (figure 8.3).[6] A small number of modified conditional cash transfer (MCCT) beneficiaries were also added to cover vulnerable populations not identified through the household survey for *Listahanan*.[7] In terms of the absolute number of households covered, *Pantawid* ranks fourth globally, behind analogous programs in Brazil, Indonesia, and Mexico.

WHAT ARE THE IMPACTS OF *PANTAWID* ON NUTRITION TO DATE?

In its early stage of program implementation, *Pantawid* had a powerful effect on nutrition, but the findings on recent impacts are inconclusive. Several studies

FIGURE 8.3

Coverage of the *Pantawid Pamilyang Pilipino* Program, 2007–19

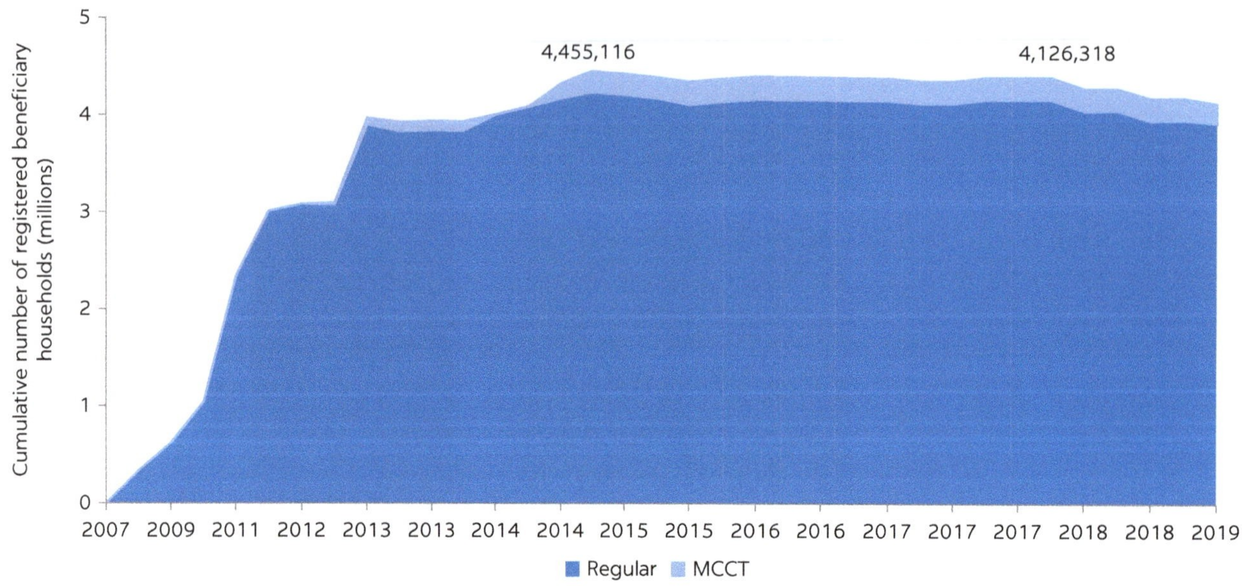

Source: Based on Department of Social Welfare and Development data.
Note: MCCT = modified conditional cash transfer.

have investigated the impact of *Pantawid* on nutrition using different methodologies over various time spans (table 8.1). The first round of impact evaluation, based on data collected in 2011 using a randomized control trial (RCT) approach, found very positive program impacts on the reduction of severe stunting.[8] Specifically, the prevalence of severe stunting among beneficiary children ages 6–36 months was 10 percentage points lower in program localities (treatment) than among children in the same age group from low-income households in non-program localities (control).[9] Using the same data, Kandpal et al. (2016) also found that *Pantawid* increased height-for-age Z scores among beneficiary children from 6 to 36 months of age. The anthropometric impacts of the program were encouraging, as they indicated behavioral changes among parents, including changes affecting their children's diet. However, the second impact evaluation, which used data collected in 2013, did not find a similar impact on stunting. Preliminary results from the third impact evaluation, using data collected during the period 2017–18, suggest that severe stunting rates actually increased among children under five. This increase appears to be driven by an increase in the stunting rate of children who were not monitored and not exposed to the program at the most effective time—during the critical first 1,000 days of life.[10]

The heterogeneous findings are, in part, due to different samples, time periods, and evaluation strategies. Evaluations based on the RCT method compare outcomes of randomly selected treatment localities (where poor households participated in *Pantawid*) and control localities (where poor households did not

TABLE 8.1 **Review of impact evaluations of *Pantawid* and findings on nutrition**

STUDY	YEAR OF SURVEY	METHODOLOGY	RESEARCH ENTITY	NOTES ON METHODOLOGY	MAIN FINDINGS ON NUTRITION
First impact evaluation; Kandpal et al. (2016); Filmer et al. (2018)	2011	Randomized control trial	World Bank researchers and DSWD	• Random selection of treatment or control group • Sample drawn from pilot districts that are relatively poor and remote	• Significant reduction in stunting and severe stunting • Improvement in anthropometric measures (height-for-age) • Increases in stunting among nonbeneficiary children
Second impact evaluation	2013	Regression discontinuity design	PIDS[a] researchers and DSWD	• Nationwide coverage of beneficiaries • Sample drawn only around the cutoff level and results not applicable to the poorest households	• No significant effect on stunting outcomes
Third impact evaluation	2017–18	Regression discontinuity design	PIDS[a] researchers and DSWD	• Nationwide coverage of beneficiaries • Sample drawn only around the cutoff level and results not applicable to the poorest households • Significant time lapse since the change in cutoff level	• Negative results among children in beneficiary households who were not monitored • No significant impact on children ages 0–2 years • Positive impact on older children who were monitored

Source: Authors' summary of the review of impact evaluations of the *Pantawid* program.
Note: DSWD = Department of Social Welfare and Development. PIDS = Philippine Institute for Development Studies.
a. Republic Act no. 11310 specifies that PIDS, in collaboration with DSWD, carry out regular impact evaluations of *Pantawid*.

participate in *Pantawid*). Due to this random selection, RCT results can be attributed to *Pantawid* with confidence. The early studies using RCT during the initial implementation phase of *Pantawid* were based on sample localities from the country's poorest areas, and the results reflect their poverty and vulnerability. After the program expanded to cover the whole country, the RCT method was no longer a viable evaluation strategy, and studies instead used regression discontinuity design (RDD). Households were assigned a proxy means test-based poverty score,[11] and only those below a predetermined cutoff score were eligible for *Pantawid*. Therefore, the RDD studies compared the outcomes of households very close to the cutoff.[12] The outcomes of *Pantawid* beneficiaries just below the cutoff were compared with households just above the cutoff, which were otherwise similar but ineligible for *Pantawid*. The RDD results were drawn from a nationwide sample, but an important weakness of this strategy is that it did not capture the impact on the poorest (households far below the cutoff) whom the program was designed to help the most. Moreover, given that the value of transfers eroded over time (discussed below), a level of impact similar to that found in earlier studies was not expected.

For intermediate outcomes, the evaluation studies found generally positive impacts. The likely pathways that may explain the positives changes in nutrition include increased use of health services among poor children and pregnant women, increased quantity and quality of food, and behavioral changes. Evaluations found a significant increase in the use of health services (see annex 8A for a summary). In particular, regardless of the methodology used, the studies found that *Pantawid* increased access to maternal and child health care, increased household consumption devoted to children's health and education, and improved dietary diversity. Parenting advice provided through FDS appears to have changed mothers' feeding patterns, so they increased the family's consumption of better-quality food (particularly dairy products), while reducing the consumption of packaged food (Kandpal et al. 2016).

Can CCTs inadvertently worsen the stunting outcomes of nonbeneficiary children? A recent study investigating *Pantawid*'s impact on stunting among nonbeneficiary children adds to the already mixed literature on the impact of CCTs on nutrition. Filmer et al. (2018) hypothesize that cash transfers could increase the price of certain nutritionally sensitive foods, which, in turn, could hurt children in the most saturated treatment localities. The negative impact would likely be particularly pertinent among nonbeneficiaries without the means to mitigate the negative impact of higher prices. Using nationwide data, the study found that price levels were indeed higher in localities with a higher share of *Pantawid* beneficiaries. The study then investigated the RCT data from 2011 to see if the price patterns were similar and if they led to changes in stunting. The RCT data showed that the higher the share of beneficiaries in treatment localities, the larger the increase in the price of perishable goods, including high-protein food, such as eggs. The higher price of high-protein foods critical for children's growth, in turn, appears to have reduced the consumption of nonbeneficiaries, leading to an increase in stunting rates.

The RCT results for the price inflation effect may be less relevant to the program today, but they provide important policy lessons. The price inflation results were found in the poorest villages where the majority of households were *Pantawid* beneficiaries and in remote villages where the supply of food—especially perishable protein-rich foods—could not keep pace with the increase in demand. Such localities represent only a small share (4 percent based on 2015 data) of households in the Philippines, as Filmer et al. (2018) acknowledge. Moreover, the price effects would be expected to dissipate over time if the real value of CCT benefits decreases and as the market adjusts supply to meet the increased demand. Finally, with the massive increase in transportation infrastructure, market connectivity today has improved significantly since 2011 when the RCT survey was conducted.[13] Nonetheless, the results are an important reminder of the need to monitor the general equilibrium effects of programs—both intended and unintended—and to adjust policy parameters accordingly.

In a similar vein, the third impact evaluation investigated the impact of *Pantawid* separately on monitored and nonmonitored children in beneficiary households. Many children in beneficiary households are not monitored because health and nutrition grants are not related to the number of children monitored. The preliminary results suggest a higher stunting rate among nonmonitored children in *Pantawid* households than in non-*Pantawid* households.

WHY IS *PANTAWID* NOT HAVING A GREATER IMPACT ON NUTRITION?

Declining share of pregnant women and young children among *Pantawid* beneficiaries

New pregnancies and newborns of current beneficiaries are often not monitored for compliance. By design, the program conditions apply only to monitored individuals. These monitored individuals are identified at the time of program enrollment, unless the beneficiary voluntarily reports updated information (such as a new pregnancy in the household). As the program matured and expansion slowed, the number of monitored pregnant women, postpartum mothers, and children under five declined significantly, meaning that succeeding pregnancies and newborns were not linked to the program's compliance verification system. Figure 8.4 shows the number of households and pregnant women

FIGURE 8.4

Number of households and pregnant women and children under age five being monitored by the *Pantawid Pamilyang Pilipino* Program, 2008–18

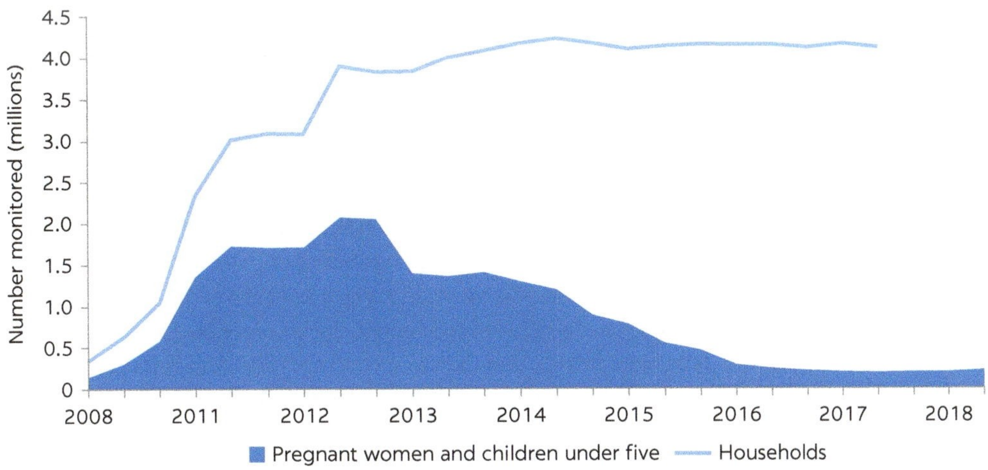

Source: Based on the program's management information system data.

and children under five monitored from 2008 to 2018. While the coverage of households has leveled off since 2014, the number of pregnant women and young children has declined rapidly. In 2018 fewer than 200,000 pregnant women and children under five were monitored for compliance with health conditions compared with a peak of more than 2 million in 2012.

City and municipal coordinators—the frontline social welfare staff of the program—encourage pregnant women and new mothers to report their children for monitoring,[14] but households have few incentives to do so. The health condition is an "all or nothing" conditionality in which a flat benefit is offered per household regardless of the number of individuals monitored for compliance (pregnant women, postpartum mothers, and children under five). Compliance is met when all individuals who are monitored satisfy the conditions stipulated. Registering newborn children in the program merely increases the burden of compliance without increasing the benefits. Historically, rates of compliance with the stipulated health conditions have been high among monitored children, but the absolute number of monitored children and pregnant women has declined rapidly, remaining low since 2015. The *Pantawid* National Advisory Council, the intergovernmental body regulating the program, issued a resolution mandating that all newly identified pregnant mothers and newborns be monitored for compliance. However, in the absence of incentives for beneficiary households, *Pantawid* staff have found implementing this new policy to be an uphill task.

Since the program reached its peak number of beneficiaries in 2014, few new beneficiaries have been enrolled. Originally, most beneficiaries were identified through *Listahanan* 1, which was conducted in 2009–10. After five years of program implementation, the plan was to enroll new beneficiaries identified through *Listahanan* 2, conducted in 2015, in place of households that left the program when their children grew older and thus were no longer eligible for inclusion. However, a moratorium on the enrollment of new households in 2015 prevented the replacement of households, as it was learned that many current *Pantawid* beneficiaries were not surveyed in *Listahanan* 2. Further, although *Listahanan* 2 includes information about pregnant women and young children in *Pantawid* households, it was not used to update official information on *Pantawid* beneficiaries. Newly identified pregnant women and young children were not able to participate in or be monitored under *Pantawid*, limiting the program's ability to tackle maternal and child health and nutrition challenges through CCTs.

Declining share of poor people among *Pantawid* beneficiaries

Failing to enroll new beneficiaries using the up-to-date registry undermines the program's ability to help the country's poorest and most vulnerable population. Using the nationally representative data from the 2013 and 2017 Annual Poverty Indicators Survey, an incidence analysis shows a clear pattern of worsening targeting for *Pantawid* (Acosta, Endo, et al. 2019). The share of the lowest-income quintile of households among *Pantawid* beneficiaries decreased from 75 percent in 2009 to 53 percent in 2013 and then to 46 percent in 2017 (figure 8.5, panel a). When compared with other major CCT programs in low- and middle-income countries, *Pantawid*'s targeting performance has regressed (figure 8.5, panel b).

The main reason that targeting is worsening is the use of an outdated registry of beneficiaries. As discussed, current *Pantawid* beneficiaries were

FIGURE 8.5

Distribution of conditional cash transfer beneficiaries in the Philippines and comparison countries, by income quintile

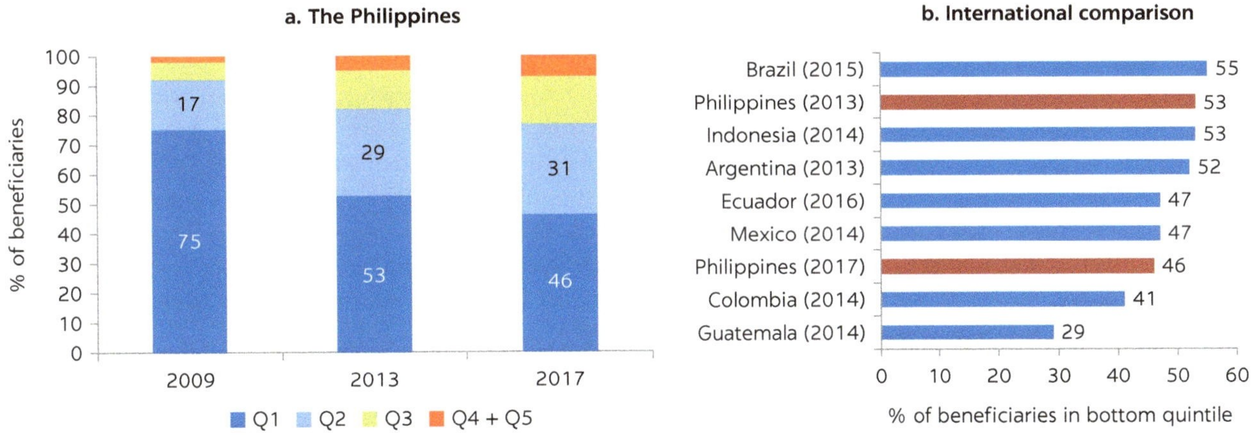

Sources: Acosta and Velarde 2015; Acosta, Endo, et al. 2019.

identified in 2009–10, and the enrollment of new beneficiaries to replace existing households did not start until 2019. Natural attrition from the program has been increasing over time, and in 2019, about 2.2 percent of all beneficiaries (93,000 households) had exited the program. As the program aims to maintain the number of households at the 2014 level (4.4 million), the DSWD issued implementing guidelines on the replacement of *Pantawid* households (DSWD 2019) and has enrolled around 300,000 new households identified through *Listahanan* 2.

With nutrition outcomes lagging significantly among poorer households, the declining accuracy of targeting indicates an inefficient use of resources in policy efforts to reduce malnutrition. The poorest households persistently have the highest prevalence of low weight-for-age, wasting, and stunting across the country. In 2015 almost half of all children under five in the poorest income quintile were classified as severely stunted. Moreover, pregnant women from the poorest quintile were more nutritionally at-risk, with a higher incidence of delivering low birthweight infants and other pregnancy complications, conditions experienced by about 30 percent of the poorest pregnant women. The prevalence of low birthweight is also highest (17 percent) for the poorest households. There is substantial room for improvement in channeling assistance toward the most needy individuals at crucial stages of health and nutrition, where assistance could make the greatest difference.

Low and declining cash value

The real value of benefits has been low and declining with inflation. Multiple analyses suggest that the benefit amount is too low to have a significant impact on important outcomes. When the program started, the benefit amount was estimated at 23 percent of beneficiary household income. The grant amount has remained the same, and its value has eroded with inflation over the years. The average *Pantawid* benefit was around 10 percent of the pretransfer income of households from the lowest quintile of the income distribution in 2017, despite the additional ₱500 for high-school children introduced in 2014.[15] Compared with CCT programs in other countries, this share is at the lower end of the spectrum (27 percent in Ecuador in 2016, 20 percent in Brazil in 2015, for instance).

Recognizing the low real value of benefits, the government made *Pantawid* beneficiaries eligible for additional assistance from other programs and later introduced a modest increase in CCT benefits as well. Cash benefits from rice subsidies and universal cash transfers have been distributed through *Pantawid's* payment delivery system. But these benefits are relatively small, temporary measures, serving as top-up benefits. The *Pantawid* Act (enacted in 2019) increased health and nutrition grants by 50 percent (from ₱500 to ₱750 per month), which was implemented beginning with the last payment of 2019. The increase in the benefits amount is likely to help households invest in their children's human capital.

Weak service delivery

Offering a wider range of topics in family development sessions may inadvertently affect the dissemination of information on nutrition. *Pantawid* requires mandatory participation in FDSs, targeting behavioral changes in health, nutrition, and education. In the early years, *Pantawid* offered only six modules focusing exclusively on these three areas; now more than 40 modules and submodules are offered on multiple topics. Some of the new topics include climate change mitigation measures and financial literacy and entrepreneurship. While the expansion of topics covered has been necessary, it has weakened the relative emphasis on the core health and education topics. In addition, the program does not have a system to monitor how effectively these sessions are delivered to beneficiaries. In a qualitative assessment of the impact of *Pantawid* on nutrition outcomes, the Economic Policy Research Institute (2019) found that, while some positive behavioral changes were associated with FDS attendance, perspectives on its implementation were mixed. Some beneficiaries found the sessions to be informative and applied what they learned, especially in diet and food preparation. Others did not find the sessions to be particularly helpful, noting that the lecture-based format allowed little time for interaction between the speaker and participants.

In the Bangsamoro Autonomous Region in Muslim Mindanao (BARMM), significant implementation challenges undermine the potential of CCTs to improve nutrition outcomes. Delays in payment delivery have been significant in BARMM, where the prevalence of both poverty (53 percent in 2018) and stunting (44 percent in 2015) is the highest in the country. Since the beginning of *Pantawid*, data errors and payment delays have been common in the region. In August 2019, for example, after more than a year of waiting, beneficiaries in Lanao del Sur received their full-year payment for 2018, while others in BARMM still await the 2018 payments. Several reasons were identified for the recurrent overdue *Pantawid* payouts: problems with the system's data cleansing of duplicates and fraudulent beneficiary profiles; a low proportion of cash card distributions, with the majority of beneficiaries relying on over-the-counter payments; and an insufficient number of conduits for the delivery of cash grants (such as the Land Bank of the Philippines). The delay of payments defeats the program's purpose of helping the poorest make ends meet.

There is scope for health services to be used further. Despite the program's health conditionalities, beneficiaries use health services to varying degrees.

The uptake rate for prenatal care is quite high, and there is robust evidence that *Pantawid* has increased the take-up rate among its beneficiaries. The latest impact evaluation suggests that about 86 percent of pregnant women in *Pantawid* households received at least four prenatal checkups, in line with Department of Health (DOH) guidelines, which is 11.8 percentage points higher than the average for pregnant women in non-*Pantawid*, low-income households.[16] However, the use of other health services, such as postnatal care, children's immunization, and growth monitoring, is not as high. For instance, the latest impact evaluation found that only roughly one in three children under five had visited a health facility within the past two months.

HOW CAN *PANTAWID* STRENGTHEN ITS IMPACT ON NUTRITION?

On the basis of the issues identified and discussed in this chapter, the following recommendations are offered to strengthen *Pantawid*'s impact on nutrition outcomes (table 8.2).

First, the CCT program needs to serve the most nutritionally vulnerable populations: pregnant women and young children. This population can be reached by adopting the updated registry to identify vulnerable populations and by developing a more dynamic system to update beneficiary information frequently. As discussed, many children under five, particularly those living in poverty, do not benefit from the program because new households are not being widely enrolled. Once the new round of *Listahanan* becomes available, *Pantawid* should immediately use it to enroll newly identified poor households and ensure coverage of pregnant women and young children. Furthermore, efforts are required to make the social registry more dynamic. A dynamic social registry would allow regular updates of key information to reflect the changing socioeconomic well-being of a household and identify new poor and vulnerable households so that they can be considered for relevant social safety net systems. Implementing a more dynamic *Listahanan* in the near future has been discussed, as it would facilitate the assessment, identification, and registration of new poor and vulnerable households. Furthermore, discussions have also suggested using a

TABLE 8.2 ***Pantawid* challenges and proposed solutions**

CHALLENGES	PROPOSED SOLUTIONS
Declining share of pregnant women and young children	• New enrollment through an up-to-date social registry • Incentives for reporting pregnancies and registering newborns and young children
Declining targeting performance	• New enrollment, recertification, and exit through an up-to-date social registry • Regular monitoring of targeting performance (in collaboration with research institutes such as PIDS) and dynamic social registry updates
Declining cash value and unintended price effect	• Regular monitoring of price impact (in collaboration with research institutes such as PIDS) • Adjustments in benefits possibly by indexing the benefits level to inflation
Weak service delivery	• Refinement of the family development session curriculum to emphasize core health and education goals and improved delivery • Efforts in service delivery in BARMM

Source: Authors' summary of key challenges and proposed solutions of the *Pantawid* program.
Note: BARMM = Bangsamoro Autonomous Region in Muslim Mindanao. PIDS = Philippine Institute of Development Studies.

community-based monitoring system to update beneficiary information more frequently.

Second, it is necessary to create the required incentives to encourage households to report pregnancy and newborns for monitoring under the program. To this end, the program could redesign the flat health benefit level linked to health criteria and instead increase payments according to the number of eligible household members (pregnant women and children). The structure of benefits could be designed so that the incremental benefit for each additional child decreases with the number of children in the household. This approach would offer households an incentive to enroll an additional child for monitoring, while minimizing concerns about encouraging higher fertility. If increases in benefits are not feasible on account of fiscal constraints, shining a powerful spotlight on commitment could be considered. Some studies argue that clearly informing beneficiaries of the intention and purpose of grants can be as effective as imposing stringent conditions (Benhassine et al. 2015; Heinrich and Knowles 2020). *Pantawid* could introduce a stronger commitment to monitoring children's health, with monetary consequences for noncompliance. Given that all beneficiary families are required to sign the oath of commitment, the oath could include a clause on registering all subsequent pregnancies and eligible children, with a clear indication that noncompliance would entail the termination of benefits. In addition to adjusting the benefit structure or requiring stronger beneficiary commitment, using relevant information from the DOH database (birth, health checkups) could be considered. The timing of initiating young children into monitoring programs matters. Evidence shows that cash transfer programs tend to have greater benefits for children enrolled at younger ages than those enrolled at older ages (Manley, Gitter, and Slavchevska 2013; Sánchez, Meléndez, and Behrman 2016). Enrolling children on time means initiating treatment when they are younger, providing more key nutrients (or medication), exposing them to improved nutrition during the critical early-life window, and offering growth-monitoring sessions plus vaccinations.

Third, it is important to renew the health and nutrition messages of the FDS and to improve the delivery and monitoring systems. The FDS social and behavior change communication strategy on the health and nutrition of mothers and newborns could be repeated in refresher sessions. Moreover, the delivery of the parenting modules could be improved. Evaluations have shown that parenting interventions can improve child development outcomes, notably in cognition and language development. Evidence from successful parenting programs points to multiple key features for success (Arriagada et al. 2018), including (a) targeting both parents (not just mothers); (b) including demonstrations with children and opportunities to practice and receive feedback during the training sessions; (c) investing in strong program protocols and materials to ensure consistency; (d) establishing a frequent and supportive supervision scheme, including on-the-job training and coaching for field staff; and (e) investing in a monitoring and evaluation system for quality assurance.

Fourth, a mechanism is needed to monitor inflation and price impacts on consumption, especially food security, and to adjust the level of cash benefits and coverage accordingly. The *Pantawid* Act aims to protect beneficiaries from the risk of inflation by mandating regular reviews of the real value of benefits over time. Benefits need to be adjusted periodically to offset inflation. The *Pantawid* implementation rules and regulations also recommend regular updates of benefit levels, although the recommended frequency (six years) may need to be reconsidered, depending on the policy environment and economic conditions. In addition, given the potential increase in the price of food items in poor and remote villages with a large proportion of beneficiaries and imperfect local markets, the program could monitor beneficiary saturation rates with a view to examining the prevalence of negative spillover effects in such localities. Fundamental solutions would include better connectivity through infrastructure in remote areas and better livelihood activities to increase the production of perishable goods. Meanwhile, *Pantawid* could use digital payments to smooth out transfers and reduce market-day price spikes, along with an option to include all villagers to reduce the unintended impact on nonbeneficiaries.[17]

Fifth, service delivery needs to be improved in the BARMM, where nutrition outcomes are poor and poverty is prevalent. While there is ample anecdotal evidence about inefficiencies associated with payment delays in the region, there have been no clear strategies to tackle the implementation challenges peculiar to BARMM. A thorough assessment of the geographic distribution and reliability of cash delivery points is needed. Moreover, FDS and messaging for health and nutrition could be refined, taking BARMM's cultural context into consideration.

ANNEX 8A. IMPACT OF *PANTAWID* PROGRAM ON HEALTH AND EDUCATION

Impacts on health

The mothers and children who are beneficiaries of *Pantawid* have better access to maternal care and basic health services as a consequence. Results from the second impact evaluation study found that more *Pantawid* mothers had institutional deliveries in the past five years, with 7 in 10 live births among *Pantawid* mothers compared with 5.5 in 10 births among nonbeneficiary mothers. This finding is in line with the first impact evaluation, which showed that more poor mothers in *Pantawid* villages were receiving antenatal care services than poor mothers in non-*Pantawid* villages; they also made such visits 60 percent more frequently than mothers in non-*Pantawid* villages. Similarly, the use of postnatal care at home within 24 hours of delivery was 10 percent higher in *Pantawid* villages than in non-*Pantawid* villages.

Pantawid children have access to basic health services, such as vitamins and mineral supplementation, that are vital for improving health outcomes: 86 percent of *Pantawid* children ages six months to six years reported receiving vitamin A supplementation compared with 73 percent of nonbeneficiaries. Among beneficiaries, 35 percent reported receiving iron supplements compared with 23 percent of nonbeneficiaries.

The program has increased and successfully sustained regular weight and growth monitoring, as found in each impact evaluation study. Similarly, significant increases in intake of deworming pills have been found since the first evaluation of the program.

The first impact evaluation found that the program helped improve the long-term nutritional status of younger children (6–36 months old) by reducing severe stunting 10 percent compared with areas that did not receive the program.

The program changed the spending patterns of poor households, with beneficiary households spending more on health and education than poor households that did not benefit from the program.

Impacts on education

School enrollment was higher among children in beneficiary households. The first impact evaluation found that enrollment increased 10.3 percent among preschool and day care–age children (3–5 years old) and 4.5 percent among elementary school–age children (6–11 years old). The second evaluation found gross enrollment of elementary school–age children (6–11 years old) was equally high for both beneficiaries and nonbeneficiaries (98 percent).

Increased school attendance was found across all school-age groups, suggesting that *Pantawid* is meeting the objective of keeping poor children in school. The first evaluation found that school attendance in *Pantawid* areas was 3.8 percentage points higher among children ages 6–11 years, 4.9 percent higher among children ages 12–14, and 7.6 percent higher among children ages 15–17. The second evaluation found a positive impact on preschool attendance: 94 percent of preschool *Pantawid* children were attending classes 85 percent of the time compared with 55 percent of non-*Pantawid* children.

Pantawid also keeps teens in high school. The gross enrollment rate for teens (12–15 years old) was higher for *Pantawid* children living near the poverty threshold: 95 percent compared with 89 percent of non-*Pantawid* children. The program keeps children in school during the critical stage when they are otherwise most likely to drop out in order to earn a living.

Finally, *Pantawid* reduces the time children spend working and encourages parents to invest more in their children's education.

NOTES

The chapter is based on a Social Protection Policy Note prepared by a World Bank team led by Yoonyoung Cho and comprising Jorge Avalos, Yasuhiro Kawasoe, and Ruth Rodriguez (Cho et al. 2020). Considerable support and insight were provided by the research and *Pantawid* teams at the Department of Social Welfare and Development.

1. See Acosta, Avalos, et al. (2019) for a summary of the program.
2. DSWD Memorandum Circular no. 6, Series of 2017: Guidelines on the Provision of Rice Subsidy to *Pantawid Pamilyang Pilipino* Program Households (DSWD 2017).
3. DSWD Memorandum Circular no. 3, Series of 2018: Implementing Guidelines for the Unconditional Cash Transfer Program (DSWD 2018). The universal cash transfer benefits will likely end in 2020, as they constitute a temporary mitigation program to support *Pantawid*, the Social Pension Program for Indigent Senior Citizens, and other poor households who have been adversely affected by rising prices, despite the benefit of lower income taxes from Republic Act no. 10963: Tax Reform for Acceleration and Inclusion (TRAIN) Law. The TRAIN Act is the initial package of comprehensive tax reforms signed into law on December 19, 2017 (Congress of the Philippines 2017).
4. Some nutrition-specific interventions aim to reduce extreme stunting by transferring nutritional supplements, providing access to clean water, and promoting nutrition-supporting behaviors (hand washing and breastfeeding).
5. FDS modules include lessons on exclusive breastfeeding, good feeding practices, remedies for children with diarrhea, child stimulation and positive parenting, and access to and use of other social services.

6. As a share of population, relative to other countries with large CCT programs, *Pantawid* has the third largest coverage in the world, behind Colombia and Mexico, each covering 22 percent of the population (Acosta, Endo, et al. 2019). The size of the CCT program is determined by the number of individuals covered (World Bank 2018). Only the top eight largest CCT programs with coverage data for the last five years are included as comparison.
7. Beneficiaries for MCCT were selected not through *Listahanan*, but through community identification. The intention was to reach out to families who are vulnerable and in need of assistance but not covered by the regular CCT because they were not captured by the enumeration of *Listahanan*. The beneficiaries comprise homeless street families, indigenous peoples, and families in need of special protection. Since the program was introduced in 2011, the number of MCCT beneficiaries increased, reaching 200,000 households in 2014, with similar levels maintained subsequently.
8. Measured as height-for-age < / −3 standard deviations, applying the World Health Organization child growth standards.
9. An impact of a similar magnitude was also found in Indonesia's Program Keluarga Harapan.
10. A parallel study that revisited the original RCT sample households from the first evaluation found that receiving program benefits during the first 1,000 days of life resulted in better nutrition outcomes (lower likelihood of being severely underweight) than receiving program benefits later.
11. Proxy means test is a statistical model that aggregates multiple proxy indicators into a single score that represents the household's welfare level. See Fernandez (2012) for a discussion of the design and implementation of the Philippines' targeting system.
12. RDD is a quasi-experimental method of evaluating program impact that is applicable when observation units (households) can be sorted using some continuous metric (proxy means test score). Program eligibility is defined using a predetermined threshold or cutoff point of the metric. In RDD, observations just below the cutoff are similar to, and therefore compare well to, those just above the cutoff.
13. Multiple sources of data suggest that infrastructure in the Philippines has improved significantly over time. For instance, the World Economic Forum's global competitiveness index reports that the score for infrastructure increased from 3.19 in 2012 to 3.43 in 2015 with better road, port, and transport infrastructure; the proportion of paved roads and total length of arterial roads also increased significantly during the same period.
14. Measures were taken to strengthen the engagement of city and municipal coordinators, such as the revision of the oath of commitment from beneficiaries to report all children in the household and to develop a task force—Malusog na Batang 0–5—to address child malnutrition.
15. According to the last three benefit incidence analyses of the program. The second impact evaluation found that benefits represented 7 percent of total household expenditure in 2014.
16. This finding is based on fuzzy regression discontinuity results within a coverage error rate bandwidth.
17. In this case, the high saturation and remote location of a village should qualify it for rule-based program implementation.

REFERENCES

Acosta, Pablo, Jorge Avalos, Arianna Zapanta, and Francesca Ma. 2019 [per CMOS 15.29]. "*Pantawid Pamilya* 2017 Assessment: An Update of the Philippine Conditional Cash Transfer's Implementation Performance." Social Protection Policy Note 18, World Bank, Washington, DC, September.

Acosta, Pablo, Isaku Endo, Jose Antonio Garcia Garcia Luna, Aisha de Guzman, and Yuko Okamura. 2019 [per CMOS 15.29]. "Making Payments More Efficient for the Philippines Conditional Cash Transfer Program." Social Protection Policy Note 20, World Bank, Washington, DC, September.

Acosta, Pablo Ariel, and Rashiel Besana Velarde. 2015. "An Update of the Philippine Conditional Cash Transfer's Implementation Performance." Social Protection Policy Note 8, World Bank, Washington, DC.

Arriagada, Ana-Maria, Jonathan Perry, Laura Rawlings, Julieta Trias, and Melissa Zumaeta. 2018. "Promoting Early Childhood Development by Strengthening Linkages between Cash Transfers and Parenting Behaviors." World Bank, Washington, DC.

Benhassine, Najy, Florencia Devoto, Esther Duflo, Pascaline Dupas, and Victor Pouliquen. 2015. "Turning a Shove into a Nudge? A 'Labeled Cash Transfer' for Education." *American Economic Journal: Economic Policy* 7 (3): 86–125.

Capanzana, Mario, Gabriel Demombynes, and Paul Gubbins. 2020. "Why Are So Many Children Stunted in the Philippines?" Policy Research Working Paper 9294, World Bank, Washington, DC.

Cho, Yoonyoung, Jorge Avalos, Yasuhiro Kawasoe, and Ruth Rodriguez. 2020. "Optimizing *Pantawid* for Nutrition." Social Protection Policy Note 21, World Bank, Washington, DC. https://openknowledge.worldbank.org/handle/10986/34784.

Congress of the Philippines. 2017. "Republic Act no. 10963: Tax Reform for Acceleration and Inclusion (TRAIN) Act." Congress of the Philippines, Manila, December 19, 2017.

DSWD (Department of Social Work and Development). 2017. "Memorandum Circular no. 6, Series of 2017: Guidelines on the Provision of Rice Subsidy to *Pantawid Pamilyang Pilipino* Program Households." DSWD, Batasan Hills, the Philippines.

DSWD (Department of Social Work and Development). 2018. "DSWD Memorandum Circular no. 3, Series of 2018: Implementing Guidelines for the Unconditional Cash Transfer Program." DSWD, Batasan Hills, the Philippines.

DSWD (Department of Social Work and Development). 2019. "DSWD Memorandum Circular no. 12, Series of 2019: Implementing Guidelines on the Replacement of *Pantawid Pamilya* Households to Reach the Annual Household Coverage." DSWD, Batasan Hills, the Philippines.

Economic Policy Research Institute. 2019. "Rapid Qualitative Assessment of the Impact of *Pantawid Pamilyang Pilipino* Program (4Ps) on Nutrition Outcomes in Beneficiary Households in Selected Municipalities." A study commissioned by UNICEF Philippines, Metro Manila, May 14, 2019.

Fernandez, Luisa. 2012. "Design and Implementation Features of the National Household Targeting System in the Philippines." World Bank-Philippines Social Protection Note 5, World Bank, Washington, DC.

Filmer, Deon, Jed Friedman, Eeshani Kandpal, and Junko Onishi. 2018. "Cash Transfers, Food Prices, and Nutrition Impacts on Nonbeneficiary Children." Policy Research Working Paper 8377, World Bank, Washington, DC.

Galasso, Emanuela, and Adam Wagstaff. 2018. "The Aggregate Income Losses from Childhood Stunting and the Returns to a Nutrition Intervention Aimed at Reducing Stunting." Policy Research Working Paper WPS 8536, World Bank Group, Washington, DC.

Heinrich, Carolyn J., and Matthew T. Knowles. 2020. "A Fine Predicament: Conditioning, Compliance, and Consequences in a Labeled Cash Transfer Program." *World Development* 129 (May): Art. 104876.

Kandpal, Eeshani, Harold Alderman, Jed Friedman, Deon Filmer, Junko Onishi, and Jorge Avalos. 2016. "A Conditional Cash Transfer Program in the Philippines Reduces Severe Stunting." *Journal of Nutrition* 146 (9): 1793–800.

Leroy, Jef L., Marie T. Ruel, Jeanne-Pierre Habicht, and Edward A. Frongillo. 2014. "Linear Growth Deficit Continues to Accumulate beyond the First 1,000 Days in Low- and Middle-Income Countries: Global Evidence from 51 National Surveys." *Journal of Nutrition* 144 (9): 1460–66.

Manley, James, Seth Gitter, and Vanya Slavchevska. 2013. "How Effective Are Cash Transfers at Improving Nutritional Status?" *World Development* 48 (August): 133–55.

Martínez, Rodrigo, and Andrés Fernández. 2008. "The Cost of Hunger: Social and Economic Impact of Child Undernutrition in Central America and Dominican Republic." Documentos de Proyectos 144, Economic Commission for Latin America and the Caribbean (ECLAC), Santiago.

Qian, Rong, Mara K. Warwick, Ndiame Diop, Birget Hansl, Kevin Thomas Garcia Cruz, Markus Bruckner, Kevin C. Chua, et al. 2018. "Growth and Productivity in the Philippines: Winning the Future." Working Paper 130056, World Bank Group, Washington, DC. http://documents.worldbank.org/curated/en/586871537541775427/Growth-and-Productivity-in-the-Philippines-Winning-the-Future.

Sánchez, Alan, Guido Meléndez, and Jere Behrman. 2016. "The Impact of the Juntos Conditional Cash Transfer Programme in Peru on Nutritional and Cognitive Outcomes: Does the Age of Exposure Matter?" Working Paper 153, Young Lives, London.

World Bank. 2018a. *The State of Social Safety Nets 2018.* Washington, DC: World Bank.

9 Local Governments as the Key to Tackling Malnutrition

ABSTRACT The Philippines' national nutrition program seeks to establish an organizational structure at all levels of government. The National Nutrition Council is responsible for national planning, coordination, and strategic development of nutrition policy. Meanwhile, regional, provincial, municipal, and barangay nutrition committees are responsible for implementing and managing nutrition programs at the local level. However, significant gaps exist in the delivery of nutrition programs. The major gaps include maternal nutrition (balanced energy protein supplementation) during pregnancy, complementary feeding of infants, continuous monitoring of children's growth and development in rural health units, and provision of other health and nutrition interventions. These gaps weaken the ability of local government units to address the problem of malnutrition among Filipino women and young children.

BACKGROUND

In 1991 the Republic Act no. 7160 (also known as the Local Government Code) was enacted into law (Congress of the Philippines 1991). The code devolved basic services, giving responsibility for health (as well as agricultural extension, forest management, services, barangay [district or neighborhood] roads, and social welfare) to local government units (LGUs). At the same time, LGUs were granted administrative autonomy to raise local revenue, to borrow, and to determine local expenditure, including expenditure on health care. The act sought to enhance the provision of services at the grassroots level as well as to improve the efficiency of resource allocation. Further, it sought to widen the decision-making space by encouraging the participation of stakeholders, especially at the local level.

In order to mobilize communities to accept and practice good nutrition, a properly selected and well-trained cadre of volunteers is necessary. In 1978 Presidential Decree no. 1569: Strengthening the Barangay Nutrition Program specified the provision of at least one nutrition scholar in every barangay

(Government of the Philippines 1978). Barangay Nutrition Scholars (BNSs) undergo intensive training in the delivery of practical nutrition services, including monitoring the growth of preschool children, communicating simple nutrition messages to parents, particularly pregnant and lactating women, and delivering food and pharmaceutical supplements to targeted women and children. The work of BNSs is further strengthened by another volunteer, the Barangay Health Worker (BHW). These volunteers provide primary health care services, including nutrition, to a cluster of 20–30 households in every barangay (DOH 2020).

The Philippines' national nutrition program seeks to establish an organizational structure at all levels of government. The National Nutrition Council (NNC) is responsible for national planning, coordination, and strategic development of nutrition policy. Meanwhile, regional, provincial, municipal, and barangay nutrition committees are responsible for implementing and managing nutrition programs at the local level. These committees are headed by the most senior political leaders in each LGU. The barangay, as the smallest governance unit, is the designated focal point for planning and implementing the nutrition program. With the assistance of a designated municipal nutrition action officer (MNAO), the municipal mayors and nutrition committees plan, coordinate, and manage the nutrition programs of the barangays in their municipality. Both the municipality and the barangay receive a share of the allotted internal revenue as well as social development funds, of which a certain percentage may be used for social projects, including health and nutrition projects. The municipal and barangay local chief executives and their legislative bodies determine the amount to be allocated for such purposes in their area (Solon 2006).

The enactment of Republic Act no. 11148 in 2018 and the release of its implementation rules and regulations the following year provided a fresh mandate for a more systematic and vigorous implementation of the nutrition program, this time with a clear focus on preventing stunting during the first 1,000 days of life (Congress of the Philippines 2018, 2019). The law and its implementation rules and regulations specifically call for implementing the program at the barangay level through health centers, rural health units, and barangay health stations, under the direct supervision of the city or municipal government (Rule 7, Section 1 of the implementation rules and regulations). Moreover, with the law came the prospect of increased LGU financing, involving the use of a larger share of national government revenues than had ever been allocated. This led to the April 10, 2019, Supreme Court decision ruling in favor of a petition that the LGU share of national government revenues should include all revenues, rather than only internal revenues (as had been done since 1992).[1] However, a widely discussed element still missing in law, and consequently at the local level, pertains to key personnel at the rural health units (such as nutritionists or dieticians) specifically tasked to provide technical guidance on nutrition.

The NNC's 2014 assessment of the operational gaps in implementation of the Philippine Plan of Action for Nutrition (PPAN) observed that, for many LGUs, nutrition program activities revolved around weighing children, feeding children in day care centers and schools, and participating in the July Nutrition Month celebration (NNC 2013). A review of LGU programs among persons who had received awards from the NNC for outstanding performance in nutrition revealed that, prior to 2015, the child nutrition intervention was intended to reduce the prevalence of low weight-for-age in children under five, in line with the relevant Millennium Development Goal. In 2015, with adoption of the

Sustainable Development Goals, the indicator was changed to the prevalence of stunting (and wasting). From this standpoint, it is understandable that the LGU response would focus on child-feeding programs, especially at the ages and in the settings where children are readily accessible (day care centers and schools).

Therefore, in order to understand the possible associations between nutritional outcomes and the local-level policy environment, in 2016 the World Bank commissioned a review of nutrition policy formulation, program planning, and implementation at the subnational and local levels in four provinces. The four case studies were carefully selected to represent the three main island groups (Luzon, Mindanao, Visayas) and the prevalence of stunting among children under five (FNRI 2013; table 9.1).

The PPAN was reviewed to identify key monitoring and evaluation indicators of program implementation. Records from local development offices were reviewed to determine whether nutrition had been incorporated in development plans. Key informant interviews were carried out with local chief executives and planning development officers at the provincial, municipal, and barangay levels to understand the local-level policy environment with a focus on nutrition. The interviews covered topics on the planning and implementation process, funding sources, manpower resources, and program monitoring and evaluation. Focus group discussions were also held among members of provincial, municipal, and barangay nutrition councils to determine whether the councils were functional, whether food and nutrition concerns were being prioritized, and how program planning was being undertaken. The focus groups were intended to complement and substantiate data obtained from the interviews. This chapter is based on the findings from three of the provinces in that review.

RESULTS FOR RIZAL PROVINCE

Rizal Province had a prevalence of 18.6 percent for underweight and 21.6 percent for stunting among children from birth to age five (FNRI 2013), indicating a relatively low prevalence of undernutrition. The provincial nutrition committee was not functioning, having never held a formal meeting. However, the

TABLE 9.1 **Levels of site selection**

LEVEL	NUMBER OF SITES	CRITERIA
Province	5	• Stunting prevalence ranked from highest to lowest, with acceptable coefficient of variation values • Four provinces with at least 40% prevalence of stunting • One province with less than 25% prevalence
Municipality	10	• Two municipalities from each province that have the highest and lowest prevalence of low weight-for-age based on the 2013 Operation *Timbang* (OPT) results
National Capital Region (NCR)	2	• Two districts from NCR that have the highest and lowest prevalence of stunting
Barangay	24	• Two barangays from each municipality and two from NCR, one with the highest and lowest prevalence of low weight-for-age based on the latest OPT results

Source: World Bank.

municipal committee did meet in 2014. At that meeting, committee members consolidated the municipal nutrition action plans that had been submitted to the council and formed part of the Philippine National Aquasilviculture Program and then forwarded the consolidated plan to the regional nutrition committee. The key informants admitted that nutrition had not been a priority at either the provincial or the municipal level.

The municipality of Tanay: Low prevalence of underweight and stunting

The 2014 Operation *Timbang* (OPT) for Rizal revealed that the municipality of Tanay had the lowest prevalence of low weight-for-age in the province. For Tanay, the key informants were primarily the municipality's health officer, nutrition action officer, and planning and development officer. According to the key informants, during every new mayoral term, the municipal nutrition committee was reorganized, creating instability. Moreover, the planning and development officer, not being an active committee member, could not recall whether or not the committee was functional. However, the health officer and the MNAO deemed the committee to be functional, despite the small number of members, inasmuch as it had approached the mayor to request a nutrition budget.

According to key informants, each committee member had a specific role in implementing nutrition programs in the municipality. As reported by the municipal health officer, representing the municipal Health Department, the following nutrition and health programs were being implemented: deworming, *Garantisadong Pambata*, a feeding program, immunization, provision of ferrous sulfate for pregnant women four months before delivery, and BNS activities. The feeding intervention followed a protocol, commonly involving deworming of children and checking and treating those with tuberculosis primary complex. The health program also included a program for adolescents, with a teen-friendly clinic, to inform them of their rights and educate them on human immunodeficiency virus (HIV)/acquired immunodeficiency syndrome (AIDS).

Program planning

The MNAO reported that the committee members discussed the causes of malnutrition in the municipality and concluded that the possible causes were laziness and lack of money to buy food. The solutions identified were to offer feeding programs at day care centers and to request that nongovernmental organizations (NGOs) sponsor them. The MNAO also reported that the prevalence of underweight children was reduced but could not quote an exact figure.

Implementation of programs and services

The municipal nurse at the health unit described other programs and projects implemented in the municipality, highlighting the promotion of breastfeeding among pregnant women through the establishment of breastfeeding corners for the benefit of waiting patients. The health unit's initiative to promote breastfeeding was reportedly successful, even though breastfeeding was not monitored or followed up. For pregnant women, each barangay held antenatal consultations every Thursday, at which iron supplements were distributed. The key informant reported that municipal iron supplementation reached relatively few recipients, owing to limited supplies at the national and local levels of government.

The municipality also held nutrition education sessions for pregnant women and promoted the use of iodized salt. Likewise, mothers received advice on complementary feeding. During *Garantisadong Pambata*—the biannual regular health program, which is held in April and October—deworming medicines, vitamin A, iron supplements, and iodine testing kits were distributed. However, it was reported that iron supplements, iodine testers, and immunizations, which were provided by the national government, were in short supply. Micronutrient powder provided by the United Nations Children's Fund (UNICEF) was also distributed.

The municipal Agriculture Office, by contrast, distributed seeds to the BNSs for their respective barangays and offered lectures, demonstrations on container gardening, and livelihood training, such as making banana chips and banana bread. The municipal Department of Social Welfare and Development and Department of Education implemented supplementary feeding in day care centers and in schools, respectively. The feeding program in schools was usually funded by NGOs. The municipal planning development officer (not being involved in program implementation) was not aware of the nutrition programs and projects for 2011–15, but provided verbal assurances that these programs were funded.

The municipality of Angono: High prevalence of low weight-for-age and stunting

Angono had the highest prevalence of low weight-for-age in Rizal, based on the consolidated 2014 OPT data. Flooding in 2012 due to Typhoon Habagat had affected all barangays in the municipality.

The key informants affirmed that the executive order was the legal basis for creating the municipal nutrition committee, but that no related documentation had been provided. The municipal nurse, who was responsible for the tuberculosis program and Department of Health (DOH) medicines for *Pantawid* beneficiaries, was designated MNAO in August 2014 and attended a five-day training on nutrition program management conducted by the NNC in October 2014.

The key informant from the health sector explained that the composition of the municipal nutrition council is similar to that of the local health board, which is composed of the mayor as chair, the municipal health officer as vice chair, alongside the budget officer, planning officer, president of the Association of Barangay Captains, BHW president, and an NGO representative. The council includes the MNAO (who is usually designated), a municipal social welfare officer, a representative of the *Sangguniang Bayan* (the municipal council) on health, a municipal agriculture officer, a representative of the Department of the Interior and Local Government, a municipal accountant, a municipal treasurer, and the mayor. Each member has specific roles and functions. The municipal health officer acts as adviser to the council and is responsible for implementing and monitoring the nutrition program. In the absence of the mayor, the municipal health officer chairs the meeting.

Program planning

According to key informants, the basis of the data or information for the nutrition program was unclear, other than that the target beneficiaries were children under five, according to the municipal nutrition action plan. The OPT served as the basis for reaching malnourished children in the supplementary feeding element of the program, which targeted the barangay with the most malnourished children. The MNAO admitted that no joint planning had been undertaken and that the municipality had a nutrition action plan for 2013 and 2015, but not for 2014.

Agencies represented on the municipal nutrition committee have the following roles and functions:

- The Budget Office allocates funds for nutrition programs.
- The Department of Interior and Local Government supports the proposed nutrition program through advocacy at the budget office and approval by the mayor.
- The Department of Social Welfare and Development provides data on malnourished children covered in the day care feeding program.
- The Sangguniang Bayan on health facilitates the passage of policies and regulations related to health and nutrition.
- The Barangay Chairman is the focal person for BHWs, who implement the program at the local level.
- The Agriculture Office is responsible for the food production component of the program, specifically the distribution of seedlings and organization of livelihood training sessions.

The municipal planning development officer said that the council met twice a year, especially during nutrition month and every round of annual investment program planning. All plans submitted by the departments were integrated into one municipal annual investment program, which followed national guidelines. Budget allocations for projects depended on the national programs and guidelines of the Commission of Audit. Strict compliance with these guidelines was required to prevent the misuse of funds. However, the municipal planning development officer also admitted that the municipality had no separate plans for nutrition, apart from the annual investment program. For 2016, the municipality's annual investment program included the establishment of a breastfeeding station in the waiting area for patients of the rural health center as well as in the public market (an initiative inspired by breastfeeding stations established in shopping malls).

Implementation of programs and services

The health and nutrition programs are incorporated in primary health care services like *Garantisadong Pambata*, medical missions, and blood testing. For maternal nutrition, the program activities included counseling and lectures for pregnant women, a free laboratory for indigent families or mothers during *Buntis* Congress (an annual one-day health drive), and setting up of breastfeeding stations in every barangay health station. For children, activities included the OPT, *Garantisadong Pambata,* and supplemental feeding programs. Children were dewormed and weighed before enrollment in the feeding program. Some key implementation challenges were highlighted for this municipality:

- *Limited financial support.* Programs for implementation depend on the LGU budget, which was limited, particularly for nutrition. The key informant reported that the annual budget for nutrition amounted to ₱50,000, which only covered promotional materials, food, and office supplies for launching activities. Feeding programs for malnourished children were usually funded by NGOs with support from the barangay.

- *OPT data.* The key informants said that the result of the 2014 OPT was inaccurate due to the use of bathroom weighing scales and lack of supervision. The MNAO reported that this issue had been relayed to the municipal nutrition committee and that the use of bathroom weighing scales was not approved by the NNC.

RESULTS FOR ZAMBOANGA DEL NORTE PROVINCE

The 2013 National Nutrition Survey revealed a very high prevalence of low weight-for-age (26.3 percent) and stunting (44.2 percent) among children under five in Zamboanga del Norte (FNRI 2013). Members of the provincial nutrition committee agreed that the committee was not functional, as demonstrated by the absence of program planning and the convening of only two meetings the previous year (2014). At the time of the study, the current administration and committee members were not updated on their roles and functions. Moreover, despite the presence of the 2014 Philippine National Aquasilviculture Program, a provincial committee member had never been invited to any program planning session and therefore considered that no planning had taken place.

The municipality of Polanco: Low prevalence of underweight and stunting

Polanco is an agricultural municipality with 70 percent of its land area devoted to crop production. As in most regions, rice, corn, and coconut are the most common crops. At the time of the survey, the municipality was considered a model for LGU implementation of nutrition and health programs. Polanco had a functional municipal nutrition committee, as demonstrated by the holding of regular quarterly meetings of its 26 members and special meetings when needed. The committee had prepared a two-year local nutrition action plan (2012–14), independent of the annual municipal plan. The committee had strong support from the local chief executive and the *Sangguniang Bayan* members.

Program planning

As the municipal health officer, the MNAO of Polanco presided over the planning session for the municipal nutrition action plan, as instructed by the mayor. The officer related that, during planning, the committee had analyzed the nutrition situation of the municipality using a problem tree. The planning reportedly was based on NNC guidelines and the results of surveys conducted on priority programs needed in the municipality. Based on the nutrition situation in each barangay, the data were consolidated during the planning session, common problems were identified, causes and outcomes were determined, and the program to be pursued was decided.

Each agency on the committee incorporated the nutrition program and activities into its own plans. For instance, nutrition activities were coordinated and delivered alongside the activities of the municipal Health Department. The target beneficiaries were infants ages 0–5.9 months, children ages 6–23.9 months, and pregnant and lactating mothers.

Implementation of programs and services

The LGU had implemented all of the national programs for health and nutrition, as indicated in the Field Health Services Information System (FHSIS) for 2007–10 and 2012–14. The key informants specifically mentioned the focus on the first 1,000 days, micronutrient supplementation for women of reproductive age, antenatal services, family planning, OPT, and *Buntis* Congress. Interviews with key informants identified the change of political administration every three years as being a major problem. After each election, a new BNS is installed and has to undergo training on how to implement and manage the program.

The municipality of Godod: High prevalence of underweight and stunting

Godod is in the interior southern part of the province and part of the Third Congressional District. The municipality is an agricultural area with farming as the main source of income. About 80 percent of the total land area is used for agricultural production. The major agricultural crops are rice and corn, with perennial commercial crops such as rubber, coconut, and plantation trees of various species of fruits.

The municipality is classified as geographically isolated and disadvantaged, with inaccessible households. Two barangays can be reached only by passing through three municipalities; they cannot be reached from inside the territorial boundaries of Godod. The provision of safe water is a problem, as are poor communications (especially internet access).

Godod has the second highest prevalence of malnutrition in Zamboanga del Norte. Local records show that the municipal nutrition committee was created through Executive Order no. 21, signed by the mayor on July 21, 2011. The committee appeared to be functional, judging by the regularity of its meetings, although only three meetings were reported for 2014. Likewise, the LGU had drawn up the municipal nutrition action plan (2014–16), which served as the basis for program implementation.

Program planning

In Godod the designated MNAO was a nurse from the rural health unit. The municipal nutrition committee usually met as a group, bringing their individual plans and discussing programs and activities to be included in the municipal nutrition action plan. During meetings and annual program planning, the mayor was supposed to serve in person as the committee chair, but often sent a deputy instead. The budget for nutrition activities was usually taken from the mandatory Gender and Development Fund.

Implementation of programs and services

Nutrition programs and services implemented in the municipality were related to capacity building, including training for the BNS, training on feeding infants and young children, and training on issues such as growth monitoring (OPT) and *Pabasa sa Nutrisyon* (Fight against Malnutrition through Education). Other national programs and services included school fruit and vegetable gardening, vitamin A supplementation, iron supplementation, use of iodized salt, salt testing, supplementary feeding, antenatal services, immunization, and deworming.

The lack of availability of early prenatal services was attributed to the geographic inaccessibility of some barangays in the municipality. As in the municipality of Polanco, key informants in Godod identified the frequent replacement of the BNS as a problem in program implementation.

RESULTS FOR ALBAY PROVINCE

Albay Province is primarily agricultural (87 percent). The majority of its people depend on agriculture and fisheries for their livelihood. Food security in the province is regularly threatened and affected by erratic changes in climate, such as the eruption of Mayon Volcano in 2014.

The provincial nutrition committee was created on the basis of Executive Order no. 2007-15: Reactivating the Albay Provincial Nutrition Committee, which was signed on December 14, 2007 at Legazpi City. The executive order stated the composition, functions, term of office, meetings (at least quarterly), and funds for the activities and projects of the committee. The committee has 12 members, excluding the chair and vice chair, who are the governor and vice governor of the province, respectively. The Secretariat is headed by the provincial nutrition action officer, who can designate the coordinator for each of the three districts of the province to serve as technical assistants for the provincial nutrition action officer. The executive order stipulates that the province shall ensure nutritional improvement with a focus on the most nutritionally needy and depressed areas of the province. Specifically, the provincial nutrition committee shall formulate local food and nutrition policies, strategies, programs, and projects for nutritional improvement; coordinate the planning, implementation, monitoring, and evaluation of the integrated local food and nutrition program; and coordinate between local government and concerned agencies on generating resources and other assistance as the need arises. Respondents in the province said that Albay was lucky to have a dedicated governor, who exemplified good governance and good leadership, gave high priority to health and education, and budgeted rewards for good works in health and education.

The 2014 PPAN annual report for Albay Province showed excellent progress in the programs and projects related to health and nutrition. The province adopted the national programs on nutrition, such as micronutrient supplementation, immunization, a referral system, maternal care, promotion of exclusive breastfeeding, distribution of seeds, supplementary feeding, a promotion campaign on the use of fortified products, and a campaign to draw on the services of the Philippine Health Insurance Company. The nutrition program was implemented in all municipalities in the province.

The municipality of Malinao: High prevalence of underweight and stunting

The municipality of Malinao had the highest prevalence of low weight-for-age in Albay Province in 2014 and is also classified as low income. The major source of income is derived from real estate taxes. The municipality is abundant in agriculture, especially rice production, but the area is prone to typhoons. Almost all of the barangays were affected by Typhoon Juaning (in 2011) and Typhoons Glenda and Ruby (in 2014).

Program planning

The key informants deemed the municipal nutrition council to be functional, as it convened on a quarterly basis. Attendance at committee meetings usually ranged from 8 to 10 members (out of 14). The nutrition action plan was a combined plan for 2013–14, as required by Intervida Philippines Foundation, an NGO that implemented the nutrition program in six barangays in Malinao for three years from 2012 to 2014.

The MNAO admitted to experiencing some difficulties because her permanent appointment was with the municipal Agriculture Office as agricultural technologist. Her designation as MNAO started in 1997, when she was tasked with coordinating municipal nutrition programs and initiating regular committee meetings. In the absence of the municipal mayor, she chaired the committee meeting.

Implementation of programs and services

The programs implemented for 2011–15 were nutrition education, *Pabasa sa Nutrisyon*, cooking demonstrations in the barangay, and training of BNSs on nutrition program management sponsored by Intervida. Also implemented were programs conducted by the Philippine Health Insurance Company, *Garantisadong Pambata* during the months of April and October, feeding of infants and young children, micronutrient supplementation such as the distribution of vitamin A and iron, provision of prenatal and postnatal care, promotion of iodized salt, construction of toilets, construction or rehabilitation of water systems, health and nutrition education advocacy, a campaign on food production in schools and communities, supplementary feeding, nutrition advocacy, implementation of the no-home-birthing policy, and livelihood programs. A key problem highlighted during the key informant interviews and focus group discussions was the lack of appropriate government funding.

The municipality of Tiwi: Low prevalence of underweight and stunting

The municipality of Tiwi is dependent on crop production, livestock and poultry raising, and fishing. It is also known for the production of ceramics and for its geothermal plant. The municipality does not produce vegetables, and such supplies are brought in from other municipalities. At the time of the study, Executive Order no. 2013-14: An Order Reorganizing the Municipal Nutrition Council was signed, specifying the council's functions, composition (including Philippine Geothermal Production Company and Intervida Philippines Foundation as NGO members), and overall role. Under Circular no. 2013-89: Adoption of the Philippine Plan of Action for Nutrition, PPAN was used as a basis for the municipal nutrition plan from 2011 to 2015. No problems were identified with regard to the budget allocated to the programs because the legislative and executive bodies had agreed that program plans would be supported regardless of political affiliation.

Program planning

During interviews conducted for this study, the MNAO described the process of planning as follows: "The coverage should be above 80 percent and should be completed by the end of April every year; the results of the OPT were analyzed with the BNS." After this validation, the OPT results were presented to the municipal nutrition council. Beneficiaries were chosen on the basis of those data. By June of that year, and in preparation for budget discussions, the previous plan on health and nutrition was presented to the members, and decisions were made on the projects or activities to be sustained or modified. Programs and projects were subsequently integrated in the municipal development plan for approval. The community-based monitoring system survey data also served as a basis for targeting, giving priority to nutritionally depressed barangays.

Program implementation

The target beneficiaries were underweight children and their parents, pregnant and lactating mothers, and the elderly. Priority was also given to nutritionally depressed barangays. Some of the programs and projects accomplished in 2012–14 were supplementary feeding of day care children, center-based feeding, maternal health care, production of foods such as cassava and seaweed, medical consultations, *Pabasa sa Nutrisyon*, distribution of micronutrient supplementation, promotion of food fortification, livelihood assistance like microfinance, and livelihood training on eco bag making, ceramics, and chicken raising. A 120-day supplemental feeding program was implemented in all day care centers regardless of nutritional status (though funded by the Department of Social Welfare and Development, not the LGU). A seed distribution program was implemented for parents of underweight children to help them cultivate a kitchen garden. The BNSs were paid an allowance when attending training.

Some key implementation challenges mentioned during the discussions were the replacement of trained BNSs due to political conflicts during elections, lack of budgetary support in some barangays, attitude of beneficiaries (lack of cooperation), and insufficient production of local crops.

CONCLUSIONS

The provincial case studies covered three provinces classified as having high and low prevalence of low weight-for-age and stunting among children under five, based on the National Nutrition Survey (FNRI 2013). The local policy environment (including how programs are planned, translated, monitored, and evaluated on the ground) was examined through interviews and focus group discussions with provincial and municipal officials. Households were asked about their participation in government programs, food security, dietary diversity, and food expenditure.

For the local government units as a whole to have a measurable and sustained impact on stunting, a very large number (if not all) of the more than 1,500 LGUs should be providing the whole continuum of nutrition interventions at the required "dosage" to the target population of mothers and young children. It is not enough merely to note that some LGUs are performing very well.

For national impact, scale is important. Unfortunately, gaps are evident in the delivery of nutritional health. The major gaps include maternal nutrition (balanced energy protein supplementation) during pregnancy; complementary feeding of infants; continuous monitoring of children's growth and development in rural health units; and provision of other health interventions. Gaps are also evident in the delivery of specific components of a particular intervention. For example, nutrition counseling is often lacking in prenatal consultations. While micronutrient supplementation is provided, the supply given to pregnant women is less than required. Popular LGU programs that are classified as part of the nutrition program include feeding programs in day care or in schools (which naturally cannot influence stunting during the first 1,000 days of life) and programs such as gardening, livelihood training, and poverty reduction.

What factors or deficiencies might determine the LGU's choice of interventions? Public understanding of stunting is still limited, as emerged strongly in the evaluation of PPAN, especially at the barangay level. By contrast, certain programs tend to be popular because they are visible and relatively easy to organize (such as feeding programs).

Program planning

The municipal nutrition action plan is a product of planning sessions that the municipal nutrition committee conducts as a group. Unfortunately, not every LGU undertakes planning by means of that committee, as observed in this case study. The municipalities that conduct structured nutrition planning sessions are mostly in areas with a low prevalence of undernutrition, like Polanco and Tiwi. These municipalities follow the planning process and the guidelines of the National Nutrition Council, as noted by a key informant (in Polanco). While informants from other municipalities did not mention that any planning guidelines were being followed, they claimed that "planning is a collaborative effort" and the planning process is conducted by the members of the municipal or city nutrition committee every first quarter of the year (in Muntinlupa City, Taguig City, and Tiwi). In the municipalities where planning was not conducted by the municipal nutrition committee, the key informants shared that each department conducts its own planning and that the plans are consolidated by the municipal planning development officer. The agency departments sometimes meet and bring their plans and programs for further discussion; these proposals are then incorporated in the annual investment plan. In municipalities where a separate budget is not allocated for nutrition, the municipal nutrition committee does not conduct nutrition planning. Instead, the nutrition programs and projects planned are consolidated and form part of the municipality's medium and annual investment plan.

Programs and services implemented

The case studies revealed that programs and services originating at the national level are delivered to and adopted at the provincial and municipal levels down to the barangays. However, the continuous implementation of these programs depends on the initiatives of the local chief executives. Municipalities where nutrition is a priority, with active, full-time MNAOs or a part-time person with support staff, are able to deliver more programs and services. Moreover, these municipalities receive most of the nutrition and related programs of private and nongovernment organizations.

Case study areas with a low prevalence of malnutrition are able to manage and efficiently implement health and nutrition programs, especially national programs. Interventions like feeding programs for malnourished children are usually funded by NGOs. The municipalities of Tiwi in Albay and Polanco in Zamboanga del Norte demonstrated exemplary performance, marked by the receipt of a series of awards recognizing their effective and efficient management of nutrition programs. These municipalities implemented all of the national programs for health and nutrition, as indicated in FHSIS (2007–10 and 2012–14).

In contrast, municipalities with limited budgets and weak support for the prioritization of nutrition fail to implement some planned programs. In the absence of sufficient funds from the LGU, partnerships with NGOs for the implementation of nutrition programs are the only available options for delivering high-priority services (such as feeding interventions). The failure to deliver services is also due to geographic location, natural calamities, and lack of personnel or community workers.

Challenges in implementation

Municipalities face three common problems in the implementation of nutrition interventions, particularly in municipalities with a high prevalence of childhood undernutrition: the allocation of insufficient budget for nutrition programs, the absence of a full-time MNAO, and the scarcity of health personnel. Nutrition often has to compete with a long list of other infrastructure projects in the budget priorities of the LGUs. Nutrition is rarely a priority for LGUs, and NGOs are therefore asked to fund nutrition programs. The designated MNAO overseeing the implementation of nutrition programs often has a full program of activities to undertake simultaneously and hence cannot allocate a sufficient amount of time for nutrition and nutrition-related responsibilities. In addition, nutrition committee members have heavy workloads, resulting in their failure to participate in nutrition-related meetings and to implement other nutrition-related activities.

Another notable problem is that the LGUs do not have reliable information systems regarding the true magnitude of their nutrition problems and progress made toward achieving outcomes. The OPT data are "plagued with quality issues," making them unreliable for resource allocation. For coverage of interventions, the FHSIS provides information on micronutrient supplementation for mothers and children and related information on child health care (treatment of diarrhea and pneumonia, immunization, and deworming); child feeding (breastfeeding and the introduction of solid food); and family planning. The FHSIS also contains household-level data on environmental sanitation (potable water and sanitary toilets). The FHSIS data are reported at the barangay, municipal, and city levels and are consolidated at the city and provincial levels.

The common belief at the local level, which is allegedly common among the general populace, local officials, and even program implementers, is that "stunting is not a problem." This belief constitutes an important challenge. Instead, the short stature of children is ascribed to genetics, while the consequences of stunting for cognitive development remain unrecognized. While there have been some shifts in mindsets as a result of LGU mobilization efforts, the fundamental misperceptions remain a problem that needs to be addressed constantly.

Other problems include (a) the termination of BNS services due to political conflict and changes in political administration every three years (a problem observed in all areas) and (b) indifference on the part of clients, a common problem that implementers said results in low participation rates, especially in the immunization and backyard gardening programs. Beneficiaries particularly dislike the provision of ferrous sulfate and micronutrient powder.

RECOMMENDATIONS

The results of these case studies highlight local issues and concerns that could explain some of the challenges facing LGUs in delivering nutrition programs and services on the ground. These challenges weaken their ability to address the problem of malnutrition among Filipino women and young children. The following recommendations emerge from the findings of the case studies:

- Both executive and legislative bodies in the municipalities need to prioritize and vigorously support nutrition interventions. As indicated in the case studies, LGUs that strongly support nutrition programs tend to perform better and have low prevalence of undernutrition among children under five.
- Increasing the budget allocation and providing a separate budget for nutrition would demonstrate strong support for the nutrition agenda of the LGUs. Only with the availability of dedicated budgets can nutrition programs be implemented and sustained.
- The inclusion of standard, reliable, and high-quality monitoring and evaluation systems in every nutrition and health-related program would be useful in assessing the effectiveness of the intervention programs.
- The personnel who oversee the implementation of nutrition programs should be technically competent, with proper health and nutrition experience and the time and energy to focus on the job. If possible, the LGU should fund an MNAO who would be housed on a permanent basis in a municipal agency or department. This person would oversee the nutrition program and serve a term different than that of the municipal mayor so that the implementation of nutrition programs could be sustained.
- The status of volunteer workers (BNSs and BHWs), who are the major players in implementing nutrition programs at the barangay level, could be safeguarded by (a) providing protection from being replaced due to changes in political administration; (b) offering more material incentives; and (c) providing continuous capacity building through training, particularly on measuring the weight and height of children, computing age in months accurately, keeping records, and assessing maternal weight gain during pregnancy.
- For the effective implementation of Operation *Timbang*, it is important to procure standard, appropriate weighing scales (with regular calibration and maintenance) and height boards. It is also important to train volunteer workers in their proper use.

NOTE

1. The Supreme Court ruled that the "just share" of local government units must be computed and sourced from all national taxes, not just from the national internal revenue taxes. But

the Supreme Court also ruled that the new and expanded basis for calculating the LGUs' share of national government revenue will first apply in 2022. See http://sc.judiciary.gov.ph/3726/.

REFERENCES

Congress of the Philippines. 1991. "Republic Act no. 7160: An Act Providing for a Local Government Code of 1991." *Official Gazette,* October 10, 1991.

Congress of the Philippines. 2018. "Republic Act no. 11148: An Act Scaling up the National and Local Health and Nutrition Programs." *Official Gazette,* November 11, 2018. https://www.officialgazette.gov.ph/downloads/2018/11nov/20181129-RA-11148-RRD.pdf.

Congress of the Philippines. 2019. "Implementing Rules and Regulations (IRR) of Republic Act (RA) no. 11148." *Official Gazette,* May 2, 2019.

DOH (Department of Health). 2020. "Barangay Nutrition Scholar (BNS) Program." DOH, Manila. https://doh.gov.ph/health-program/BNS.

FNRI (Food and Nutrition Research Institute). 2013. *Eighth National Nutrition Survey.* Taguig City: Department of Science and Technology, FNRI.

Government of the Philippines. 1978. "Presidential Decree no. 1569, s 1978: Strengthening the Barangay Nutrition Program by Providing for a Barangay Nutrition Scholar in Every Barangay, Providing Funds Therefor, and for Other Purposes." *Official Gazette,* June 11, 1978.

NNC (National Nutrition Council). 2013. "Philippine Plan of Action for Nutrition (PPAN)." NNC, Taguig City, December 3, 2013. https://www.nnc.gov.ph/plans-and-programs/philippine-plan-of-action-for-nutrition-ppan.

Solon, Florentino S. 2006. "Good Governance for Nutrition in the Philippines: Elements, Experiences, and Lessons Learned." *Food and Nutrition Bulletin* 27 (4): 343–52.

10 Opportunities to Improve Data for Nutrition Policy and Programs

ABSTRACT Designing, monitoring, and evaluating actions that result in impact are impossible without adequate knowledge of who is affected by malnutrition and why. Nutrition data and information systems play a critical role in ensuring that valid, reliable, and timely data are available, accessible, and used by key stakeholders to inform decision making. However, despite considerable recent progress in alleviating malnutrition among children in the Philippines, gaps still exist in the data needed to identify the direct and underlying causes of malnutrition on a geographic basis and improve the targeting of nutrition programming and interventions.

INTRODUCTION

The government collects data on nutrition through household surveys and administrative data. The National Nutrition Survey (NNS) is the primary source of official statistics on nutrition. Operation *Timbang* Plus (OPT Plus) is an administrative monitoring system that supports planning and policy formulation at local levels (*timbang* is the Tagalog word for "weight" or "weigh"). The Philippine Field Health Services Information System (FHSIS) is the government's major resource for managing public health data. FHSIS data are used for policy analysis and planning at all levels of the public health system. Most FHSIS data originate during patient care at barangay (district or neighborhood) health stations, city and rural health units, and hospitals. This chapter discusses the features of these data sources and opportunities for improvement. (See annex 10A for comparisons of the three surveys.)

THE NATIONAL NUTRITION SURVEY

The nationally representative NNS has been conducted by the Food and Nutrition Research Institute (FNRI) of the Department of Science and Technology (DOST) since 1978. Executive Order no. 128, Section 22, mandates that FNRI undertake research on citizens' nutritional status, especially the causes and effects of malnutrition, and on alternative solutions to nutrition problems (Government of the Philippines 1987). Executive Order no. 352 designates the NNS as the means of generating official statistics on the Philippine food, nutrition, and health situation to guide the formulation of food and nutrition policies as well as intervention and related development programs (Government of the Philippines 1996).

Beginning with just three major components in 1978, the NNS has had 10 components since 2013: anthropometry; biochemical aspects; clinical and health; dietary consumption; socioeconomic aspects; food security; participation in government programs; infant and young child feeding practices; maternal health and nutrition; and, lastly, household awareness and use of iodized salt, nutrition labels, and nutrition facts.

The comprehensive NNS is conducted every five years, supplemented by an Updating Survey conducted between successive comprehensive surveys. The Updating Survey is a simpler, more rapid nutritional assessment, comprising 9 of the 10 components. The NNS is funded primarily by the national government through the FNRI budget, with additional financial assistance from the Department of Health (DOH) and the Philippine Council for Health Research and Development. Nine NNSs and seven Updating Surveys have been conducted since 1978.

In response to the need for tracking the country's attainment of the Sustainable Development Goals, which involves more granular local data alongside more frequent national estimates, the NNS was expanded in 2018 to a three-year rolling survey, the Expanded National Nutrition Survey (ENNS). The ENNS uses replicated sampling within the 2015 new master sample developed by the Philippine Statistics Authority. This sampling allows the ENNS to generate estimates at the national level and in select provinces and highly urbanized cities (rather than national and regional estimates, as for the NNS). Over the three years to 2020, the ENNS collected sample data from about 60,000 households and 40 provinces per year. To date, results from the Eighth NNS in 2013 and the Updating Survey in 2015 have been published in full, while national and provincial estimates of nutrition and health indicators for 2018 and 2019 from the ENNS have been reported.

Preparation

Dietary researchers, anthropometric researchers, and allied health professionals are key personnel assigned to teams conducting the survey, including more than 400 staff who are trained by the FNRI. Staff are trained over four months, including a blood pressure certification class specifically for staff assigned as local researchers.

The FNRI conducts presurvey conferences for regional, provincial, and municipal coordination, including a discussion of survey needs and presurvey information. City or municipal nutrition action officers on the ground coordinate with the barangay focal person. Upon deployment, the survey team meets with local officials and aides for a briefing on the aide's responsibilities and the locations of households to visit. Field staff stay in a survey area for three to five days to ensure that members have accomplished their duties. The required data are checked and transmitted to the central office before staff depart. The interviews are generally finished within two days, and additional days are spent on editing and transmission. The data sent by field researchers are monitored by the data transmission monitoring system. Upon receipt at the central database, data are immediately validated and cleaned. Several rounds of manual and machine validations are applied to encoded anthropometry measurements before completion and preparation for the report.

Data collection

The electronic data collection system (e-DCS) was developed for the NNS, replacing the use of traditional pen-and-paper interview guides with computer-based interview schedules, except for certain components such as anthropometry, which is recorded using pen and paper prior to electronic entry and uploading using the browser-based e-DCS. Team leaders and researchers are provided with netbooks with which to use the system. Aside from facilitating data validation, the e-DCS improved the transmission of data from survey areas to the central database in FNRI for immediate data cleaning and further validation.

The anthropometric component of the NNS covers the nutritional assessment of all members of the sample household using standard measurements for weight and height, waist, hip, and mid-upper-arm circumference. The anthropometric researcher collects information about the household, participation in government programs, feeding of infants and young children, maternal health and nutrition, and food security, in addition to taking body measurements and blood pressure. Weight is measured twice using a digital double-window weighing scale and recorded to the nearest 0.1 kilogram. A third measurement is taken if the difference between the first and second weights is greater than 0.3 kilograms. The digital scale's two-in-one function key enables determination of the body weight of infants, young children, and persons not able to stand independently. The caregiver (adult) is weighed first without the child, and then the function key is pressed to display the child's weight. Height is likewise measured twice, using a stadiometer for subjects two years old and above. Length for infants and children under two is measured using a medical plastic infantometer and then recorded to the nearest 0.1 centimeter. Birthweight is obtained from the birth record of the child. If no record is available, the mother or caretaker of the child is asked to recall the weight of the newborn obtained within an hour after birth. This birthweight in grams is recorded and encoded in the e-DCS.

The 2015 Updating Survey recorded an 89 percent response rate for anthropometry (as a proportion of the eligible population) (FNRI 2015). Failure to respond includes reasons such as the child was too irritable for a measurement to be made, the person refused to be measured, or height was not taken due to disability (such as polio, kyphosis).

The instruments used for the surveys have been upgraded constantly to adopt technological advancements. For the 2015 Updating Survey, new instruments were procured for ease of data collection and accuracy. In the Eighth NNS conducted in 2013, the infantometer used was a wooden length board, since replaced by a medical plastic infantometer for 2015. The microtoise (with retractable tape) was also replaced by a stadiometer. The instruments were calibrated following standard procedures. New digital weighing scales were adjusted in the field using 5-kilo test weights.

Dietary data from the NNS have been the source of information on national food consumption. Public and private entities often cite NNS food intake as a basis for policy, programs, and even marketing. Together with questions about food security, the NNS provides information on dietary energy sufficiency and nutrient adequacy. The NNS also provides data on micronutrient status (iodine, anemia, vitamin A, and zinc status are measured on a regular basis), and this information has been instrumental in the enactment of policies such as the ASIN Law and the Food Fortification Act.[1] For example, the tracking of urinary iodine levels provided a basis for scaling back salt iodization levels from 40 parts per million or more (in 1995) to 30 parts per million (in 2013), as median urinary iodine excretion among school-age children—the index population stipulated by the World Health Organization (WHO)—reflected more than adequate levels by 2003 (figure 10.1) (Perlas et al. 2017).

Reporting

The NNS uses the WHO child growth standards and the WHO growth reference 2007 to assess the nutritional status of children. The survey reports weight-for-age (underweight or above-normal weight), length-for-age or height-for-age (stunting or above-average height), and weight-for-length or weight-for-height (wasting or overweight) by population groups, such as children under five years old, children and adolescents under 19 years old, adults, pregnant women, and lactating mothers.

In recent rounds, FNRI has released initial results of national estimates as early as six months after data collection. These data are usually presented

FIGURE 10.1

Distribution of urinary iodine excretion values among children ages 6–12 in the Philippines, 1998, 2003, 2008, and 2013

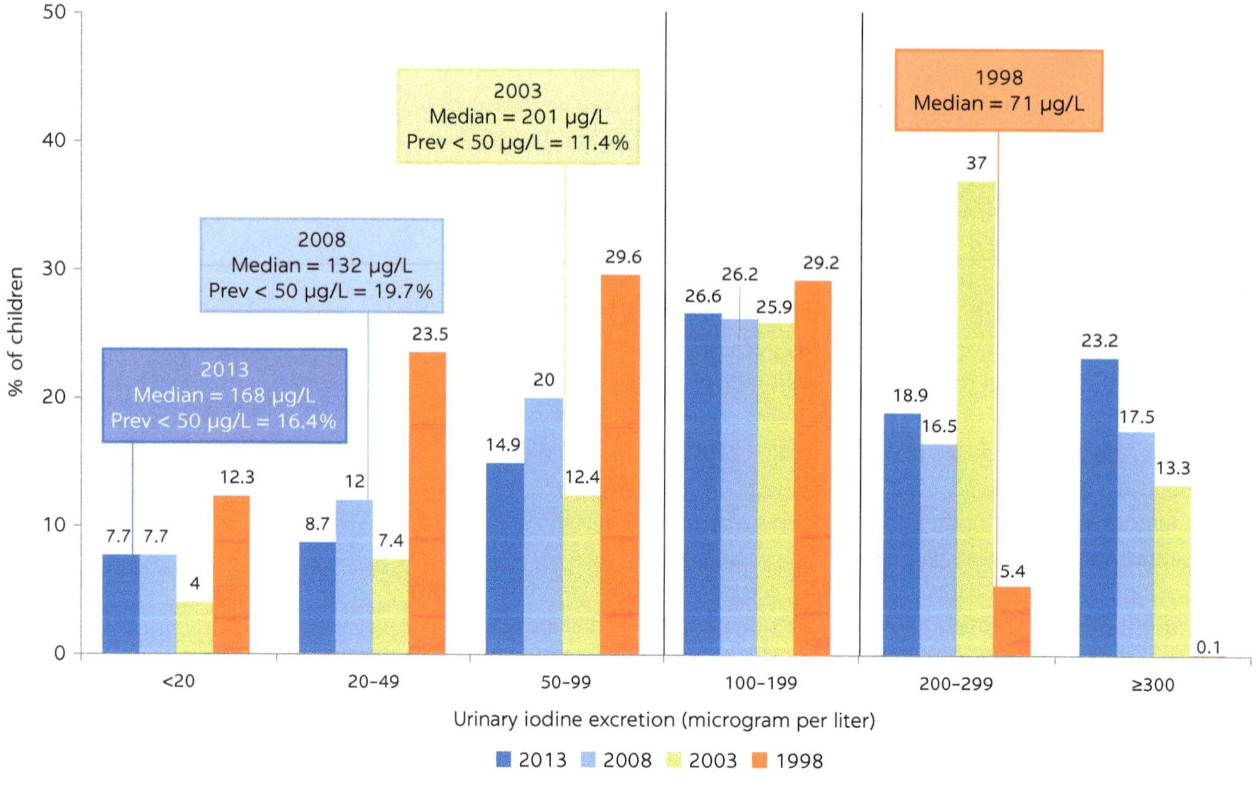

Source: Perlas et al. 2017, from National Nutrition Survey data (FNRI 1998, 2003, 2008, 2013).
Note: μg/L = microgram per liter.

to national line agencies, nongovernmental organizations, international and development partners, and other stakeholders through a forum. FNRI also organizes postsurvey conferences and seminars to disseminate results to the regions and select provinces. Full reports for each component follow thereafter.

OPERATION *TIMBANG* PLUS

The National Nutrition Council collects administrative data on anthropometry yearly for monitoring outcomes through the OPT Plus. Compared with the NNS and its Updating Survey, which are available every three to five years, OPT Plus can provide more nuanced and detailed records of select nutrition indicators within regions and provinces. The OPT system provides governments, particularly local government units (LGUs), an opportunity to assess their efforts to address malnutrition (Solon 1979). The system is used frequently, mainly for operational purposes. These data allow planners to rank the region, provinces, municipalities, and barangays according to the prevalence of underweight among children (Solon 2006).

LGUs conducted regular growth monitoring and promotion activities until Operation *Timbang* was institutionalized in 1976 with the National Nutrition Program (Heaver and Hunt 1995). Several growth standards have been used to assess the nutritional status of Filipino children through the years, among them the Philippine reference standards in 1992 and the National Center for Health Statistics international research standards in 2003. In 2006 the WHO advocated the use of the new child growth standards, and in 2010 the DOH issued Administrative Order no. 2010-0015, mandating the use of the WHO child growth standards to assess the nutritional status of children under five (DOH 2010). In 2012, following approval of the revised implementing guidelines, the activity officially became Operation *Timbang* Plus, which indicated the addition of height or length measurements for a more comprehensive assessment of children's nutritional status).[2]

OPT Plus annually registers the weight and height (length for infants or children unable to stand) of all children from birth to 59 months old (71 months old until 2016) undertaken at the barangay level and implemented by LGUs during the first quarter each year. It is the NNC's largest program, accompanied by counseling and referral, community mobilization, nutrition education, record keeping, and assistance with other child health activities, such as immunization and deworming (Berman, Downey, and Felter 2016).

The activity is the main system for identifying localities facing nutrition challenges, as it seeks to identify moderately and severely underweight preschool children and their families who need immediate intervention assistance. Children who are identified as malnourished by OPT Plus are located so that they can receive nutrition-related services on a priority basis. Annually, the NNC processes OPT Plus results at the municipal and provincial levels and generates a list of nutritionally depressed areas to inform government decisions regarding resource allocation and give priority attention to these areas in planning nutrition programming and intervention.

Preparation

At the barangay level, the rural health midwife is supposed to lead the OPT Plus team, as per the 2012 OPT Plus implementing guidelines, but this is not always the case in practice. In some areas, the Barangay Nutrition Scholar (BNS) leads the conduct of OPT Plus, sometimes assisted by the Barangay Health Worker (BHW). The barangay committee chair on health and nutrition, Sangguniang Kabataan (Youth Council) chairperson, other BHWs, day care workers, and teachers-in-charge can be asked to be part of the team. The team can request additional assistance from leaders of the purok (minizone) or mothers' groups, other community leaders, and representatives from civic organizations.

Following the OPT Plus schedule, the BNS prepares the equipment and supplies and prints the previous year's master list of preschool children, listed by purok or sitio (hamlet), for easy reference during weighing. At the city or municipal level, the city or municipal nutrition action officer supervises OPT Plus activities in selected barangays. These officers ensure the availability and use of (a) calibrated measuring tools; (b) tables based on the WHO child growth standards for weight-for-age, height-for-age, and weight-for-height; (c) OPT Plus forms; or (d) the latest e-OPT Tool software. They ensure that members of the barangay OPT Plus team are trained on the correct procedures for anthropometric measurement. However, many of the ad hoc team members (such as barangay nutrition committee members, Sangguniang Kabataan chairperson, day care worker, teacher-in-charge, purok or mothers' group leaders, or other community leaders) may not have attended OPT Plus training nor have the skills to conduct the anthropometric measurements properly (Briones et al. 2017; Felismino et al. 2018; Herrin et al. 2018; Pasion 2019).

OPT Plus trainings are handled by the regional NNC office and the provincial and municipal health or nutrition office. In view of the need for more trainers, the NNC has supported the training of trainers through the associations of Barangay Nutrition Scholars at the municipal, provincial, regional, and national levels.

Data collection

The activity is conducted by municipal and city government nutrition officers on a campaign basis, through the BNS, BHW, and rural health midwife. Health and other municipal staff in the LGU, including day care workers, members of the barangay council, and local community leaders, participate in the large public event, which is usually held in the barangay hall, day care center, or barangay health station. The OPT Plus team can also resort to house-to-house collection of data among children in the master list who are not present at the event. Aside from measuring the child's weight and length (0–23 months) or height (24 months and older), the team records the child's name, address, sex, ethnicity, and birthdate, as well as the name of the child's mother or caregiver and other household information. Based on the 2012 OPT Plus implementing guidelines, the coverage target is 80–110 percent of all preschool children in the community. The DOH prescribes the reference factors, including the population multiplier by province, to compute the projected population of children ages 0–59 months.

The midwife and nutrition scholar help conduct the anthropometric measurements. As of 2020, there were 49,779 nutrition scholars in 42,046 barangays in the country. The midwife measures length and height, while the BNS measures weight. The guidelines state that, although the midwife is assigned to measure length and height, he or she may supervise the nutrition scholar or another trained personnel to conduct the measurements. In the absence of an assigned midwife in the area, the barangay captain may assign the BNS or BHW to lead the team.

In practice, several barangays are not equipped with the correct weighing and measuring instruments, such as Salter-type hanging weighing scales and height boards (Gordoncillo et al. 2019; Heaver and Hunt 1995; Ramirez, Viajar, and Azaña 2019; Solon 2006). They have either a Detecto-type or a mechanical column scale, both of which are appropriate for use in health centers, but not for use in home visits, or bathroom scales and measuring tapes, which are not suitable and greatly affect the quality of measurements. A consultant report reviewing administrative data on health and nutrition found that some barangays had the correct equipment, but it had not been calibrated; moreover, in one province, some municipalities and barangays had not received the height boards that had been procured by the provincial office. In addition, some barangays still conduct simultaneous weighing despite a lack of appropriate equipment. Correct processes and data quality are sacrificed for the sake of speed (Ramirez, Viajar, and Azaña 2019).

OPT Plus reports weight-for-age, length-for-age (height-for-age), and weight-for-length (weight-for-height) for children under five years old. Until 2016, the coverage of the nutrition statistics included children up to 71 months old. Only from 2017 onward did OPT Plus results use measurements of children from birth to 59 months of age in full implementation of the 2012 OPT Plus guidelines. If sufficient time is available, the child's age in months and nutritional status are determined during the recording of data (Ramirez, Viajar, and Azaña 2019). If the child is obviously malnourished, the mother or caregiver is instructed to consult the barangay or rural health station.

At OPT Plus, the BNS is responsible for preparing and updating a community spot map that shows the location of houses with malnourished children. After conducting OPT Plus, the BNS encodes the measurements and new information using the e-OPT Plus Tool at the office. For barangays without access to a computer or laptop, the BNS manually consolidates the OPT Plus forms and submits the hard copy of the report to the municipal office. Included in the responsibilities of the BNS is the maintenance of OPT Plus records; however, data collected are not stored centrally in the barangay.

To consolidate OPT Plus data and improve the timelines of reporting, the NNC developed the e-OPT Tool or database in Microsoft Excel. The e-OPT Tool's features include automatic computation, such as age in months and nutritional status, and detection of errors, such as double-counting and out-of-range values. It also has preformatted report templates such as the master list of malnourished children for follow-up. The e-OPT Plus Tool assists nutrition workers in consolidating data at the municipal, city, provincial, and regional levels. It provides barangay, municipal or city, and provincial records if at least 80 percent of the intended population is covered. The e-OPT Tool user's guide, a step-by-step guide for use at the local level, has been published by the NNC and the Food and Agriculture Organization.

Reporting

The BNS presents the OPT Plus results to the barangay nutrition committee, where the indicators help form the basis for planning the nutrition improvement activities, such as feeding and other community-based programs on acute malnutrition. The barangay captain submits a copy of the results to the city or municipal officer within five working days. The city or municipal nutrition action officer then consolidates the barangay submissions and presents the results to the appropriate nutrition committee. The consolidated OPT Plus results are submitted to the provincial nutrition action officer, consolidated with the other municipal reports, and submitted to the NNC regional office. The NNC regional office, in turn, consolidates the provincial and city results and submits the consolidated report to the national office. Each level is given a month to follow up and consolidate the reports.

The OPT Plus results are published to show the estimated number of preschool children in the city or municipality, how many children are assessed, and how many are underweight, overweight, stunted, and wasted. The results show wide variation in coverage of the population; the majority of municipalities do not reach the recommended 80–110 percent coverage of children (figure 10.2). The corresponding prevalence data for measures of malnutrition may thus appear low relative to estimates obtained from an NNS conducted for the same year.

The NNC reports on the ranking of the 100 most severely nutritionally depressed municipalities in previous years or cities before 2004. The report uses a composite index of OPT prevalence of low weight-for-age (underweight) and the Commission on Audit's report on per capita income of the municipalities or cities. To date, the NNC reports data on the 100 municipalities or cities with the highest prevalence of stunting, wasting, and underweight.

FIGURE 10.2

Distribution of coverage from OPT Plus results, 2015

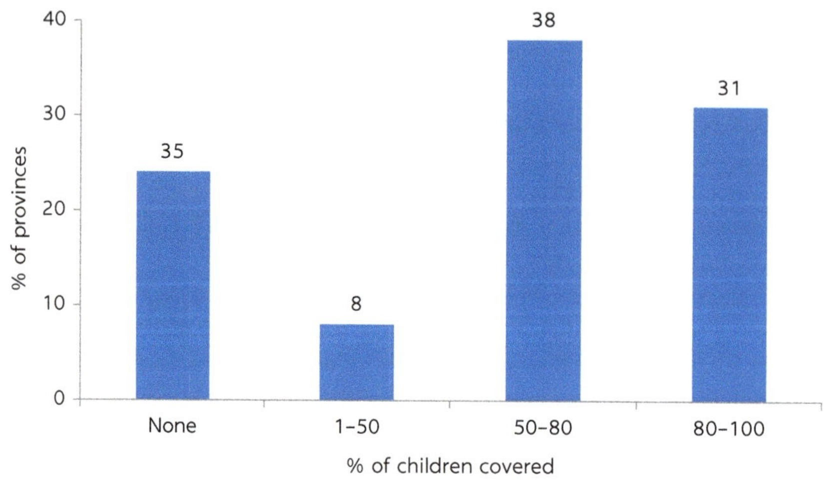

Source: Operation *Timbang* Plus 2015 results.
Note: Distribution excluding cities.

COMPARING ANTHROPOMETRIC RESULTS FROM ENNS AND OPT PLUS

The anthropometric component of the National Nutrition Surveys and Operation *Timbang* Plus are two major activities assessing the growth of children and providing important information for planning nutrition programs and formulating nutrition policy. The NNS seeks to generate data on the national and subnational prevalence of malnutrition among children. In a similar vein, OPT Plus seeks to generate data on the nutritional status of children in a barangay, municipality, or city. Given differences in other objectives, schedules, sampling design and coverage, enumerators, and funding, there are general disparities between disaggregated NNS figures and aggregated OPT Plus figures for the same years.

OPT Plus results for child malnutrition are often lower than NNS estimates (Abrigo et al. 2019; Ramirez, Viajar, and Azaña 2019). For this chapter, we use the values from 2018 and 2019 at the provincial level such that both the OPT Plus and ENNS indicators refer to children ages 0–59 months; previous OPT Plus results were for children ages 0–71 months. Figures 10.3–10.5 show prevalence indicators for underweight, stunting, and wasting, respectively, in 2018 and 2019, from the ENNS and OPT Plus. As of the writing of this chapter, 37 provinces have complete 2018 ENNS results, while 16 provinces have complete 2019 ENNS results that can be matched to OPT Plus results. For 2018, of the 37 provinces with complete ENNS and OPT Plus reporting, the 10 best- and

FIGURE 10.3

Prevalence of underweight in children under five in the Philippines: Comparison of ENNS and OPT Plus records for 2018 and 2019

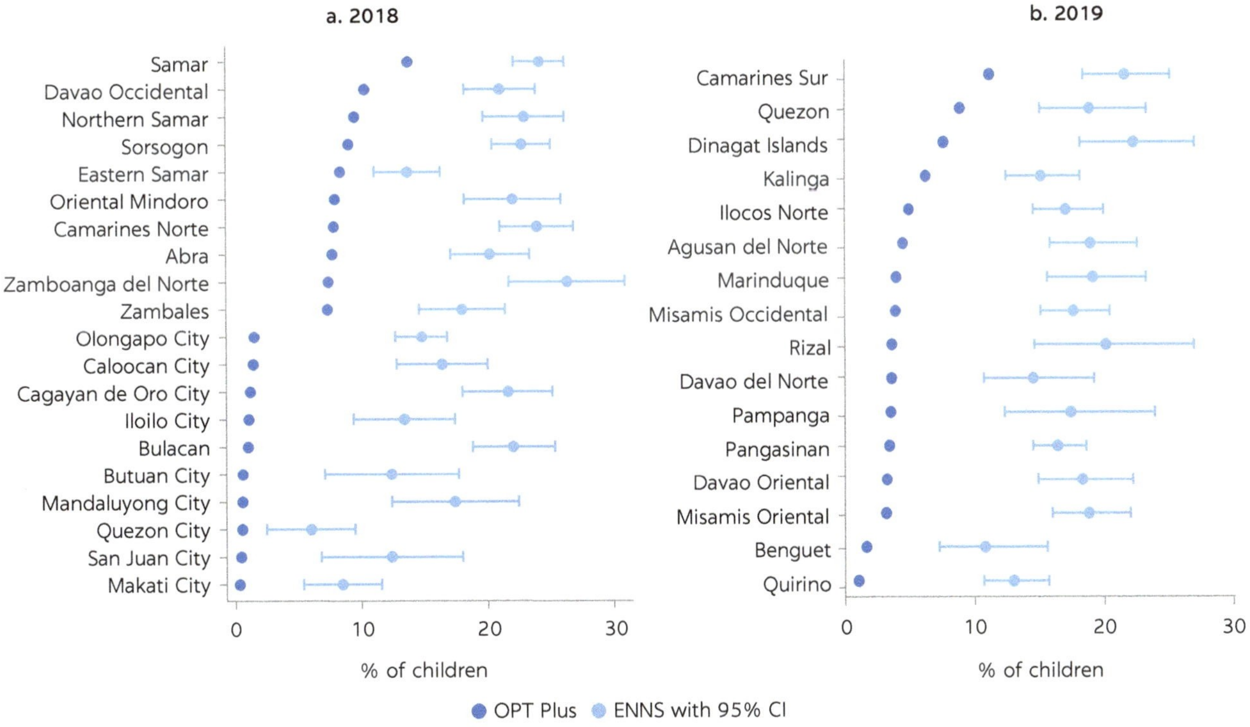

Source: OPT Plus records and ENNS estimates.
Note: CI = confidence interval. ENNS = Expanded National Nutrition Survey. OPT Plus = Operation *Timbang* Plus.

FIGURE 10.4

Prevalence of stunting in children under five in the Philippines: Comparison of ENNS and OPT Plus records for 2018 and 2019

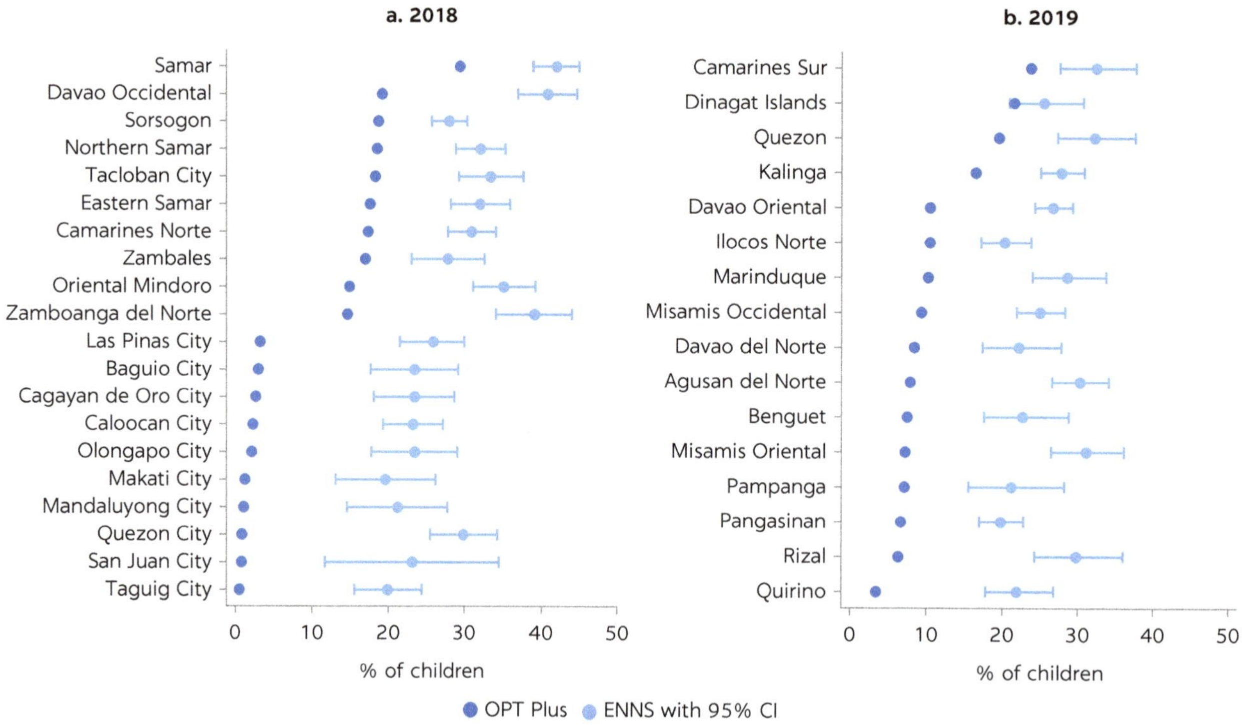

Source: OPT Plus records and ENNS estimates.
Note: CI = confidence interval. ENNS = Expanded National Nutrition Survey. OPT Plus = Operation *Timbang* Plus.

worst-performing provinces in OPT Plus prevalence are displayed alongside the equivalent prevalence and 95 percent confidence intervals from the ENNS. For 2019, all available data are presented in the figures. The simple ranking is based on OPT Plus results, not the composite index, based on prevalence of low weight-for-age and per capita income, that the NNC uses to categorize the 100 worst-performing provinces. The estimated prevalence of low weight-for-age and stunted children reported by OPT Plus is generally lower and beyond the confidence interval of the ENNS prevalence. The same is true for the prevalence of wasting for top-performing provinces. In contrast, the prevalence of wasting for the worst-performing provinces reported by OPT Plus often falls within the ENNS confidence interval.

It is not yet clear what might explain the differences between estimates from the NNS and results from OPT Plus. Aside from having different objectives and designs—the NNS is a survey, while OPT Plus is a total enumeration—one reason for the differences may be the accuracy of measurements. The survey team may have better training and adequate measurement tools than the BNS. The survey team, given its composition, is also more likely to be better supervised than the BNS and local team. Another reason might be the consistently off-target coverage of the population by OPT Plus, with several municipalities not reaching 80 percent coverage of preschool children in their area. The disparities become a concern when LGUs, Congress, and

FIGURE 10.5

Prevalence of wasting in children under five in the Philippines: Comparison of ENNS and OPT Plus records for 2018 and 2019

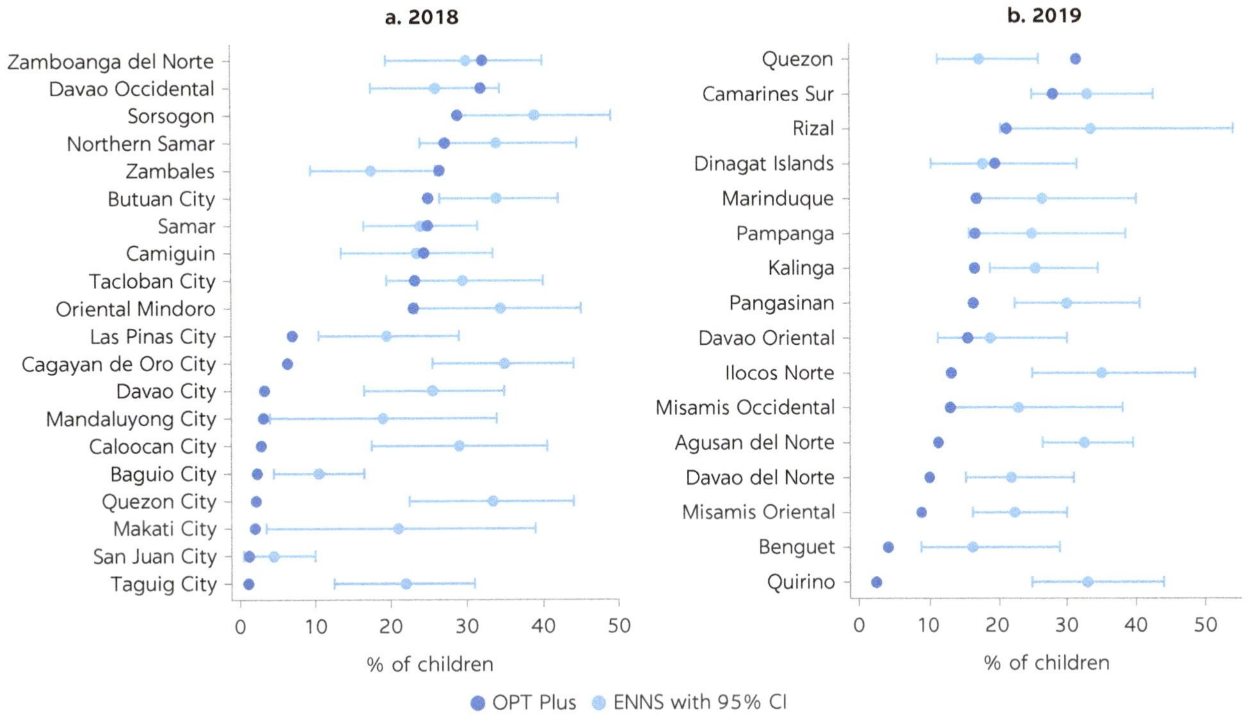

Source: OPT Plus records and ENNS estimates.
Note: CI = confidence interval. ENNS = Expanded National Nutrition Survey. OPT Plus = Operation *Timbang* Plus.

other stakeholders need local data estimates for formulating development plans, particularly at the level of provinces and specifically for highly urbanized cities. The need to reduce these discrepancies was the rationale for adoption of the annual ENNS in 2018. Clearly, it is more difficult for LGUs to place a high priority on preventing stunting if the prevalence rate is less than 10 percent than if it is close to 25 percent.

The large disparity between the estimates yielded by the different sources begs the question of data consistency. The NNS adheres to standard practices, and thus protocols are thoroughly set in survey operations to ensure comparability and validity of the data collected. OPT Plus relies heavily on the capability of LGUs to implement the data collection activities. Often, consistency in data collection is compromised. Instruments used for measuring height and weight are not standard across barangays, which rely on available resources provided by the LGU. The period of data collection also varies, as not all LGUs can comply with the allotted time frame. When data are combined and collated using pen and paper, consolidation of these reports can be cumbersome.

In 2019 the NNC conducted an in-house mixed-method study using a sequential explanatory research design to determine the awareness, knowledge, attitudes, and practices of Barangay Nutrition Scholars in Malabon City regarding the 2012 OPT Plus implementing guidelines (Salunga et al. 2019). The study also explored the reasons for the success of the activity. The information was drawn from a quantitative approach using a self-administered questionnaire and a qualitative approach using a semistructured interview with key informants. The study found that the majority of Barangay Nutrition Scholars in Malabon City were not aware of the implementing guidelines but were knowledgeable and had a positive attitude toward OPT Plus; however, most of them did not use best practices in conducting the activity. Awareness, knowledge, attitudes, and practices are interrelated. Having an enabling and cooperative environment, work and life balance, information and dissemination strategies, innovation, measuring tools, training and supervision, and dedication to work were considered factors underlying the successful implementation of OPT Plus.

FNRI also conducted operations research to investigate the factors affecting OPT prevalence rates and uncover factors that facilitate or hinder data collection for OPT (Ramirez, Viajar, and Azaña 2019). The study found that the measurement skills and capacities of the BNSs varied, which could be due to high staff turnover and insufficient training in the use of equipment, weak incentives, and lax supervision. They also noted variation when comparing wasting rates with NNS and OPT data. This phenomenon raises the possibility that the discrepancies between the two measurement opportunities may be more systematic than random. Improvements in methods could reduce the variance between the two, which would increase confidence in the use of OPT results for local policy and program development.

FIELD HEALTH SERVICES INFORMATION SYSTEM

The Field Health Services Information System was developed in 1987 and implemented nationwide in 1989 to improve the initial DOH reporting system. Implementation of the Local Government Code in 1992 involved challenges in the DOH's implementation of the FHSIS, leading to a modified FHSIS beginning in 1996. The DOH revised the FHSIS further in 2001, resulting in a decentralized FHSIS, which was piloted in six areas. These efforts failed to solve the problems of inaccuracy, incompleteness, and delay experienced with the original and the modified FHSIS. An evaluation recommended enhancing the FHSIS support systems, such as the policy and implementing rules and regulations, increasing the availability of skilled data managers, providing adequate financing, and instituting an efficient computerization of the system. The DOH discontinued the decentralized FHSIS in 2004 and started the FHSIS program enhancements in 2005. A series of consultative workshops with program managers yielded the 2008 version of the FHSIS. The e-FHSIS, a web-based stand-alone system for submitting reports, was developed in 2009. Further enhancements brought about the 2012 version, introducing new programs and indicators.

The FHSIS is intended to guide local health officers in managing the delivery of services in their area and to guide the DOH in implementing new policies and guidelines, prioritizing the allocation of resources, and improving the quality of health services. FHSIS reports on a range of nutrition-related indicators, including infants and children given vitamin A, multiple micronutrient supplementation, and iron supplementation; infants and children with diarrhea given oral rehydration solution; birthweight; breastfeeding practices; complementary feeding practices; and water, sanitation, and hygiene.

Data collection

The rural health midwife or nurse at the barangay health unit records the day-to-day transactions through an individual treatment record, a target client list, a summary table, and a monthly consolidation table. These reporting tools generate the FHSIS reports, which contain summary data from the local health facilities and are consolidated and transmitted on a monthly, quarterly, and annual basis to the next administrative level (rural health unit). The information is consolidated at the rural health unit level and then transmitted to the provincial or city level for further consolidation and transmission to the regional level. The regional FHSIS coordinator prepares the quarterly and annual reports for transmission to the national level, whereupon the DOH Epidemiology Bureau uses the data to compile the annual FHSIS. The usefulness of the FHSIS data relies on the completeness and accuracy of the data recorded by the rural midwives, FHSIS leaders, and champions at the rural health units and barangay health stations when the clients consult or seek health services from the health facility. However, many health units reportedly consider the reporting system to be burdensome and time-consuming.

Reporting

To produce the annual report, the Epidemiology Bureau of the DOH relies on submissions of the DOH regional offices, which are reports consolidated manually from iClinicSys and the different electronic medical record (EMR) systems at the municipal, city, and provincial levels. Perhaps due to the series of consolidations at successive levels, the FHSIS annual report is usually released late, much later than the scheduled first week of July of the following year. The current FHSIS annual report focuses only on quantitative measures; it does not address contexts or discuss notable results and trends. A discussion of findings was included in several FHSIS publications before 2010, but this practice was discontinued. Some DOH regional offices publish their regional FHSIS annual reports complete with discussions, but this practice is not widespread. However, the Epidemiology Bureau plans to include discussions and trends in the future. As the primary users, the DOH and its attached agencies use FHSIS data for reporting to government and international organizations. For example, the NNC uses FHSIS data to analyze the nutritional status of pregnant and breastfeeding mothers in the different regions. But issues related to the quality and reliability of data have been raised about FHSIS as well as OPT data.

Table 10.1 compares the vitamin A supplementation rates obtained from the 2017 National Demographic and Health Survey (NDHS) (PSA 2017) and the 2017 FHSIS (DOH 2017). The NDHS qualifies supplementation as persons given vitamin A supplements within the last six months, based on maternal recall. The survey methods are based on a standard protocol to enable national and regional comparisons over time. The sample selection methodology is based on a two-stage stratified sample design using the master sample frame constructed on the basis of the results of the 2010 Census of Population and Housing and updated using the 2015 Census of Population.

The differences in supplementation rates are glaring, as are the differences in age subgroups, although both systems cover the same age group overall (6–59 months). These differences cause some confusion when data are presented,

TABLE 10.1 **Results for vitamin A supplementation in the Philippines from the 2017 NDHS and 2017 FHSIS**
coverage (% of target population)

		2017 FHSIS	
AREA COVERED	2017 NDHS OVERALL	CHILDREN, 6–11 MONTHS	CHILDREN, 12–59 MONTHS
Region			
National Capital Region	66.7	94.23	80.20
Cordillera Administrative Region	88.1	117.24	67.38
Ilocos	77.0	84.17	28.98
Cagayan	78.4	95.31	46.00
Central Luzon	73.2	80.81	24.88
CALABARZON	72.1	107.18	38.96
MIMAROPA	83.0	112.46	71.11
Bicol	75.9	96.35	51.33
Western Visayas	75.0	79.25	44.46
Central Visayas	81.7	117.88	56.07
Eastern Visayas	90.2	85.86	29.59
Zamboanga Peninsula	77.4	86.39	31.05
Northern Mindanao	81.8	132.05	71.90
Davao	83.8	156.08	76.77
SOCCSKSARGEN	77.1	151.46	75.50
ARMM	44.6	70.05	18.40
Caraga	87.2	96.17	86.23
National			
Children, 6–8 months	54.6	101.69	–
Children, 9–11 months	71.1	–	–
Children, 12–17 months	76.5	–	50.99
Children, 18–23 months	74.6	–	–
Children, 24–35 months	79.2	–	–
Children, 36–47 months	76.6	–	–
Children, 48–59 months	76.6	–	–

Sources: 2017 data from the Philippine Field Health Services Information System (DOH 2017) and the National Demographic and Health Survey (PSA 2017).
Note: ARMM = Autonomous Region in Muslim Mindanao. CALABARZON = Cavite, Laguna, Batangas, Rizal, and Quezon. FHSIS = Field Health Services Information System. MIMAROPA = Occidental Mindoro, Oriental Mindoro, Marinduque, Romblon, and Palawan. NDHS = National Demographic and Health Survey. SOCCSKSARGEN = South Cotabato, Cotabato, Sultan Kudarat, Sarangani, and General Santos. – = not available.

considered, and discussed. The limitations of the FHSIS data are often all too apparent, despite the system's legally designated official status.

The FHSIS is an annual (12-month) set of routine service delivery reports aggregated monthly at the LGU level and submitted quarterly for national consolidation. The numerator (for calculating coverage rates) comes from actual recipients of vitamin A supplementation, while the denominator comes from projections of targeted subpopulations, based on population estimates provided by the Philippine Statistics Authority. The FHSIS does not include persons who avail themselves of services from the private sector.

CONCLUSIONS AND RECOMMENDATIONS

The NNS, OPT Plus, and FHSIS have been in existence for more than four decades. Over the years, changes in these respective data sources have been introduced with a view to providing relevant information in a timely manner. The NNC implemented changes in response to updated standards, and the FHSIS expanded the range of indicators measured. The NNS adopted a rolling sample to provide more frequent and more granular estimates of nutrition.

Policy research in the field of nutrition is repeatedly hampered by the inaccessibility of granular data on the subject. The inaccessibility of data has been the main criticism of the NNS as the primary data source. Recently, the FNRI made data at the level of local administrative units available to the public. Data can be requested through the e-nutrition portal. Currently, all NNS and Updating Survey data from 2008 to 2015 can be accessed. Evidence-based policy decisions must be underpinned by the wide and timely availability of such data.

OPT Plus and FHSIS operate in similar environments at the local setting, especially since the NNC is an attached agency of the DOH. The nutrition office is usually within or contiguous to the health office, and the health officer often doubles as the nutrition officer. Barangay implementers and monitors whose services are drawn upon at the local level often are the same individual (wearing different hats), such as the rural health midwife, Barangay Health Worker, or Barangay Nutrition Scholar, leading to multitasking, work conflicts, and overburdened staff. There is also pressure to comply with central reporting requirements, with tight timelines and multiple levels of consolidation. For instance, the low OPT coverage rates in a significant number of LGUs are a symptom of this problem.

The following situations are typical of both OPT Plus and FHSIS:

- Data quality is highly dependent on the staff gathering the data. For OPT Plus, some BNSs lack the skills to conduct anthropometric measurements and process data. All OPT Plus team members should be trained on the importance of correct procedures and measurements, BNSs included. Correct processes and data quality are sometimes sacrificed for the sake of expediency. For the FHSIS, data quality hinges on the completeness and accuracy of data being recorded by midwives from clients consulting or seeking health services from the health facility. Any failure on the part of the midwife or the BHW to understand the program indicators is likely to lead to inaccurate data and reports. In addition, a report is incomplete if the midwife omits certain items or if respondents do not understand certain questions (or refuse to answer).
- Validation of data quality is, in principle, usually passed up to the next reporting level. If, as is often the case, data validation at the various levels is not undertaken, then the responsibility devolves to the national level. A series of follow-up investigations ensue, further delaying release of the annual reports.
- The manual compilation of data at the different levels is a major bottleneck in the process flow. The e-OPT Tools, the iClinicsys, and the other EMR systems can provide efficient and timely data compilation, but the adoption of these technologies has proven difficult. A supportive environment is required, as is investment in training and equipment. The absence of an integrated, online

national data repository for both administrative systems increases the risks of compilation errors as the data are transmitted from the barangay and up to the different levels.

- The health and nutrition activities cannot be implemented successfully without the support of LGU officials. Success stories illustrate this point, such as OPT Plus in Quezon Province or the EMR in Pangantucan (Bukidnon Province). The Quezon provincial nutrition action officer has a clear implementation plan on OPT Plus, coordinating the efforts of the relevant municipalities to ensure data quality and smooth implementation of the activity. The rural health unit in Pangantucan, where the midwife encodes patient information using a tablet, is still somewhat exceptional, but amply demonstrates how much easier improvements become when there is LGU support. Other success stories are documented in the NNC's recently published compendium of LGU best practices in nutrition, which describes nutrition interventions since the 1990s in 11 LGUs (Nutrition International et al. 2018). In these LGUs, prevalence, as reported in OPT Plus, tends to be low, ranging between 5 and 10 percent, with only one LGU having a 21 percent prevalence of stunting among children in 2015. Nevertheless, the implementation of nutrition interventions saw these LGUs performing better in reducing malnutrition and improving health among pregnant women, mothers, and their children.

Information is key, particularly at the LGU level, where malnutrition can be monitored closely and addressed. Not only should the reliability of administrative data be ensured, but their utility to frontline workers and local decision makers also should be made clear. Doing so would entail addressing a series of issues that encompass resources, infrastructure, and operations.

ANNEX 10A. FEATURES AND INDICATORS OF THE NNS, OPT PLUS, AND FHSIS

TABLE 10A.1 **Features of the NNS, OPT Plus, and FHSIS**

FEATURE	NATIONAL NUTRITION SURVEYS (NNS AND ENNS)	OPERATION *TIMBANG* PLUS (OPT PLUS)	FIELD HEALTH SERVICES INFORMATION SYSTEM (FHSIS)
Definition of data gathered	Nutrition and health data, in the following components: anthropometry, biochemical, dietary, clinical and health, socioeconomic, government program participation, food security, maternal health, and feeding for infants and young children	Data on nutritional status of children ages 0–59 months using weight-for-age, weight-for-height or weight-for-length, and height-for-age or length-for-age	Extent of coverage of essential public health services (immunizations, family planning, infant and maternal care) mostly through the data collected when clients visit public health facilities
Purpose or use of data	To provide empirical data on the nutritional and health status of Filipinos for planning nutrition and development programs	• To inform planning nutrition interventions at the barangay, city, and municipal level • To quantify and identify preschoolers who are malnourished and locate their families so they can be the priority beneficiaries of nutrition-related services	To inform the DOH reporting to national and international organizations, donors, and partners

(continued)

TABLE 10A.1, *continued*

FEATURE	NATIONAL NUTRITION SURVEYS (NNS AND ENNS)	OPERATION *TIMBANG* PLUS (OPT PLUS)	FIELD HEALTH SERVICES INFORMATION SYSTEM (FHSIS)
Indicators related to nutrition	For several age groups: • Underweight or weight-for-age • Stunting or height-for-length • Wasting or weight-for-length	• Underweight or weight-for-age • Stunting or height-for-length • Wasting or weight-for-length	• Infants and children given vitamin A, micronutrient powder, or iron • Micronutrient intake among mothers • Infants and children with diarrhea given oral rehydration solution • Low birthweight • Exclusive breastfeeding • Complementary feeding • Households with safe water supply, complete sanitation facilities
Origin of data	Survey collection	Weight and height measurements taken by the OPT team during the barangay mass weighing	Mostly data collected from clients visiting public health facilities
Assigned LGU personnel	FNRI-hired staff, including assistance from LGU personnel: • Barangay Nutrition Scholar • Rural health midwife • Barangay Health Worker	• Barangay Nutrition Scholar • Rural health midwife • Barangay Health Worker	• Rural health midwife • Barangay Health Worker
Software and its use	e-DCS, a computer-based interview schedule that facilitates data transmission	e-OPT Plus Tools in Microsoft Excel that provide automatic computation and detection of errors and assist in consolidating data at the different levels	iClinicSys, an electronic medical record that provides required data for the FHSIS and PhilHealth reports
Technical expertise needed to operate systems	Training is required and provided in several phases, including assessments	Training is required, especially on measuring weight and height	Technical expertise is needed; the midwife and other health workers should know how to use the EMR and be well informed on the FHSIS indicators and reporting
Recording of data	e-DCS; minimal manual recording	Manual recording at the field level and then manual and electronic recording at the barangay or municipal office	Manual or electronic recording at the barangay health station or rural health unit
Flow of reporting	Field data are transmitted to the central office for validation, processing, and consolidation	OPT Plus results from the barangay are submitted to the municipality or city for consolidation and thence to each subsequent level up to the national office	Summary data from the barangay health stations and rural health units are submitted to each subsequent level up to the national office
Scope or coverage	All members of a household; households selected by PSA sampling	Children ages 0–59 months nationwide	Depends on the indicator, but mostly from public health facilities nationwide
Available data	• Province • Region • National	• Barangay • Municipality or city • Province (assuming at least 80% coverage in the municipalities and cities)	• Barangay • Municipality or city • Province • Region • National
Representativeness of samples	Nationally representative	Some cities and municipalities do not achieve 80% coverage target	Data are collected mostly from those visiting public health facilities

(continued)

TABLE 10A.1, *continued*

FEATURE	NATIONAL NUTRITION SURVEYS (NNS AND ENNS)	OPERATION *TIMBANG* PLUS (OPT PLUS)	FIELD HEALTH SERVICES INFORMATION SYSTEM (FHSIS)
Availability of report	Yearly (delayed publication release)	Yearly (delayed publication release)	Yearly (delayed publication release)
Strategies employed for dissemination of information	Conferences and seminars	Local and national media partners	None

Source: World Bank.
Note: DOH = Department of Health. EMR = electronic medical record. FNRI = Food and Nutrition Research Institute. LGU = local government unit. PSA = Philippine Statistics Authority.

TABLE 10A.2 **Indicators used by NNS, OPT Plus, and FHSIS**

MODULE	NATIONAL NUTRITION SURVEYS (NNS AND ENNS)	OPERATION *TIMBANG* PLUS (OPT PLUS)	FIELD HEALTH SERVICES INFORMATION SYSTEM (FHSIS)
Anthropometry	Prevalence of underweight, stunting, thinness, overweight, and obesity (body mass index, waist circumference, waist-to-hip ratio) among population groups: 0–60 months, 61–120 months, 121–228 months, 20 years and up, pregnant, lactating women	• % of children ages 0–59 months who are underweight, overweight, stunted, wasted, by city or municipality and province • 100 most severely nutritionally depressed cities and municipalities	% of children ages 0–59 months who are underweight, stunted, wasted, overweight, or obese
Biochemical or dietary	• Prevalence of iron deficiency anemia, iodine deficiency disorders, thalassemia, vitamin D deficiency, vitamin A deficiency, and zinc deficiency • Food and nutrient intake and adequacy at the household and individual levels	n.a.	• % of mothers receiving micronutrients • % of infants or children who completed vitamin A supplementation • % of infants ages 6–11 months and children ages 12–23 months who completed micronutrient powder supplementation • % of infants born preterm or with low birthweight who were given iron supplements
Child health	% of low birthweight children, ages 0–71 months	n.a.	• % of live births, by weight (< 2,500 grams) • % of high-risk infants or children with measles or persistent diarrhea who received vitamin A capsule aside from routine supplementation • % of diarrhea cases in children ages 0–59 months who received oral rehydration solution with oral zinc drops or syrup
Maternal health and nutrition	Maternal nutrition and child health care practices of mothers with children ages 0–36 months	n.a.	• % of pregnant women who completed the dose of iron with folic acid tablet supplementation • % of pregnant women given iodine capsule • % of postpartum or lactating women given vitamin A supplementation • % of pregnant women given complete doses of calcium carbonate • % of postpartum women who completed iron with folic acid supplementation

(continued)

TABLE 10A.2, *continued*

MODULE	NATIONAL NUTRITION SURVEYS (NNS AND ENNS)	OPERATION *TIMBANG* PLUS (OPT PLUS)	FIELD HEALTH SERVICES INFORMATION SYSTEM (FHSIS)
Infant and young children feeding	• Exclusive breastfeeding, infants ages 0–5 months • Breastfeeding initiation within one hour of birth, children ages 0–23 months old • Continued breastfeeding at one year and at ages 12–15 months • Introduction of complementary food (soft, semisolid, or solid foods) • Infants, ages 6–8 months • Children ever breastfed, ages 0–23 months • Continued breastfeeding at age 2 years • Age-appropriate breastfeeding, ages 0–23 months • Predominant breastfeeding under 6 months, ages 0–5 months • Bottle feeding, ages 0–23 months • Duration of breastfeeding • Dietary diversity (minimum dietary diversity), ages 6–23 months • Meal frequency (minimum meal frequency), ages 6–23 months • Minimum acceptable diet, ages 6–23 months	n.a.	• % of infants exclusively breastfed until age 6 months • % of postpartum women who, immediately after birth, initiated breastfeeding lasting 90 minutes • % of infants who continued breastfeeding and were introduced to complementary feeding beginning at 6 months of age
Household health and sanitation	• % distribution of households by sources of water for drinking, cooking, and handwashing • % distribution of households by sanitation facilities and waste disposal practices	n.a.	• % of households with access to basic safe water supply • % of households with basic sanitation facility • % of households with complete sanitation facilities • % of households using safely managed sanitation services • % of barangays declared zero open defecation areas • % of households using safely managed drinking water services • % of households with satisfactory solid waste management
Food security	Prevalence and magnitude of household food insecurity and household economic access to food	n.a.	n.a.

Source: World Bank.
Note: n.a. = not applicable.

NOTES

1. These statistics are discussed and referenced in chapter 7.
2. See https://psa.gov.ph/article/approving-adoption-world-health-organization-child-growth-standards-tool-generating.

REFERENCES

Abrigo, Michael R. M., Connie Bayundan-Dacuycuy, Aubrey D. Tabuga, Lora Kryz C. Baje, Carlos C. Cabaero, and Zhandra C. Tam. 2019. "Situational Analysis of Distal Factors Affecting Early Childhood Care and Development in the First 1,000 Days of Life in Zamboanga del Norte." PIDS Discussion Paper 2019-28, Philippines Institute for Development Studies, Quezon City. https://pidswebs.pids.gov.ph/CDN/PUBLICATIONS/pidsdps1928.pdf.

Berman, Eli, Mitch Downey, and Joseph Felter. 2016. "Expanding Governance as Development: Evidence on Child Nutrition in the Philippines." NBER Working Paper w21849, National Bureau of Economic Research, Cambridge, MA.

Briones, Roehlano, Ella Antonio, Celestino Habito, Emma Porio, and Danilo Songco. 2017. *Strategic Review: Food Security and Nutrition in the Philippines.* Rome: World Food Programme.

DOH (Department of Health). 2010. "Administrative Order no. 2-10-0015: Revised Policy on Child Growth Standard." DOH, Manila, June 8, 2010.

DOH (Department of Health). 2017. *Philippines Field Health Services Information System (FHSIS) Annual Report 2017.* Manila: Epidemiology Bureau, DOH.

Felismino, L. M., Maria Theresa M. Talavera, Normahitta P. Gordoncillo, and Nelson J. V. B. Querijero. 2018. "Nutrition Governance, Good Governance for Nutrition, and Nutritional Status of Children under Five Years of Age in Laguna, Philippines." *Malaysian Journal of Nutrition* 24 (3): 301–13.

FNRI (Food and Nutrition Research Institute). 1998. *Fifth National Nutrition Survey.* Taguig City: Department of Science and Technology, FNRI.

FNRI (Food and Nutrition Research Institute). 2003. *Sixth National Nutrition Survey.* Taguig City: Department of Science and Technology, FNRI.

FNRI (Food and Nutrition Research Institute). 2008. *Seventh National Nutrition Survey.* Taguig City: Department of Science and Technology, FNRI.

FNRI (Food and Nutrition Research Institute). 2013. *Eighth National Nutrition Survey.* Taguig City: Department of Science and Technology, FNRI.

FNRI (Food and Nutrition Research Institute). 2015. *2015 Updating Survey Results.* Taguig City: Department of Science and Technology, FNRI.

Gordoncillo, Normahitta P., Nancy A. Tandang, Maria Theresa M. Talavera, and Divine Grace C. Domingo. 2019. "Comparison of Height Measuring Instruments for Children Used in Two Municipalities of Laguna, Philippines." *Southeast Asian Journal of Tropical Medicine and Public Health* 50 (5): 952–65.

Government of the Philippines. 1987. "Executive Order no. 128, s. 1987: Reorganizing and Strengthening the Philippine Statistical System and for Other Purposes." *Official Gazette,* January 30, 1987.

Government of the Philippines. 1996. "Executive Order no. 352, s. 1996: Designation of Statistical Activities That Will Generate Critical Data for Decision-Making of the Government and the Private Sector." *Official Gazette,* July 1, 1996.

Heaver, Richard A., and Joseph M. Hunt. 1995. *Improving Early Childhood Development: An Integrated Program for the Philippines.* Washington, DC: World Bank.

Herrin, Alejandro N., Michael R. M. Abrigo, Zhandra C. Tam, and Danica A. P. Ortiz. 2018. "Child Stunting Prevention: The Challenge of Mobilizing Local Governments for National Impact." PIDS Discussion Paper 2018-45. Philippine Institute for Development Studies, Quezon City.

Nutrition International, UNICEF (United Nations Children's Fund), NNC (National Nutrition Council), and DOH (Department of Health). 2018. *The Ascent of Local Governments in Nutrition in the Philippines: A Compendium of Actions on Nutrition.* Ottawa: Nutrition in Action; New York: UNICEF; Manila: Taguig City: NNC; Manila: DOH.

Pasion, Patricia Anne. 2019. "'It Takes a Village to Raise a Child': Malabon City in the Philippines Mobilizes to Reduce Malnutrition Rates, 2013–2018." Global Delivery Initiative Case Study, KDI School of Public Policy and Management, Sejong City, Republic of Korea. https://archives.kdischool.ac.kr/bitstream/11125/34121/1/cs_philippines_v3a_final.pdf.

Perlas, Leah, Joselita Ulanday, Juanita Marcos, Michael Serafico, Josefina Desnacido, Maritess Alibayan, Charmaine Duante, and Mario Capanzana. 2017. "Iodine Deficiency Disorder among Filipino School Children, Pregnant and Lactating Women, and the Elderly 20 Years after the Act for Salt Iodization Nationwide Law." *Journal of Endocrinology and Metabolism* 7 (3): 86–93.

PSA (Philippine Statistics Authority). 2017. *Philippines National Demographic and Health Survey 2017.* Quezon City: PSA; Rockville, MD: ICF.

Ramirez, M. A., R. Viajar, and G. Azaña. 2019. "Operationalizing Local Children Nutrition Surveillance System: The Philippines' Operation *Timbang* Revisited; the Case of Abra de Ilog." *World Nutrition* 10 (4): 86–98. https://doi.org/10.26596/wn.201910486-98.

Salunga, Daniel G., E. R. Bullecer, R. C. Habito, L. S. Africa, H. C. C. B. Gawe, and D. V. Aguila. 2019. "A Study on the Awareness, Knowledge, Attitudes, and Practices (AKAP) of Barangay Nutrition Scholars (BNS) on the 2012 Operation *Timbang* Plus (OPT Plus) Implementing Guidelines in Malabon City, Philippines." Philippine Health Research Registry PHRR200819-002838, National Nutrition Council, University of the Philippines Manila. http://www.registry.healthresearch.ph/index.php/registry?view=research&layout=details&cid=2838.

Solon, Florentino S. 1979. "Evaluation of the Philippine Nutrition Program." *Philippine Sociological Review* 27 (1): 35–43.

Solon, Florentino S. 2006. "Good Governance for Nutrition in the Philippines: Elements, Experiences, and Lessons Learned." *Food and Nutrition Bulletin* 27 (4): 343–52. https://journals.sagepub.com/doi/pdf/10.1177/156482650602700409.

www.ingramcontent.com/pod-product-compliance
Ingram Content Group UK Ltd.
Pitfield, Milton Keynes, MK11 3LW, UK
UKHW060419100426
469794UK00007B/21

9 781464 817014